HAVE YOU EVER PRAYED & MEANT IT?

BY CAPT. PHIL GAY

ISBN: 1-4700-9162-3

ISBN-13: 978-1-4700-9162-0

ACKNOWLEDGMENTS

I would like to acknowledge my friend and sponsor George Benedict for his kindness, patience and love my 30 years of sobriety. He has been a father and older brother rolled into one. Never did he point out many of my mistakes, but instead reminded me of all my successes. My higher power and George worked together to teach me how to be an honorable man, a compassionate man, a generous man and how to do the right thing.

Annette Albano Benedict who passed suddenly on September 12th, 2010 I acknowledge for her love and being the mother I never had. The genuine love and interest she showed me gave me what I needed in life. A softer, kinder soul I have never met in my lifetime and many will miss her.

And to Glen Cuyjet my friend and therapist I thank for being there for close to 20 years to listen to me talk through the good times and difficult times. In my journey of self discovery and self awareness I have been taught a huge amount of insight that has helped me, my brother and many other people

INTRODUCTION

Kauai is a magical place. I vacation there sometimes during my winter vacation and love to sit on the wall near my condo and look out over the ocean. I love watching the whales jumping high in the air as if they are jumping just for me to see. I've always loved the sea, and that's probably why I never left the Hamptons. My house is two miles from the beach, so almost every winter these last few years has taken me to an island or a beach in Costa Rica, Mexico, Hawaii, or Australia.

Being from New York, I am not used to the morning walkers and joggers all saying "Good morning" as they go past. Why don't do that at home?

The deep blue sea washing over the Hawaiian lava rocks reminds me of a scene, but I'm not sure where I have seen it—then it comes to me. When Dad died in '92, the church handed out a folder. On the cover were the dates he lived on this earth; inside it had hymns and a picture of the sea and rocks. I had come across it a few months before, in a drawer in my house on Long Island. His name was Philip, and he had passed in April '92.

I remember him in a fond way, and it brings a warm smile to my face. I wonder sometimes if he is proud of me and the man I have become.

He was a good man, honorable and interested in all my affairs, sometimes even too much so when I was young—and now I would trade it all to just to sit and chat about things, even for just five minutes. Don't get ıg…he had his stuff too. He was an alcoholic with control issues, stubborn, a perfectionist, and even could be very manipulative at times.

I have a picture of him in his twenties, a handsome man resembling Cary Grant. At times he had a devilish sparkle in his eye, as if he knew something and wasn't telling. I built a house next door to his in Water Mill. When he used to ride his small tractor to visit, I would hide so I would not have to talk to him. I now sometimes wish I had more patience back then to just sit and talk with him. I was in my thirties then and felt there would be plenty of time.

My memory of my childhood is like many, I guess. I remember bits and pieces, but I realize today that each of my parents carried hurt and abuse from their own childhoods into our family. The old saying that people who are hurting hurt other people was present in my upbringing for many years.

Dad grew up in New York City and in the 1930s came out to the Hamptons with his family on the weekends, way before it became fashionable. His own father had died before I was born. Grandpa had owned a house on First Neck Lane in Southampton. He was a banker, and when the crash happened, he held on to most of his money. Dad came down with polio when he was two or three, and although he never said anything, it must have been tough for him growing up. His four sisters and two brothers were lucky and never came down with that awful disease.

I can remember when I was a young boy, seeing old home movies of Dad. He was in his twenties with powerful arms and a strong chest, as if God was trying to make up for his shortfall. Dad walked with a limp, but he held no cane back in those days, and in many of the movies he smiled and seemed happy.

The house on First Neck Lane had a small pond behind the house, and ducks, geese, chickens, and maybe even a cow resided there. This is something the rich and famous who live there now would never tolerate! I wish I knew more about those times. I'm not sure I ever asked; it was safer sometimes not to ask questions. He attended a school of aeronautics, and with a great ability in engineering and welding, he could repair just about anything. In the days when I grew up, he was always repairing the furnace, the water pump, the water heater, and leaking faucets and pipes. In those days, you just fixed a lot of things on your own; it cost money to call a repairman.

I was the oldest son, and my father taught me many things he loved. We were sailing, clamming, camping and fishing in the summer, and duck hunting and maybe sleigh riding in the winter. There were not many hills, but we had one we called Blueberry Hill in the field behind the house in Water Mill because of the wild blueberries that grew there in summer.

Mom grew up in Southampton; her father owned a well-known department store. I think it was said that the store had been founded in the 1800s. She was a Daughter of the American Revolution, and she made sure she told us that weekly when we were growing up.

We also used to hear the story about how, after one too many martinis, Dad hit the telephone pole across the street from my grandfather's house and came in to use the phone and there met my mom, the woman he would marry.

She was beautiful, and he was very handsome. There was electricity—probably left over from the telephone pole—and soon after they were married.

Our house was a fun place from the outside. We lived on a thirteen-acre piece of land in Water Mill. Dad bought the land from a distant relative of my mom's for $12,500. Even in 1950, that was a deal. The old white house built in the late 1700s had four bedrooms and two baths, and if anyone ran the water when you took a shower, you would get scalded or icy water. I took enjoyment torturing my family from time to time, running the water when they took a shower, especially my sisters and brother.

There were several red barns in the back: one a shop where my dad repaired broken equipment, and one long, narrow one where we kept chickens. Sometimes there were also sheep, and for a year or so, a horse that my sister would ride. There was also a garage where we kept the old antique tractor my dad had won in some sweepstakes. There were two other small buildings, one an old outhouse and another shed we called the playhouse. To the west side of the house, Dad had planted an orchard with a dozen peach, apple, and pear trees. North of the orchard we had a vegetable garden that was 150 x 50 feet.

After they bought the house, Mom, Dad, and Uncle Ted planted white pine seedlings they bought from the state for a penny apiece. There was a fire many years ago, and many trees on the north side of the property were destroyed. On the piece of land where I eventually built my house, the trees remained untouched, and today many of them are seventy feet tall. I love the sound on windy nights as the wind rushes through their boughs.

Uncle Ted was married to my father's sister, and he was a lot of fun. He always made me laugh and could make quarters appear from behind my ears, which fascinated me as a young boy. He took me fishing and duck hunting and was my best uncle. He was a lawyer, and when I was in my twenties, he became the town attorney and later the town judge. He came in handy when I grew into a teenager as I was always getting into trouble with the law.

I grew up with pet ducks, chickens, and geese from the age of four or five. I have seen photos of me as a happy boy, holding my pet chicken Wilbur or one of three Canada geese that were imprinted and thought I was their mother. We had an incubator, and I hatched them from eggs I had found in an abandoned nest. They used to land in the driveway and meet me when I came home from school, honking excitedly and bobbing their black heads up and down. The geese were allowed in the living room when my parents had cocktails at night. At least Dad said they could come in— my mother was not happy with this. Dad and I would feed them cheese and crackers because having a conversation with the geese I guess was more fun than having one with my mother. Mom would shake her head. "They are all crazy," she would say.

My brother was born in 1960, when I was six years old. A year or two later, I began helping Dad. I always had chores. I fed the chickens and helped Dad mow the lawn and the orchard and worked in the garden after school. Dad owned a gas business and delivered oxygen to welding shops and hospitals. Sometimes I got to ride along on a Saturday. Most days he would come home late, around seven or eight at night. We were always hungry, but Mom would never feed us until after they had cocktails. Many nights, it would be nine before we ate.

In the spring, I took care of the garden with Dad. We grew asparagus, lettuce, tomatoes, carrots, onions, cucumbers, zucchini, melons, blueberries, raspberries, and strawberries, and we had a small field of sweet corn.

Dad sprayed the fruit trees until I got older, and then it became my job. Some of the trees were pretty big, and in the fall I climbed up and pick the apples...I loved that part. I was allowed to sell vegetables and fruit at a small stand I set up in front of the house long before they had many farm stands here in the Hamptons. I always had to keep track of what I sold and split the money with Dad. I never liked that part; he always seemed to want to be my partner in things.

I did not know it then, but I had a huge feeling of responsibility, to the point of being overwhelmed a lot of the time. I loved to steal away when I was supposed to be mowing the lawn. I would go to the back pond a quarter mile down the back road and catch frogs. I would put them in the small pond by the house. Other times, I loved to hide in the bushes in front of the house and watch the huge grader scrape the road and remove the old pavement. The huge trucks would spray black tar and then spread sand over it. When I smell crews tarring a roof or road today, I remember those times.

It was a safe place in front of the house in those bushes; no one knew I was there. I learned that being alone was safe. It was comfortable, and I had many places that were quiet places for me.

In the fall, my favorite thing to do was to go duck hunting with my dad on Lane's Island in Shinnecock Bay. Lane's Island was a half-mile west of the Ponquogue bridge, where my grandfather actually leased part of the marsh in the forties. On the marsh, our small house slept four men. My dad referred to it as "the shanty." I was very young, maybe less than five, when Dad and I motored out in the duck boat to the shanty. As we approached, tears rolled down my father's cheeks. Someone had lit it on fire overnight. A pile of smoldering ash was all that remained. The duck blind was on a channel on the west side of the island. It was a good spot, and in the right wind, northeast or northwest, the duck shooting was good.

My father was a good waterfowler and knew every species of duck in flight from half a mile away, and when we saw ducks I had to be very still. I never moved a muscle as Dad blew his duck call, and the ducks would circle the duck blind until at just the right moment, he would shoot. There were few times when less than two ducks would fall from his three shots fired from his model twelve shotgun. He tried being a professional waterfowl guide for a year or two, but I think physically it was too much for him.

I would help Dad with putting out the decoys and hiding the boat, and when it was low tide, there were many times I pulled the boat over the mud flats in shallow water. Dad and our dog would sit inside the cockpit. Our dog Gunner was a Chesapeake Bay retriever, and he loved to retrieve the ducks. He was a powerful dog with the head of a lion, maybe 120 pounds. I know his head well, as when I was small I liked to bite his ear to see how much pain he could withstand. I was demented back then. I still have scars on my lip and the back of my head from when the huge dog bit me, and my whole head fit in Gunner's mouth. Mom found me in a pool of blood on the front porch. I never messed with that dog's ears again.

I started toting my own 410 shotgun when I was seven years old. I became a good shot, and Dad spoke of me to his friends, telling them how good I was and that my duck calling was getting pretty good as well. A year or so later, Gunner died, and we got a black Labrador named Black Watch. We called him Watts.

One day on a late December morning, the wind was southwest and light. It was cold, just above freezing, and Dad and I had just brought the duck boat up on the beach after hunting. He went to get the jeep and boat trailer. He turned and told me to anchor the boat. I said okay as he walked back to the jeep, and I pulled the boat up on the beach. I decided to play with the dog instead of anchoring the boat. While throwing a stick far out in the water for the dog, I heard Dad yell from the truck, "You better get that boat." I looked back to the boat and saw it had drifted off the beach and was heading out for deeper water. With my short legs and hip boots, I could not get close to it. All of our decoys and guns were in it. I started to panic, running faster with cold water coming over the tops of my boots. I stopped.

"I can't reach it!" I yelled to Dad.

He said, "You better swim for it."

I began to cry because the water was freezing. I was a scared boy and never thought I would reach the boat, which seemed so far away. But I did get it, crawled on board, and made it back to Dad and a long lecture. You would think after that I never forgot to anchor a boat again, but not true. A few years back, my dog was in a boat, I pulled it up on the beach and I got sidetracked and it started to drift away. Again, the water was deep and I swam for it, and my dog looked at me as if to say, "Did you not learn your lesson yet?"

I went to school and played with the other kids—had a few friends I think—but I loved spending time with my Dad. That was always fun... well, maybe not always. There were many lessons. He was a great teacher about the sea, nature, the weather, and he told the best stories of anyone I have ever known. He was a kind man with a good heart, and although he was making $150 a week in the sixties, he was a success. He worked hard and came home late most nights; he had four children and a mortgage.

One thing about Dad: he said what he meant, and he said things that would take years to figure out. He was a bigot, a lot like Archie Bunker, and as matter of fact, he never missed a show. It was his favorite. He seemed to have something to say about every nationality, all negative. Our family was in a book called the *Blue Book*. It listed every blue blood in Southampton, many of which belonged to the Meadow Club and Beach Club. I never understood why we were in the damn book. We had no money. It was a sham, I thought.

Mom, on the other hand, was the enforcer. She punished us for bad deeds or gave us a "just wait till your father comes home." She had a ring with a blue stone in it. I disliked the ring for years as she backhanded me with that fucker all too often. She had a way of talking to us children like we were second-class citizens, and it didn't stop until I was in my thirties. She had a habit, more so when she was drinking, to point her finger a foot from your face and say, "Now you are going to listen to me." Most of the time she didn't know what the hell she was talking about, but she thought she knew everything! Her condescending tone cut deep wounds in all of us children over the years, wounds that we would have to spend thousands of dollars and hundreds of hours in a therapist's office the rest of our adult lives trying to overcome.

Her favorite punishment was washing my mouth out with soap, which seemed to happen a lot until I was big enough to fight her off. And then there were the times she ignored us. I later came to terms with that: silence abuse, it was called. I always felt she was unhappy because of me, I thought I was defective. My sisters thought it was them, and later my brother took on that guilt.

Now Dad, on the other hand, had his own tools. His cane took me down on more than one occasion. He was often amused by the sound it made when it hit my skull, but he would do it in a loving way so I would think! Because of his polio, he couldn't run me down. My Mom usually did that for him, but once his strong grip had me, there was no escaping until the punishment was over. Sometimes he was angry, and I would get either the slipper or the spanking paddle. It was humiliating having my pants pulled down to be spanked. The paddle was flat, about two feet long, and made of wood. There was a cartoon of a boy being paddled over his father's knee on one end and a handle at the other. I hated it. There came a day, though, when I was strong enough to snap it over the bed post—and that day came when I was twelve.

There were days we were rounded up and herded the doctor's for polio shots. As children, I don't think we understood what polio was and feared we would come down with it like my father. The shots hurt, and I used to try and hide. A few years later, they came out with the medicine on a sugar cube, and the days of holding me down in the doctor's office were gone.

I think if Mom knew all that was entailed in raising children, she would have bailed, but of course no one knows. I can look back now, after years of therapy and self-discovery, and know that her self-centeredness came from wanting to be the star attraction, maybe from not getting what she needed as a child either. It created many problems. Unfortunately, she was not happy being married nor having us kids, and it seemed that pointing out to each of us as many faults as she could find made her feel better in some demented, twisted way. My Dad was a perfectionist, but he struggled with procrastination, as strange a mixture as it may seem. He always told me, "If you had listened to me, none of this would have ever happened." Affirmations, as I would come to realize, were almost impossible for both of them. It wasn't until I was in my forties that I heard many of the things I longed to hear growing up, and then it seemed too late. Carrying resentment is ugly, like a festering cancer. It eats at you from the inside, and the bitterness that you despised in one or both of your parents becomes part of you and you don't even know it is happening.

The most accurate way I could describe growing up in my house is that it was inconsistent. I never knew what would happen; sometimes it would be nothing and other times I had to duck. I remember being pushed away a lot. Mom would be in the kitchen and I'd be pulling on her apron and asking a question, and she would push me away. She was always too busy or thought that what I had to say was unimportant. Nothing I did or said was ever validated in a positive way from either of my parents, but especially from my mother. Later in life, I realized what an impact this had on me. Feeling inadequate and being rejected were major issues I had to deal with for he rest of my life.

But I did have some memories that still bring a smile to my face.

One was from a day when I was around eight years old and in the kitchen watching Mom cook. Dad was at work a lot, and I was fascinated by watching her cook. My Dad always told us that she couldn't even boil an egg when he met her. I am not sure how true that was, but if it was true, she sure learned to cook after they were married.

She was making creamed spinach in a blender. They didn't have food processors back then. She stuck the spatula in the blender while the motor was chopping up the spinach and it hit the blade. Creamed spinach flew everywhere, on the cabinets and the ceiling, but the best part was that when Mom looked up, her whole face was covered in green. I started laughing and she chased me around the house to beat me I guess, but she never caught me.

There was another time my Mom was changing my brother's diapers when he was two years old. My brother was standing on a table, and all of a sudden he urinated a stream in my mother's face like a garden hose. I was maybe seven years old, and I laughed at her. Maybe it was amusing, maybe I felt she deserved it for being the witch she was. Who knows? But I had quick feet, and she seldom caught me.

I was a normal, twisted kid, I guess, doing strange stuff like putting the cats in the dryer. I liked to hear them bumpity bump around and around. Or throw them up in the air to see if they would grab a limb or just fall fifteen feet to the ground.

There were a couple of summers when the family went to Maine for a month. Dad would rent a house from my uncle in the woods, miles away from anyone. My aunt and uncle had lived there for years and owned several homes and over fifty thousand acres of forest.

The land was practically untouched and beautiful. There were deer, bear, wolves, and moose. It was so sad years later when I heard that when he died the family had to sell it all just to pay the estate taxes. An old man named Maurice Rodrick lived up the hill from our house. He had been a fly fishing guide years ago, and my uncle introduced my father and I to him. He spent hours teaching me how to fly fish, the names of the different flies, and how to tie them to the leader. I remember one called the devil bug. It was his favorite, and I think he tied them himself. I would sometimes fish with him in the pond by our house. He was kind and patient with me.

A pond stocked with trout lay a few hundred yards from our little house. In the center was a small floating platform. Almost every night at sunset, I headed there alone to fish. I would swim to the platform with my fly rod in my hand, holding it high above my head so it would not get wet. The wind always seemed to drop off at sunset, leaving the surface of the pond glassy except for the bugs that danced on the water and splashes where the trout rose to feed on them. Some nights I caught a dozen trout, some close to a foot long. I was proud when I brought them home for dinner, thinking of how good a fly fisherman I was.

A few years ago, in a drawer in my house, I found an old picture of my father, my brother, and me in bed with pajamas on in the Maine house where we used to summer. My dad read stories to us from a book. I smiled to myself, thinking how innocent and easy life was there in that little green house on those summers. We had no television, no radio, and we would visit from time to time to have dinner at my aunt and uncle's house. Otherwise, we cooked all our meals at the house. On occasion, we would go into Phillips, a small town fifty miles from Augusta. I would always head to the drug store with my brother while my mom did some shopping. Back in those days, there were soda fountains in most of the drug stores. My brother and I would each get a vanilla milk shake. They were the best on those hot summer days and cost only twenty-five cents.

I always was sad when we headed back home to Long Island. I missed the picnics, the days spent hiking, and the fishing. My family was just different there…it was simple, and my parents got along and showed more affection toward each other.

I attended public school across the street from my grandparent's house in Southampton. The best part of my day was coming home to see Grammy for lunch. My grandparent's house smelled strange, it had that smell that old people do, a musty smell of old woman's perfume and pipe tobacco. She was a short, round woman who loved to cook and eat some too, I guess. Grammy loved me unconditionally and was the only human being who loved me that way. I trusted her attention, her interest, her smile, her touch. I knew it was real, and it was safe there. I would sit and she would ask me about my day, my friends, what I was doing in school. She thought I was smart, and I trusted her. She always greeted me with a hug and a smile; she was genuinely interested in me. Sometimes my grandfather was there on his lunch hour from the department store. He was a workaholic, I realized later, but he said very little. He never did anything with me, never took me fishing, which he liked to do alone, and never played with me. When my grandparents came to dinner at our house, he would never drink. My grandmother would have a drink, but never finish it.

There were times I would go to a friend's house after school. It was always like visiting a foreign country. The parents, or maybe just their mom, would be home. They would ask me how school was and would I like a cookie and some milk. Sometimes they hugged their children when they came through the door. Maybe it was a WASPy thing, that coolness and silence when you walked through the door to my home, but I knew there was something different from the other kids' houses, and I did not want them to see it. Part of it might have been my dad and his polio. Back then, it was called "the disease." Was I ashamed of him? Who knows exactly why a child does what he does.

As I went through grade school, things started to change. I'm not sure I can put a reason to it other than reality and growing up in the '60s. I was scared a lot. I remember not wanting to go to school the first day; we all remember that. My dad had gone to work, and I was scared. I told my mom I was scared, and she angrily said, "So what? You are going anyway. You are a baby to be scared."

I started to learn that whatever I was feeling was not to be talked about or trusted, and God forbid anyone answer a child's question. I learned not to ask. I do not know if it was the '60s or what, but we did not talk about much in our house. I later found out I was not alone.

My mother, who was hurting inside, hurt us. She did not know how to stop it. Dad did it too, but not as much. He was a perfectionist—you tried your hardest, but he would always find something wrong and point it out. When I brought home report cards, if there were As and Bs and maybe one C, guess where he always focused? You got it—on the C.

If I was working on a bike with Dad, I would hold the wrench wrong. There was always something wrong. I'm not sure if it was the criticism so much as the way my dad and mom talked to me. It was cutting and harsh. I know that demeaning tone well. I am so bothered when I sometimes let it pass my lips with friends and workers. Old habits, I guess, they die hard, even as ugly as they are

It was around this time my father went into the hospital for knee surgery. The doctors thought he would walk better if the cartilage was removed from his knee. He walked with a metal leg brace the rest of his life. My mother and his two sisters told me one day after the surgery, "Now your father will never be able to take you duck hunting again, and there are many things around the place you will have to do. And if your father does something and hurts himself it will be your fault."

That was a hell of a thing to tell an eight-year-old kid. Guilt and shame were common feelings for me. I was confused a lot. I never asked too many questions and thus I never came to grip with the truth until decades later. Dad told the story of having a business, a factory near the train station, in Southampton in 1944. The government had granted him a contract to build parts for the landing gear on bombers used in the war. He took a loan out and bought lathes and expensive presses. The war ended the following year, and the government cancelled his contract. He was forced to file bankruptcy. The property and house was put in my mom's name so it would not be lost.

Then there was the company he owned where he delivered oxygen and other gases to hospitals and welding shops all over Long Island. I think that folded up when I was six or seven, and the way Mom talked to him was degrading at times. She reminded him almost nightly of his failures. She was always good at pointing out where we screwed up. So I carried shame and embarrassment, although I didn't realize it then. I was embarrassed at my father's polio.

Some nights before dinner, they had cocktails in the living room, sitting on a lima bean green sofa that was in that room until the day he died. I often sat on the floor in the hall and overheard their conversation. I was always curious about they were talking about. Dad was always working; Mom was always looking sad, angry, and mean. It must have something to do with me, I thought back then, so I wanted to know what I was doing wrong. I remember him saying to her, "You will have to ask your father for money this week, we can't afford…" They always could not afford something. Mom always said the same thing: "I am not going to go to my father and ask for money again." She would get angrier each time my father brought it up.

She would later ask my grandfather, get some more money, and things would work out until the next time. I did not know it then, but I felt Dad was just not able to provide, not able to walk like other fathers, and thus came a lot of shame. Then I would think I should not feel that way and there was something wrong with me, so guilt would take over. It was so confusing with no one to talk to.

I still struggle at times. After a hernia surgery in my fifties, I went into a depression, and my life seemed to fall in on top of me. The surgery was a success. I was unable to lift anything for a few weeks and had to rely on people to help, but felt more and more that I was a failure, inadequate, useless, and fat.

I tried to move something in my garage one day and needed someone. It angered me. At times as a child, I saw my father struggle while working on the tractor or mower in the back yard. He would never ask for help—he was either too proud or too stubborn—and it was me now, except I lived alone with no one to help me. It frightened me. It bothered me so much that, in a matter of days, I was talking about it at Glen's, my therapist's, office. I remember Dad trying to move something in the yard, cursing with anger. I would see him and go to help him. I was good that way, but sometimes I resented that I had to help him. The mind is fascinating, and unknowingly I had made up my mind that I would always be self-sufficient. Never would I have to rely on someone, especially physically. This is probably one of the reasons I work out at the gym four days a week and take spin classes three to four days a week. I was also going through some financial fear: my taxes had come back, and my catering business was off 50 percent that summer.

It began a day earlier on a gray, rainy February afternoon when it all caught up with me. I was angry and uncomfortable—the surgeon had screwed the mesh into my stomach muscles a week before, and when I bent over the pain was strong. That afternoon, I had bought a bottle of vitamins at the store and I had them in my jacket pocket. I heard a voice telling me to take them out of my pocket, and when I bent over to pick something up in the garage, they fell to the floor and the bottle shattered. The funny thing was that I told myself I should take out the vitamins. If they broke, I knew I was going to snap. Now I look back and thank God I snapped, walked into my office, and sobbed for a half hour. I said I was a loser, going nowhere in life, that I was alone because I was a failure at relationships, on and on.

I called a friend, and we talked for a while. I felt better, and it came to me a day later at my therapist's office what was coming up. I realized I was carrying a lot of fear related to what I told myself when I was eight. I have spent thousands of dollars sitting on my therapist's sofa, close to twenty years of it, but in that session I got every dollar's worth. The mind is fascinating—how it hides, how it protects you from hurt—lies seem to be as true as the stars in the sky until the day you find out what has been hiding there. Many times I have found that beneath the anger is fear, and it hides the hurt in a very cunning way. It takes a good therapist who knows you well to bring it out. I do not even know what I was saying that day to Glen about my childhood—it was about my dad, my guilt, my fear of being like him one day—but the tears wouldn't stop. It was more work I had not done. I spent a couple sessions with him, and the fear and guilt lessened. I found out more about who I am.

THINGS APPEAR DIFFERENT

One November afternoon in 1963, while I was walking home from school, I heard that President Kennedy had been shot. I ran to my grandmother's and watched in disbelief on the television and could not understand how or why they would shoot the president. My Grammy was crying, and I sat with her. She held my hand and said, "How terrible. How could this have happened?" She said it over and over again. "He was such a good man and was doing wonderful things for this country."

Things changed in the world and my life around that time. The protected environment I had been living in, with pet geese, chickens and ducks and an apple orchard, was not really what the world was about after all. It was more unsafe than I knew.

My two older sisters had their own struggles back then, and much of the time they were not around.

I had somewhat of a normal childhood, whatever that is. I went through my public grade school in Southampton and until I was in fourth or fifth grade. I was a good kid, but then I started acting out. I was getting in trouble, skipping class and hanging around kids who were considered troublemakers. One friend, Brian, was bigger than me, and he and I got caught doing all sorts of stupid shit. One day, he was being a bully. He had broken his arm and had a hard white plaster cast. I remember being pinned on the ground, with Brian sitting on my chest and hitting me in the head with his cast. He wanted me to say that I surrendered, that he was the best. There was no way I would say it. I spit in his face, and he hit me harder and harder in the head. The rock-hard cast kept whacking my head over and over again. It hurt, and I was in rage and wanted to kill him. I never surrendered and ended up chasing him with one of those sticks with a nail in the end they used to pick up papers on the school grounds. I chased him around the schoolyard sticking him in the back and the ass, any place I could get him, until a teacher grabbed me.

Being eleven or so, I did not fully understand why I was acting out and getting into trouble. It was nothing big, just little shit. Getting negative attention was better than getting no attention.

I remember many report cards saying, "Philip does not work well with others." Boy, this was the understatement of all time. "Philip does not respect authority." Really? No shit! Around the mid-sixties, my mom wanted me to transfer to a new private school in Bridgehampton called the Hampton Day School. My sister was also acting out: she was a teenager and seemed to love dating anyone my parents told her not to. My father disliked most nationalities and had names for them all, except for being English and French as that was our heritage.

I think she was beginning to smoke pot, and Mom wanted us out of the public school. I did not want to go, but I was forced to.

It was confusing. I went to public school, but in the summer my family belonged to the WASPy beach club, and we went there almost every day. It was a lot of fun, and we would go to kid's houses on the very wealthy part of Southampton, including First Neck Lane, Ox Pasture, Meadow Lane, and I was always ashamed to bring any of them to see where I lived. Then school would start, and I would not see the rich summer kids again until the next summer. I think that at times the local kids thought I was a little rich kid, too. It was confusing to say the least and the beginning of a long struggle of not feeling I belonged.

A private school was founded near my house when I was twelve. It was great, not like school. It was disorganized, and lots of kids who were getting in trouble were now together in one place now! I went to the school for two years, and as I look back, I met one of the first girls I had a crush on there. Tina was maybe thirteen and was sexy and acted older than her age. I remember spending a spring afternoon rolling around on a beach and kissing for hours. God, she felt and smelled so good, and my heart would race whenever I saw her. It never worked out because she was dating an older guy who had drugs and a car. She was the first girl who hurt me by telling me she did not want to see me anymore. Rejection was something I never seemed to deal with well. I thought about her for years and wondered what it would be like if we had became close. Then one sad day, I heard a rumor that she died from smoking coke. I wasn't sure if it was true, but she was gone.

At the school, I made friends with a boy named Drew. He was the only child of some sort of scientist who lived in Southampton.

Drew's Dad had invented this liquid the government bought the patent for. He made the stuff in a laboratory that was attached to the house. It was some sort of liquid that was added to the crankcase of a car engine so it could run thousands of miles without any oil.

Drew was a genius at the age of twelve, and we used to make fireworks and explosives in his father's lab. It was wild. We loved blowing up shit! His house was up on a cliff, and one day we used pipes as mortars and sent a few shells out over a few fishing boats sixty feet below us and a couple hundred yards offshore in the Shinnecock Bay. They exploded in the air, and some in the water, sending up geysers of water. I don't know how we did not get caught. Can you imagine what would happen today!

Anyway, Drew was a smart kid—a little twisted, but I liked that about him. We had a still we made in the science lab, and he told the teacher it was something other than a still. We made vodka out of potatoes and tested it on the hamsters. We saw they didn't die, so we thought it was safe to drink. We drank it a few mornings before school, and finally we got caught by the teacher. He never made a big thing out of it, though, probably because he was so embarrassed that we had developed a still right under his nose!

Drew taught me different formulas for making explosives and fireworks; I loved blowing holes in the ground.

One time, my parents were away and my grandmother was staying with us. There was a huge rock that weighed a couple hundred pounds in the cellar. They had poured the floor around it when the house was built. My father always wanted to get rid of it, so I thought I would do him the favor. I drilled a hole in the rock and poured some explosive powder in the hole. I placed a steel rod in the hole and, with a heavy hammer, struck the rod, thinking this would split the rock in half.

There was an explosion. Smoke filled the cellar and wafted up the stairs into the laundry room where my grandmother was folding clothes. The steel rod had blown straight up and was stuck in the ceiling. I don't know how I didn't blow that house off the foundation as I look back now.

Years later, Drew appeared from time to time downtown. He was much crazier by then, with hair almost down to his waist! He used to fly around on a Norton 750 motorcycle with the pockets of his leather jacket filled with homegrown pot. He was growing pot in the '70s under grow lights in the lab. One night he was high, driving the bike not far from his house, and drove straight into a railroad bridge and died.

THE TASTE

I had drunk a few times before the hooch in the lab at school, maybe stealing a beer from Dad. I liked that warm and fuzzy feeling, and then the magic would happen. The magic was this: fear would disappear, and I was smarter, looked more handsome, and felt that whatever I lacked I had when drunk. I liked it so much that when I was eleven or so, I broke into a few houses near home, stole liquor, and hid it above the garage where we kept the tractors. The ladder was attached to the side of the building, and I knew no one would ever climb up there. Many nights, I would have some drinks; the once shy, inadequate boy was gone, and with liquid courage running through me, I would dial up some of the girls from school and talk to them, something I could never do when I saw them in school.

You know, I have thought back sometimes and wondered how an eleven-year-old child could be drinking without his parents knowing. Many times, I am not sure if they did not care, or maybe they were drinking themselves and did not even see it.

Nevertheless, I had found it—the feeling I had been missing. I did not need to ask questions anymore; I had the frickin' answers!

In 1967, after two years in the local day school, my parents told me I was to go to a private boys' boarding school in Massachusetts in the fall. Although both parents told me this, I knew in my heart that Dad did not want me to go and that it was mostly my Mom's idea. I felt many times that I was a problem, and in many ways I guess I was. Maybe I was acting out to get attention—there were four of us, and being a middle child I often felt lost or I acted out because I was angry and felt that no one understood me.

The summer before I left for boarding school, I had fun. Hell, I was thirteen years old with no responsibilities and girls were looking better and better and I started going to parties. I was introduced to smoking pot that summer, but booze was what I liked. I remember one of the first dances I attended was at a local tennis club in Southampton. It was a tennis club for the rich and famous, and although I did not fit either category, I crashed it. I started with a friend, drinking some of his parent's vodka. We drank vodka and tonics—my first and last for a long time.

Long story short, I just wanted to get that buzz, be able to have fun and be the life of the party, find a young girl and then…well, I did not even know what I was to do with her, but I am sure it would have been great! Great it was not—that evening, I was found on the sofa in the club with vomit all over me. I was asked to leave. I was asked to leave a few places that summer at thirteen years old. I would be at a party having fun, then it would be three in the morning and I would wake up. Not one person would be left, and I would walk home. Amazingly, back then I rarely felt bad the next day, but I would not drink for a day or two.

I started surfing that summer, and many days I rode to Montauk with my cousin in his parent's VW bug convertible to catch the waves. I always had some weed; it made us better surfers, or so we thought. We would stop in Amagansett at the same Coke machine every trip and put in a dime, pull the handle, and a glass bottle of Coke would drop down with a thump. With our cottonmouth, Coke was like some magic elixir that gave us a boost to be ready for the waves. The summer went by pretty fast, and in late August, I packed and got ready to take the trip to boarding school. At home, my sisters had left and were working in NYC, and my brother Eben was maybe seven years old. I don't remember anyone seeing me off and wishing me well when I left.

That September of 1968, I arrived at boarding school and had no idea what I was getting myself into. I showed little emotion to my parents as I gave them a hug and they left. The dress code included a suit and tie with a blue blazer, but I did not even know how to tie a tie. One of the boys in the dorm helped me each morning to tie my tie before breakfast. My room, at eight feet by eight feet, was less than half the size of my room at home and had a wall around each side that went up six feet. Above that there was a second floor with glass, where on occasion you could see one of the boys from the second floor of the dorm peering down at you, sometimes in the middle of the night. It spooked me. I cried myself to sleep for weeks, it seemed. I cried into my pillow so the other boys would not hear me and think I was a wimp.

I had never made my own bed, done my own laundry, or cleaned up after myself. Abandonment wreaked havoc in me. "What could I have done so wrong to be sent away like this?" I thought. I felt and thought that I was bad. I felt that way about myself for fourteen years.

I learned quickly about how to take care of myself and made some friends. Two of the boys I knew from back home at the beach club went there, so I at least knew a couple boys. They told me to watch out for this one blond boy; he had a habit of molesting the other boys. This blond-haired kid was a big fat kid, and I remember his eyes being close together. Many of the boys feared him. I learned how to have a crazy look in my eye. Part of it was a bluff, and part of it was true. I was a little crazy. He stayed away from me, and later in the school year I heard that a bunch of the boys went into his room in the middle of the night, tied him up, and rubbed Bengay all over his balls for messing with one of the younger boys.

The school year seemed to crawl by. At Thanksgiving, my parents said they did not have enough money for me to travel back to Long Island, and I stayed at school. There were a couple other boys there also. It hurt that money was more important to my parents than I was. It bothered me a lot, but I never would speak of what I was feeling to anyone.

I was caught always doing something against the rules. I hated rules and authority for years. I was allowed to go to my Uncle Bill's place in Dedham one weekend, but the rest of the time I had demerits. My punishment was to sit in study hall and pick up papers in the yard with a stick with a nail in the end of it.

Uncle Billy was a great guy. I loved him, and he always brought us the best Christmas presents. The gifts were always unique and special, and we knew that thought went into each gift. Uncle Billy wore the same clothes and had the same car for many years; he made very little money. He was single—his wife had been an Olympic figure skater and had committed suicide years before, and he never remarried.

When I stayed there one weekend, we went sightseeing and then he cooked dinner. Actually, his girlfriend came and cooked, and Uncle Billy did the drinking. After dinner, she left and I went up to bed. Around midnight, I was awakened by a huge crash downstairs. Scared of what I might find, I slowly stepped down the stairs and found poor Uncle Billy on the kitchen floor. He had tipped over the table and was muttering something while on his back. I thought he was hurt, but he wasn't. He was just real drunk. He yelled at me and told me he was fine and to go back to bed. I left him there and went back upstairs to my bed.

It terrified me. I had never been with anyone in that condition. He was my uncle. Would I find him dead on the floor in the morning? I kept worrying as I tried to fall asleep.

The next morning I woke up and was scared to go down to the kitchen. I heard noise downstairs, so I walked down to find his girlfriend cooking breakfast and everything cleaned up like nothing ever happened.

It was my first insight to see what a real drunk was. Uncle Billy was a sweet man with a great heart, but he had the awful disease of alcoholism and never had a chance to get sober. He wore a patch on one eye later in life from a fall he took in the apartment. He had fallen and took out his eye on the corner of the coffee table.

It was a family thing, I suspect. When something happened because of drinking or being inappropriate, you said nothing as if it never happened.

The school year went by fairly quickly after Christmas. As far as sports went, I was on the soccer, basketball, and lacrosse teams. I enjoyed sports and was good at them. I had a shorter than usual temper, though, and sometimes it got me in trouble. We played prep school kids who were several years older and a lot stronger and bigger than we were. I'm not sure of the reasoning for playing these teams, but it is what we did.

Lacrosse is a tough game. I played defense and was good at it. Being a defensive back, it was my job to keep the other team from reaching the goal. One day, a bigger kid took me out a couple times and blindsided me once so they scored. Another time, he swung his lacrosse stick across my shins when the ref was not looking and the ball was nowhere near us. I went down hard and got up and chased him down. I knocked him down and swung the stick over and over at this kid until they pulled me off him. I was ejected from the game and my coach yelled at me, but I did not care. I knew I had hurt him, and that was good in my book. I left the game.

Once in a while, there would be a school dance and some girls from a neighboring girls' school would be bussed in. I had gone a couple times to local charm school dance on Hill Street back home and it was the same.

The large room was lined with chairs where the boys sat on one side and the girls sat on the other.

We would have a dance every other month. I hated them and was always one of the last boys sitting before a teacher would make me ask one of the remaining girls to dance. By that time, all the cute girls would be dancing, and I would get stuck with one of the leftovers. I was a shy boy anyway, and it was funny once I started dancing to think, "What was I worried about anyway?" The other boys were used to it. They had been in boarding schools there whole lives, but it was all new for me.

After the dance, we would all lie about how cute the girls were and some of us would claim to have kissed the girls outside during the dance.

In May 1969, I received a diploma from private school, and my parents were happy that I had graduated. My grades were not perfect, of course, but they were good enough for me to go home to Long Island and enjoy the summer. In the fall, I was to attend a prep school in Connecticut. That boarding school has sent me alumni letters for over forty years now, and they all have been thrown in the garbage can. There are no fond memories of that school and nothing I want to remember. Something did happen that year—maybe it was being alone, maybe it was good to have discipline— but I wanted no responsibility that summer.

I was so relieved and felt more free than I had ever felt when I returned to Long Island.

The day after I came home from school I said to my parents, "ok, I have done what you asked and went to private school, now I am going to do what I want to this summer".

They never said anything. I was fourteen, and I meant what I said, dammit! Now girls were looking really good, and besides the dances up in school, I had not even seen a girl my age in over a year and had not had sex yet. There had been a time the year before when one of the hottest summer girls in town asked me to meet her at the beach one night. There were rumors that she was into sex, and I went there with every intention to get her naked. We were both thirteen, and with a bottle of wine, I hoped it would happen. Everything went as planned. We did end up naked together on a blanket under the stars. What was not planned was that she did not drink so I finished the bottle, and thanks to whiskey dick, I remained a virgin that summer.

Anyway, this summer would be different, and even though I had no idea exactly what sex was all about, I wanted a lot of it, soon.

It was late May when I get home, and I often went to town in the early evening. There were a lot of young kids hanging around what we used to call "the corner." I bumped into a guy who had sold me a nickel bag of pot the summer before, along with a few other guys, and that was where it all happened. The kids my age were still in school and had to be home early, but I hung out with the older guys and girls. Some had Ramblers or VWs, some had vans, and we would meet and take a drive, maybe to the woods, maybe to the beach, to smoke pot and drink.

Since I had left for boarding school, a lot of things had changed around town—most of all, I had changed. I was in a strict school that made me cut my hair every two weeks and wear a damn tie and blazer, along with shoes that had to be shined every week. I had to wake up at 6:00 a.m., make my bed, and go to classes all day. Now I was waking up when I wanted and doing what I wanted, wearing bell-bottom jeans and T-shirts full of burn holes. Back then, we did not clean the seeds from pot so they would pop while smoking joints and embers would hit your shirt. Sometimes you would be smoldering, and if you were good and stoned, you might not notice it until the ember burned through your shirt! You could always tell who got stoned a lot.

An amazing thing happened that I had never felt before: a sense of having friends, a sense of being accepted, a sense of belonging. I was cool, and my friends had many names for me. They called me "Philip the Pipe" or just "The Pipe." I always had the best weed, hash, or something else.

There were concerts everywhere. In New York City, I saw Led Zeppelin play in Central Park. At the Filmore East, I saw many concerts, including Mountain with Leslie West, the Steve Miller Band, Canned Heat, and Santana. There was a club called the Playground in Southampton that opened up, and on July 3, I saw Jethro Tull. On the Fourth of July, I even saw Johnny Winter and Edgar Winter play, and I gave Johnny a joint rolled in a red, white, and blue rolling paper. He said, "Thanks, kid," and lit it up while tuning his guitar. He was awesome that night, and somehow I the joint I gave him helped him be great.

The best bands in decades were all making music: Creedence Clearwater, Jefferson Airplane, the Doors, Janis Joplin, Jimi Hendricks, the Stones, the Allman Brothers. Many would die from drugs: Janis, Jimi, Stevie Ray, Jim Morrison—they were dropping like flies. I can remember doing a hit of LSD sunshine that summer while listening to Led Zeppelin and actually floating out of a car window. My friend grabbed my foot as I hung in the air over the roof of the car. It was an adventure each day, and I would bump into someone with a new drug and have some great hash or trip on something.

There was one period when I lived in the woods with some other hippies. We would surf or hit the town during the day and come to the campsite at night.

It was said that marijuana led to other drugs. We all used to say that was horseshit. All I know was that summer I did something with three letters or three numbers every day: LSD, DMT, PCP, MDA. Then there were downers like reds, yellow jackets, tueys, 714s, or Quaaludes. The real ludes, or lemons, were called leg spreaders or gorilla biscuits—we had names for all of it. And then there were uppers like dexies, white crosses, black beauties, crystal meth, and on and on. Pot was named for where it was grown, with names like Panama Red, Michoacán, Acapulco Gold, and Thai sticks. There was hash, too, usually in blond, red, or black, plus hash oil. It was endless. I tried almost all of it that summer, even heroin, cocaine, and opium. I think smoking good opium was my favorite high. It had a cool menthol taste; then a numbing, sleepy state took over, and everything had a blue haze around it.

There was LSD in many forms: blotter, barrels, wedges, cubes, and more. MDA was another favorite drug. It made you love everyone and everything—now they call it ecstasy. It was endless, and in the middle of all of it there was a girl.

The first time I met her she was in a friend's car. She wore a red headband and bell-bottom jeans with a Grateful Dead T-shirt. She had long brown, shining hair and dark brown, doll eyes that seemed not to have any pupils even when she was high. She had the look of an Indian until she spoke, and then her Italian twang from Brooklyn would ring out. She was sexy, and I had never seen a body like hers.

"Hi, my name is Nancy," she said.

I shook her warm, soft hand and said, "I am Philip." I was stoned that whole summer, including when I met Nancy, so I can't really say how many times we had sex that summer, but it was a lot. Some days we did not even say much to each other. We got high, had sex, and laughed a lot—we called them the ho-hos. We'd be so stoned and laughing so hard that tears would roll down our cheeks, and we just could not stop laughing. They were fun times back then, things were easy.

I am not sure exactly what happened. It was not like we were making dates to meet each other. We just sort of bumped into each other and then we'd end up in my bedroom at my house. You didn't call it a relationship. It was just known that Nancy was my girl, and if she did have sex with someone else, I never knew it because I was stoned or tripping every day. There was never a feeling that I was in love, it was all so new to me. Having a girl, having sex almost every day, and being stoned to the bone was all a blur.

Nancy and I went out for a few months. I lost contact with her a couple years later, and in the '80s I heard she had gotten some pure heroin and overdosed and died.

I was fourteen years old when I went to Woodstock...what a show. I don't mean the concert as much as all the people—it was something I had never seen before or since. There were four of us who went: Robert, a guy named Al, Bazooka, and me. Robert was maybe twenty at the time; he had red, curly hair and a handlebar moustache that was on the verge of being orange. He was heavyset and maybe six feet tall. Robert and I always hung out that summer. I knew where to get the best drugs, and if I didn't, he did.

Al knew where we could get some pot for the trip to Woodstock, so on the way upstate we stopped in a pizza parlor in Queens to pick up some weed. We got there, and Al did the purchase. At the counter, he told the guy he wanted a pizza with double mushrooms…that was the code. The guy told him to wait in the back parking lot. The parking lot in the back held about forty cars, so we stood by Robert's green Javelin and the guy with the weed walked over. Just as he showed us the four ounces of weed, three unmarked cop cars pulled into the lot with the tires squealing, sending hippies and narcs running. Our guy dropped the pot at our feet and jumped over a fence with two narcs chasing him. We just stood there, never moving a muscle. A cop ran up to us and told us not to move. We didn't, and he ran after some guy. After a minute, we picked up the quarter pound and jumped in the car and took off. I can remember we were all laughing, smoking the bong, and hooting as we were going over the Throggs Neck doing over a hundred miles an hour. We got away with it again. That seemed to be the way it was back then—the excitement was all about doing it and getting away with it all. We loved it.

As we drove up to Woodstock, you could barely see in the car because of all the smoke. Filling a car with smoke is what we did a lot. Some nights, four or five of us kids would get together in one of their father's car and park in "the pit" and smoke for hours. I remember smoking twenty-six joints one night with the windows rolled up. It was amazing we didn't suffocate. His dad used to yell at this kid the next day because his car would smell like duck shit.

We arrived a few miles from the concert and had to walk as the New York State Troopers would not let us go any further. There were lines of people walking past the "hat man," as we called the troopers. The troopers were told not to bust anyone as the powers that be did not want to start a riot. Hippies were smoking pot and blowing smoke at the troopers as they past. When we arrived at the gate, there were hundreds of people swaying the twelve-foot chain link fence back and forth. We had no tickets, and neither did many others. I will never forget the people standing on top of other people's shoulders, with more people on top of their shoulders. The fence swayed back and forth, and with the weight of all the people, the fence had to come down, and it did. There was a rush of hundreds, maybe a thousand, people cheering and running into the concert area. A few minutes later, an announcer said, "Woodstock is now a free concert," and everyone cheered.

There were green, rolling hills and a deep bowl, maybe a half-mile across, with a huge bandstand at the bottom and scaffolds that held speakers almost a hundred feet in the air. It was an amazing sight. There were several thousand people sitting on the ground near the bandstand, so we just followed the masses and joined them down below. It was a hot, humid, cloudy afternoon, so we wore our bell-bottom jeans and T-shirts. Most everyone was dressed the same way. Some were not as stoned as we were and had thought about bringing chairs, and some even had umbrellas.

We sat down, and Al and Bazooka said they would be right back. They walked back up to the top of the bowl. There were food concessions and bathrooms there, or so someone had said. We never saw them again.

The bands were tuning instruments and getting the sound right while Robert and I smoked a few bongs. A couple hours went by, and I told Robert I was heading to the bathrooms. When we had sat down, we were in the last row. Now I stood up and was stunned to see three hundred rows of people behind us. Robert said, "Forget it. You will never find your way back." I said I would find my way back and started walking up the aisle and tried to remember where I had come from. I found the bathrooms—they were disgusting, as you can imagine—and started my way back. It was getting dark. I had looked for Robert for a half hour when I gave up and sat down next to some hippie dude. He handed me a joint, and I sat there wondering what would happen to me. Just at that moment, I heard a familiar cough and laugh. I looked down the row, maybe thirty or so people down, and there he was. I couldn't believe my eyes.

All I can tell you is that we danced in the rain, got high, and slept in the mud. No one seemed to mind. It was warm, and lying in the mud felt kind of good. There was an announcement: "We have a warning, please do not take the brown acid." Hundreds groaned in the crowd around us. "It has strychnine in it." There was more groaning, then the announcer said, "Please proceed to the medical tent." Strychnine was used sometimes to cut acid. It was rat poison and gave you a bad trip. We were lucky and just smoking that day. The announcer introduced another band, and the loud music began playing again. People danced in the rain, cheered, and sang.

One band after another played through the night. We danced, drank, smoked, and smoked some more, and finally I passed out in the mud with the hundreds of thousands who had come to be there at Woodstock. I awoke the next morning around sunrise. It was raining harder, and we both were shivering. I'm not sure who was playing, maybe Jefferson Airplane. The rest is still a blur.

If you were at Woodstock, you were cool, and I did not wash my bell-bottoms for two weeks as they had mud stains up to the knees. It meant you were part of that great time. Two weeks later, this kid Ed showed up at the corner wearing muddy jeans. He had taken a detour to California in a VW van with some people who had some good mescaline he said.

That summer lasted an eternity. It seemed every day was an adventure with my new friends. I felt accepted and loved for the first time in my life. I fit in, and I felt important and appreciated. I made people laugh, and they listened to what I had to say. It may or may not have been real, but it did not matter. We all knew each other, and we hung and clung to each other. We had what we felt and needed so desperately at that time in our lives. It was love.

I knew a kid from boarding school who knew where to get drugs in New York City, and he took me there one hot July morning to the Lower West Side and introduced me to his connection. The guy looked like a member of the Grateful Dead. His name was Bruce, and we sat down at a table and he asked what we wanted. Before I knew it, the bearded man dumped a pile of coke on a mirror and said to try it and went into the other room to make a phone call. I had a line or two, and my friend must have snorted a gram in two hits. The dealer came back and most of the pile was gone. My friend's eyes were watering. He said he had no money, and the guy kicked him out. The dealer said I needed to go too, but I told him I had money and that I barely knew this guy. I kicked my friend under the bus. My new connection closed the door and let me stay. I saw him at least twice a week that summer and took the train back to the Hamptons with a suitcase half full of pot, hash, and sometimes cocaine. I was fourteen and making more money in a day than my father made in a month at his full-time job.

A few weeks later, my dealer left me alone in his living room, and I stole a couple grams of coke. He sensed I was nervous. He confronted me, and I denied stealing it. He took a pistol out of his desk and loaded a bullet in the cylinder and gave it a spin, then put it to my head and waited for me to react. I didn't, and then he pulled the trigger. The hammer fell in an empty chamber and went click. I jumped from the table, went nuts, and told him he was crazy and headed for the door. He grabbed me and said it was just a test, that if I had stolen coke I would have folded, but I didn't. He laughed, put the gun away, and we became business partners.

You would think I would have learned my lesson and never stolen from him again, wouldn't you? A year or so later, when he went in the other room of his apartment to talk on the phone, I reached into a trunk that held two hundred bricks of Michoacán and stuffed two of them in my pants. I was wearing a long rain coat. That was the last time I did business on West 17th Street.

There were some funny times where we were high. I can remember a hot summer day when Mom and Dad were at the beach and four of us were tripping on MDA It was a great drug and made you love everyone and everything. It looked like an antacid tab. When you ate one, an hour later you became a child again, and all the world was new and beautiful. It was not like acid or mescaline, when someone could turn into a werewolf or their face would start melting right in front of you. This shit was the "love drug," and I never heard of anyone having a bad experience with it.

Well, there were four of us on that hot summer day, naked, yelling, and laughing like children while running up and down in the lawn sprinkler. Nancy, another girl, Robert, and I were just doing what we felt was perfectly appropriate for that hot day. At least until my parents came home and walked out to the orchard and started yelling at us! We bolted through the back, grabbed our clothes on the way, and I did not come home for several days. Nothing was said to me about the sprinkler incident.

There were a couple other concerts I went to that summer. One was in Powder Ridge, Connecticut. It headlined lots of great bands, and a friend named Gary and I decided it would be great to go there by bicycle. It seemed a good idea at the time. I had a bottle of white crosses (speed), so we took a few at five o'clock that hot August morning and started peddling. We took the ferries across Shelter Island to the North Fork, and then from Orient Point to New London. That was the easy part. We stopped on the way, took more white crosses, drank some water, and kept peddling. I think we each did fifteen or so each by the time we got to Powder Ridge, which was a ski area in the winter. As we got closer to the mountain, we walked our bikes because it was so steep. We arrived a little after dark, and when I laid on the ground for the first time in sixteen hours, my body ached from exhaustion yet my eyes were open so wide you would have thought I grabbed a 220-volt line!

The next day, we could barely walk. Our legs had cramped up something fierce.

It was the strangest thing—you would always bump into people you knew from home at these concerts, and it never mattered how many thousands of people were there. Nancy and a couple of other girls had hitchhiked up there, and we decided to go down the road where we had seen a waterfall and take a dip. It was beautiful. I am sure we were stoned as we walked down the rocks. And there, with bars of soap and naked, we washed each other in the cool, clear water of a twenty-foot waterfall only fifty yards from the road. We were there for a while when a cameraman and a woman with a microphone came through the bushes and announced they were from some news network and wanted our permission to interview us. We answered questions they asked, and they interviewed us for five minutes. We thought it was cool, being TV stars and all.

I am not sure which friend's house or what camping trip I told my parents I was attending that weekend, but they knew after the nightly news exactly where their fourteen-year-old son was: the Powder Ridge Music Festival, naked as a jaybird in a waterfall with some hippies! That one I heard about. "You have disgraced the family" Mom said. Dad disapproved, too, but with the twinkle in his eye and the laugh wrinkles that showed in the corner of his eye, I knew he got a kick out of seeing me there.

That summer, I never worked and always had money. Whether I stole money or dealt some drugs, it all seemed innocent enough, and I never thought I was hurting anyone. Most of all, I had friends and felt more independent than I had ever had in my life.

Sex, drugs, and rock 'n' roll were here to stay—at least I thought so.

When I was fourteen years old, someone introduced me to snorting heroin. There were times I would head into the city with Nancy and a couple of black guys and go into Harlem. I remember getting out of the car one night with these guys in Harlem and thinking it was all over. I did H with other guys. Many of them have died since, some from AIDS, some from hep C, and most from overdosing. At first I snorted it, then I began mainlining it. A month or two went by, and my habit grew to fifteen bags a day. I loved the warm and fuzzy feeling that came over me after booting it. I started needing lots of money and was too stoned most of the time to work, so I stole what I could. I began feeling out of control, obsessed with not having enough. My skin would crawl when I did not have enough in my system, or I would be sick like never before. This desperate feeling of being mentally and physically dependent was not right. People knew and tried to talk to me. Many other kids who were doing smack went on methadone to help with the withdrawal. I knew of many who had been doing methadone for years. I decided to go cold turkey. I sweated, puked, shook with fever, and poured sweat like bullets. It lasted for several days. They said I only had a chippy. I would never touch that shit ever again.

I liked smoking weed and smoked a UPS truck of it until I was twenty-seven. It was safe. So I liked pot and the booze that I trusted would be my friend forever—I was to find out later that it would become my downfall. Blow was another story. I loved the high I got when I was going to cop it, the rush I got when I snorted the first line, but then it was all catch up and I never caught up. I was trying to recapture the high of the first rush and never could, and I would spend all the money I had to try and get there.

One late August day, my parents and I had a talk about school. There was a private boys school in Connecticut where good little WASP boys went to become smart little WASP men.

I screamed, yelled, stamped my feet, and said I wouldn't go, but I was told that my grandfather would lose $3,000 unless I attended. My hair at this point was down to my shoulders, and they wanted me to cut it all off. I said there was no fucking way anyone was touching my hair, it was part of who I was now and that would take away my coolness. "You will not use that language to your mother," Dad said. I knew he realized that I was more than he could handle, so grabbing me wasn't going to happen. In my early years, Mom would wash out my mouth with soap, but those days were long gone as well.

I finally said that I would go and that was the end of that. The last few days, I spent saying good-bye to my new friends. I felt closer to many of those kids than my family. They knew me, accepted me, and I thought loved me. Plus, it was an all-boys school, and I was not digging that either. But I said good-bye to Nancy and readied myself for the dreaded trip back to boarding school.

It was a cool August day when my parents drove me to boarding school. As usual, silence permeated the car the whole ride, and I started to feel like the broken toy or damaged goods, always embarrassing the family name. I felt like I was being put in a place that would teach me some manners and responsibility. They would not have to deal with me anymore. I would be out of their hair once and for all.

At this point, I was a true rebel and hated authority and any system that told me what to do, when to do it, and how I was supposed to do it. I hated it all: parents, cops, teachers, even other kids who were conforming to the system. That night, and many nights after, I cried myself to sleep. The abandonment and rejection were so strong I wanted to die. I would call my parents and cry, telling them I hated it there and that I wanted to come back to public school where my friends were. My mother hurt me by saying that I had to stay two more weeks or Grandfather's $3,000 would be lost. She kept mentioning the money each time we talked. Finally, after two weeks, they came up and got me and brought me home. I tried not to be happy in the car ride home, but I was jumping for joy. There were tons of rules living at home. I broke them all in the first month probably.

I always wonder what would have happened if I stayed at that boarding school, gone to collage, gotten a yuppie job afterward, and conformed to that yuppie way of life, with a plastic personality full of ass-kissing and falseness. I have seen many of them at the beach club in the summers, ass-holes with flowered lily Pulitzer pants and a pink, puke green, or bright yellow golf shirt. They used words like "Mummy" and "Daddy" even though were thirty or forty.

Adjusting to public school took time, but there were many friends from the summer there. I was hospitalized in the early fall as I had a bad trip, and from that point forward I stayed away from acid. It was at the Fillmore East in New York City, front row of the balcony, watching Mountain. I had taken a hit of blotter, and after an hour I was not coming on to it, so I took two hits to make sure I would enjoy the concert. I had taken too much shit and was having a bad trip. It was like seeing a horror movie, but you are in the leading role. I was standing on my chair, and I fell and hit my head on the brass rail of the balcony. I got a concussion while peaking on the acid.

After the concert, I was with some of my friends as we headed to the subway. We walked down the stairs and everyone was putting a token into the turnstile and walking through. I was so stoned that I could not put it together, and no one helped me, so I walked under the turnstile. It did not take long before the cops grabbed me and my friends left me...some friends. I remember bits and pieces. The cops beat me up pretty good, like they enjoyed doing to guys with long hair. They asked me my name, but I could not remember it, nor where I lived, so they beat me with sticks over and over again. I finally was put on the street, where I walked from midnight until seven Sunday morning. My legs throbbed from muscle cramps, probably from the drugs and all the walking. There were knots on my head the size of lemons, and several of my ribs ached from the clubbing. I kept walking, trying to find some number or street I would remember. I walked from the West Side to the East Side, all the way downtown and all the way up the nineties. The fans that blew air from huge buildings made me imagine that the buildings were somehow alive. During that night, there were lots of crazy people and perverts who wanted me to come with them. I came out of a blackout at one point in some guy's apartment, not knowing how I got there, and I ran out of the place. To this day, I am not sure what had happened there. I kept walking. My legs ached from the combination of exhaustion and the strychnine in the acid. I was in the mid-sixties around Third Avenue when I finally started to remember my name and numbers, and I eventually found my friend's apartment. I was in a bad way, babbling a lot. Later that afternoon, when my friends dropped me off, I could barely speak and my pupils were completely black, even in the daylight. I looked like Charlie Manson.

My so-called friends would not leave me at my driveway—the left me on the lower road several hundred yards from my house. When I walked to the back field behind the house, I looked up into the blue sky. I had an out-of-body experience and saw myself from what seemed twenty feet, and then I looked down at my body from a hundred feet, then higher, until all

I could see was darkness and the blue earth below. Then I fell back into my body and collapsed. When I walked into the house, I spoke a couple words to my mom and dad and was sent to the hospital, where I did the Thorazine shuffle for a few days. My parents freaked, and I started seeing a shrink for a while, although I hated him. He was full of very stupid questions.

Mostly, he asked me why I got high and drank the way I did. My answer was simple: it made me feel good. I don't know if was the cost or my lack of interest, but after a few months I stopped going.

In the first year of high school, I was stoned every day on something. Most of the kids I hung with were toast as well. I often snuck out late or had a girl come to the house late at night and slept through most of my classes the next day. I had study hall before lunch and used to sell joints for a dollar each. Kids would stand in a line by my desk, and the teacher would look the other way. I had passed algebra in boarding school, but I took it as a freshmen in high school again and failed it. I failed most of my classes that year. I sold a lot of pot and hash and was making over a thousand dollars some weeks.

A year or so later, cars were looking good to me. The cool kids had cars—most of them drove their dad's—but they still had their own cars, something all boys approaching sixteen looked forward to. It was the spring of 1970 when I passed my test and started driving my dad's red Oldsmobile Cutlass. I think it was a 1968 and had a 350 with 325 horsepower. Burning rubber was something of a status symbol. You developed a knack for it: just let it coast in reverse and then drop it into gear and ride the gas and burn rubber. The right rear tire would go bald after a few days of this, so I would change tires and two weeks after my Dad had gotten new tires they were all bald again. He would complain to the tire guy that he was selling defective tires. Today I look back: my father was making $150 a week maybe, and a set of tires probably cost half a week's pay.

The '68 Olds did not last long after I received my driver's license. I hit both guardrails of the Seven Ponds Bridge by my house, a fire hydrant going forty in reverse, and many mailboxes as I dozed off driving home. The cops found an opened quart of vodka in the car the night I hit the bridge. They let me go and told me to walk home, and the car was towed. One night a couple months later, I got in a fight with a girl I was dating. She told me she did not want to see me anymore. Feeling rejected and abandoned, I left the party driving like a madman. I wanted the pain to go away. I was angry and had no idea what hurt I was feeling. Driving faster and faster, I remember looking at the speedometer approaching a sharp corner—it read 90 mph. I slid sideways and hit a pole, snapped it in half, and then hit the biggest oak tree on my road. The tree, five feet in diameter, did not move, and my friend who was in the passenger seat got a lot of facial cuts when the hood rolled up into the windshield. I ducked to the floor when I saw the tree coming, and it saved my life as the steering column drove into the driver's seat as the car struck the tree. I was lucky and needed some stitches in my knee, but that was it. This began a series of car wrecks that lasted until I was twenty-seven, for many of which I never got a ticket from the police.

After that night, I would not be allowed to drive my parents' cars, for good reason, and Dad took a total loss on that car. He had taken the collision insurance off just a month before.

Before my mom left when I was nineteen, she tried to enforce some laws, but no one listened. We were like "wild Indians" back then, always getting into trouble. They would find drugs, or I would be in trouble in school. She was always unhappy, but she had been unhappy for years. Mom talked to us in a mean, condescending way and did hurtful things to get even.

I remember a sad time when I was sixteen or seventeen and I was looking for old Black Watts, our black Labrador. He was having trouble walking and was almost twelve years old. He had hunted with my dad and me when I was a young boy. Watts loved me and would do anything for me.

I remember years before, I was with my dad on a cold gray day down at the pond where we hunted. The pond was frozen, and I saw a duck out on the ice. I sent the dog to retrieve it. As Watts ran out on the ice, Dad yelled at me to stop the dog as the ice was not very thick. I yelled to the dog, but he never stopped. Watts was one hundred yards from shore when he fell through the ice. He thrashed around, but he could not get back on the ice. Each time he tried to climb back up on the ice, another piece would break off and he would slide back into the cold water, his front paws clawing at the ice again and again. I wanted to run out there and save the dog I loved. He would have done it for me. But Dad yelled, "Don't you go out there!" Then he yelled, "If that dog drowns out there, it will be your fault." With tears streaming down my face, I called and pleaded for Black Watts to not give up. Sick with panic, fear, and guilt for what I had done, I stayed there for an hour until the dog made it back to the shore and I helped him back on the ice.

Watts was completely exhausted when we got him back to the jeep, and the poor dog could hardly walk. I held him in my arms all the way home and talked to him, telling him he would be all right. In the background I could hear my father scolding me for what I had done. There was no room for mistakes growing up—they were not allowed, you did things right. I hated making mistakes and found later in life that not finishing tasks or ideas was easier because no one could say I had failed. Procrastination became a way of life for me, just like it was for my father. We got back to the house and lit a fire and dried off Watts. He stayed by the fire and slept for two days. I tried to feed him, but he would not drink water or eat food.

So here I was, years later, searching for Watts. I looked around the house and outside and could not find him. I asked my mother if she had seen him, she said, "It's about time you missed him, we put him to sleep a week ago." I think my brother was there too; we both broke down and cried. I felt guilty, sad, and ashamed all at the same time. No one ever talked about the dog again, and I never forgave her for doing that to my friend. She was so cruel and hurtful at times, like she enjoyed it all in a sick, demented way. Some of what she said may have been true—not caring and being stoned, a week would go by, and it was possible not to notice Watts. Many years went by before I forgave myself, and that may be the reason I have loved all my dogs since and why I panic today when my dog is missing even for five minutes.

When I reached seventeen, I liked having my own car. I worked after school sometimes, on weekends, and in the summer. I worked at a lot of things like painting houses and carpentry, but clamming, scalloping, and fishing were always my favorite. It did not seem like you were working out there on the bay. And I could always sell a few ounces of weed to put money in my pocket.

That summer, I met a girl who worked as a nanny for a rich family from the beach club. She was seventeen and had strawberry blonde hair, blue eyes, and a beautiful face with freckles. She had a firm, young body that would not quit. I think it was the first time I fell for a girl in that way; I wanted to walk into the sunset with her. When I was with her, I was on my best behavior, I would try not to be too high and not drink to excess. I would say, "No kidding" instead of "No shit."

Lindsay and I never had sex. We came close a couple times, and I wanted her in the worst way. That's what I began to feel that if we had sex, I had "sealed the deal" and she was mine and would never leave me. Being rejected and abandoned was something I did not know about back then, and I almost never let my guard down and let a girl get too close, but Lindsay was different. She was smart, classy, and had a wonderful smile that lit a fire in my heart, and I spent many hours thinking of us together. When that summer ended, we made plans to see each other again in a week or two. I remember driving to her parent's house in New Jersey on a rainy night in my Fiat "lunch box" as I called it. It was a four-door that I bought for $500. It was the only car I owned that I didn't destroy while drunk. There was always something needing repair in that car. The day I drove to her house in New Jersey, a fuse had blown in the windshield wipers and I could barely see the wet highway. I had to roll the window down to see where I was going, but I knew what awaited me and I could not stop. Now, you have to picture me with shoulder-length hair, coming from a middle class family, and going to high school. I was wearing bell-bottomed blue jeans and a T-shirt that probably said something derogatory on it with burn holes in the front, thinking I was going to impress her parents. As I pulled up the driveway, I saw that Lindsay's house was nicer than mine and there were a couple of new cars in the driveway.

Lindsay met me at the door and gave me a hug. Then I met her parents. As I remember, I did not feel all warm and fuzzy about their reaction in seeing me. It was Saturday night, and after meeting her parents we sat in her room and talked some, then her parents showed me where I was to sleep that night. Lindsay and I hung out and watched a movie and kissed a little. Sunday afternoon came quickly, and when I was leaving, Lindsay wanted to sit outside and talk, which we did. It was a warm September afternoon, and I was about to have the wind taken out of me. She gave me a line I would use many times later in life, about how we were different and how it just would not work out. We lived too far from each other. I said I understood, but I just wanted to end our talk. I felt a lump in my throat and a familiar knot in my stomach. I felt I had been punched, but I knew I could not show any emotion. I left her house and turned down the road and it hit me. I cried for the whole three hours from New Jersey. At times, I could not even see the road and did not really care if I hit someone or not. The next few weeks were a drunken mess, but I told no one about what had happened, lest they think I was a loser. I kept it all inside and drank as much as I could to make it go away. I thought it went away eventually, but this and many other things would all come back one day tenfold.

I somehow made it through high school and graduated at the age of nineteen. There were some fun times, but I was happy to be done with school. I now was called "Cool Phil from Water Mill" and had some friends, but I always had that aching feeling that I did not belong and was on the outside looking in. I was a chameleon and acted the way each person would like me to be; I never knew who I really was. I was a good-looking kid in high school. I almost never had acne, and I had dark brown, puppy dog eyes and chestnut colored shoulder-length hair. I was lean and starting to fill out with a chest and strong arms like my dad. I dated some of the hottest girls in school, and my ego loved it.

I told them what they wanted to hear so I could have wild and crazy sex, but I never wanted to get too close.

Through my senior year, I dated a girl who wanted more from me, a commitment she called it. I was not sure what that was, but it scared me. It cut off my air supply. I felt I was choking just talking about it, and I told her I needed some time. This would be the beginning of a huge fear of commitment. It would be something I would struggle with for decades.

I remember my high school graduation as a blow-out. Many of us got drunk or high the afternoon before the graduation ceremony.

I came out to the parking lot after graduation to find a six pack of beer on the seat and a note. The note read, "Because you are such a lush, you will need this right now." I had been called a lush before—it meant you were a sloppy drunk—and I did not like it. I said something derogatory about the girl and cracked a beer—after all, they were cold—and drank one down as I drove from the school parking lot for the last time. A few hours later, I came to in the bushes near my driveway. I had begun having blackouts, where I would come out of one and not know exactly how I got there. It was dark, and my girlfriend was coming to pick me up to go to the graduation parties. I heard her voice in the driveway calling my name. I tried to speak, but I was so wasted that the words came out like a whisper. I raised my head. It felt like it weighed a hundred pounds. I tried again. She drove off, and I passed out. I missed that night. It would be followed by many other things I would miss in years to come.

I bought a 1971 four-wheel drive Chevy Blazer that summer, a red convertible. I had my first car loan. I worked painting houses for a guy for two months, then realized he was making the money and I was not making enough. I started working for myself painting houses, and within a month, I was making almost a thousand a week. It was 1973, and I liked having my own money. My brother and I were living at home; he was fourteen, and I was nineteen years old. He had started smoking some pot that year, and there were times we got high together.

It was late afternoon, maybe a Saturday, when Mom called us both into the living room to talk. As usual, my dad was sitting as far to one side of the big green sofa as possible, while my mom sat at the opposite end, as far away as possible. Their beds were set up in a similar way, twin beds that were five feet apart. Even as a young boy, I knew it was something, maybe Dad's leg or his disease of polio, that had pushed their beds apart. I was never really sure and tried not to think about it. They hardly ever touched, hugged, or kissed any more, and for all I knew they had sex four times, once for each child. Dad's face was serious and sad. He did not look up, but stared at the floor. Mom did all the talking, and in an unfeeling tone that was cold as ice, she said, "I want you boys to listen to what I say and not react for a minute. I am not happy here and have not been happy for years." This was no surprise to me. I knew I had caused all of the problems, but now what? "I have told your father that I do not love him, have never loved him, and we are getting a divorce."

There was silence that seemed to go for an eternity; time stood still, my stomach felt like I had been was punched. My brother began crying and saying, "No, no, please, there must be a mistake, you can't leave." She told us we had to be strong and help Dad and that she would live at her parent's house (my grandfather had died a few months before) in Southampton.

Dad began to cry, I had seen Dad cry before, but not like this. He tried to reassure my brother and me that it would be all right and we had to stick together.

Eben ran out of the house, crying and yelling that it was unfair, and I ran after him to the apple orchard, where he finally collapsed on the ground. I grabbed him and tried to hug him, but he kept pushing me away. "Leave me alone," he said over and over. Finally, he let go, and we cried for a while, holding each other tight like we had never done before. We made a pact that afternoon in the apple orchard that we would be close and be there for each other forever and that we would get through it. Being only fourteen, I think Eben was affected more than I was. Dad kept saying that she would be back, that any day she would return. Denial was always thick in that house, and this was no exception.

After Mom had gone, Eb and I were like wild Indians in that house. Dad would be watching Walter Cronkite at cocktail time each night, and we would either be smoking a bong next to him or drinking with him. My brother and I would argue, and there would be a brawl from time to time. Whether it was a table, a door, or a window, something would need repairing when we were done. One night, in an argument about God knows what, Eb grabbed me and my ass went through the six-over-six pane window in the den while my father was watching the news. I was stuck because every time I moved, the wooden mullions dug deeper and deeper into my ass. Dad always said the same thing: "Stop. You are both crazy." An hour or so later, Eb and I were laughing about it and smoking a joint.

Back then, the Hamptons were a very different kind of place. There were hundred-acre fields, and up toward the north, it was all trees. We used to ride bikes in the dark for a couple miles and not see a car. Back then, it was country. Today, most of those huge fields have been replaced with multimillion-dollar mansions for the rich and famous. I am sad sometimes when I think back on how beautiful it was back then and how all the city people wanted to be out here because of its beauty, and now they have built so many houses that the beauty slowly is disappearing.

After high school, I had some great parties in the back field. Tall brown switch grass grew in the fields, and the white and black pines made it a private place. There were several keg parties over the years, but one stands out. We organized it as a benefit for muscular dystrophy. We were doing in 1973 what they do in the Hamptons every summer weekend now. It was a

Saturday in August, and we had been advertising the party on a radio station for two weeks. People came from everywhere. We were charging $4 per person for a band, food, and all the beer you could drink. It was a deal!

A bandstand was built with a parachute over the top. We had a big refrigeration truck to keep the kegs of beer cold, along with barbecue, clams, and food. We had security working the front by the road, and they collected the money.

Before the party started that afternoon, my aunts stopped by and thought it was great that all these kids would be drinking in one place and not driving around. I don't think they thought about them all driving home afterward. Over seven hundred people showed up that night, and the party ended the next day on Sunday around midnight. We drank over thirty-one kegs of beer, a couple dozen cases of beer, a few cases of liquor, and whiffed up a case of "whip-its" (nitrous oxide), not to mention all the drugs that were consumed.

I was in my element at nineteen. After all, it was my party, and I could be with as many hotties as I could find. There was always another guy or girl who would turn me on to coke and some Thai stick. It was like a mini-Woodstock in my backyard—how could I not be Cool Phil from Water Mill? The cops came the first night and walked down to the party to tell the band to turn off the music for the night. It was around midnight, I guess. It was wild—a rock party/orgy/barbecue—and the two cops couldn't believe what was going on, between the empty beer kegs stacked fifteen feet in air, the hot girls running naked through the darkness, and people having sex in the bushes or smoking some sort of drug. It was a scene, and I loved it!

The party went on till almost sunrise even without the music. I awoke around ten on Sunday morning, and we started it all up again. We finally shut it down on Sunday night, but not before I had been given a ticket for holding an illegal outdoor performance without a license. It was a horseshit ticket the judge did not even know what to do with. He fined me $50, big deal. We partied like animals that weekend!

In those days, I had stamina and resilience and could knock down twenty or thirty drinks and a number of shots and get up Sunday morning, smoke a joint or two, and not shake and not feel bad. It just felt like everything was in slow motion until noon or so, and with a couple beers or a Bloody Mary or six, I would be good to go.

I got my first DWI when I was nineteen. I had gotten into an argument with a girl I was dating and had four or five drinks, left the bar, and got pulled over for speeding. I attended "cocktail collage," a class that taught you about alcoholism. I never went to the class drunk, nor did I go to the parking lot and have a couple beers at halftime, although there were some guys who did. I knew they had a problem, but not me—I was nineteen and much too young to be an alcoholic. There were things I heard that made bells ring in my head, like drinking in the morning. Well, that was okay if it was close to noon, but drinking straight through from the night before did not count. I'd had plenty of blackouts too. And needing a drink at certain times of the day or craving a drink…it made me uncomfortable to think I was an alcoholic, so I told them what they wanted to hear and didn't look back until years later.

In 1973, I started a waterfowl guide business and took lots of men goose and duck hunting that winter. I loved hunting and fishing and getting paid to do it seemed perfect.

From the time I was nineteen, I almost always was my own boss and enjoyed working my own hours. During the hunting season, I had to get up at 4:00 a.m. some days, so I tried not to drink from November through January.

A wealthy man who hunted with my father and I helped me get started in business and bought me duck decoys and a boat with an outboard engine, and all I had to do was take him hunting when he wanted to go for free. At the time, I was good at hunting but I had no idea what was in store for me.

* * *

It was the spring of 1974 and a good friend, Scott, talked me into working on the lobster boat he was working on. I was to start as "the master baiter." I did not like the term, but I figured it couldn't be that hard. One or two days at sea followed by five or six days off, then back to sea. I would make $110 for one-day trips and $200 for two-day trips. It was 1974. I had a commercial shellfish license also and would go clamming on my days off. It was a great life, being on the water all the time was always an adventure, and with plenty of time off, there was always time to enjoy the beach and lots of drinking and drugging.

Our captain, Brian, looked like a cross between a pirate and Bluto from the Popeye cartoons. He had huge arms with tattoos all over them, and his face was rough and weathered. He probably had more tattoos, but he never took off his shirt, even when it was close to a hundred degrees. He was a tough man and had seventeen years in the Merchant Marines; he was a redneck and let you know what the rules were. One was no drugs on his boat and no drinking on board. There were a few times we smoked some Thai stick on the way back in when it was his turn to sleep, but overall we behaved. It was dangerous, and you could get hurt badly, especially when it was rough—and it was rough a lot.

It seemed that he took great enjoyment in sailing on the nights we were hurting from all the partying, which was most times we hit the dock. After each trip, it took a day to sleep and regroup, then we were off to the races. One July afternoon, Scott and I dropped mescaline. It was blowing 20–25 knots out of the northwest, and we thought that he would never sail offshore as it was blowing too hard. At six we got the call and had to head for the dock. As usual, we were told to load the bait and get ready to sail. It was around seven at night, and we still didn't think he was going to sail. We were peaking on the shit when the boat broke the inlet sailing south toward the Hudson Canyon eighty-five miles off. Once we cleared the inlet, the sea calmed down a bit, maybe it was four- to eight-foot, but the wind was still blowing twenty-five knots. As usual, I had the first watch, and I stared into the green glowing radar screen for a few hours. If we were on a course with an approaching vessel, I was to alert my captain so he could change course. There were nights I was so sick, I would be throwing up out the wheelhouse window. If it got bad, the bile would burn my throat.

This night, I was wide awake and the radar seemed to hypnotize me. Occasionally, I would snap out of it when spray from a wave would crash against the wheelhouse. Brian had this rule that we only had to pull one pot, and if we could not work because the sea got too rough, we were paid for the trip anyway. It had happened once early in the season when a north-wester came up at the canyon and it blew thirty knots or more. It took us seventeen hours to get home in an eighteen-foot head sea.

The sixty-two-foot boat used to roll and pitch when the sea was above six feet. I think the boat was shrimp boat from the Gulf. To steady the boat, Brain put fifty foot steel poles called outriggers which were equipped with steel triangle planers, or birds as they were called, that were connected by chain to the rigger. At sea the outriggers were lowered, the resistance of the bird pulling through the water when the boat pitched in a heavy sea stabilized the vessel so it did not rock as much.

Suddenly, the boat pitched on the next wave and there was a crash. The pirate jumped from his bunk and wanted to know what was going on, as if I knew. He slowed the boat to five knots and opened the starboard door to the wheelhouse and with a searchlight looked up. The chain from the bird had somehow wrapped around the tip of the outrigger, and it was pulling the steel bird out of the water and sending it crashing into the rigger with each wave, making a huge clanging sound. "That's it," he said, "we'll have to turn around and head in." Now, I knew we only had four more hours and we would be pulling pots. Or we could steam home at five knots and take ten hours to get there and spend two hours cleaning up the boat and putting all the bait back in the cooler and not get paid. That would suck.

"I'll crawl out there and clear the chain, fuck heading in," I said.

Brian said, "You are nuts. You will never make it out there. It's over sixty feet to the end of the rigger."

I was still pretty stoned on the mescaline, but I wanted to do it. "I can make it, I can do it." The pirate thought a minute or two. By this time, the other mate Scott had come up from his cabin to see what was going on. He also said I was nuts.

"Okay, but if you can't make it, come right back, no bullshit," said the pirate.

The moon was pretty full so I was not in the dark completely, and it was only sixty feet. A walk in the park, I thought. The rigger was about eight to ten inches in diameter where it attached to the boat and narrowed further out. I shimmied out; it was just like crawling out on a limb in my father's apple orchard when I was picking apples. "I can do this," I said to myself. "I can do it." Forty feet out, I wondered if this was a good idea. I stopped for a second, maybe it was a minute, I couldn't tell. They yelled from the boat to come back. Their voices seemed distant, but I was determined to do it. I am not sure how much was courage, how much was determination, or how much was the fact that I was tripping my balls off and every time the boat rocked and my feet would almost touch the water and then be thirty or forty feet in the air, I felt my balls were in my throat. The mescaline was telling me that I was on a wild ride at the carnival, that it was not real, then I would bring myself back to reality and slide another few feet closer to the end of the rigger.

I could see it now, I was almost there, five more feet to go. Shit, a big wave, and my feet were in the water. I'm falling. I grabbed the steel outrigger and hugged it like a bear, then I was forty feet in the air again. I wanted to puke.

I could hear them from the boat faintly, but I could not make out what they were saying. I knew they wanted me to quit. Reaching out again, I pulled on the chain. It was tight and wouldn't budge. I figured I would wait till the boat rocked and there was slack enough to unwrap the chain from the rigger. I timed it. This was it! I pulled. There was slack but the chain smacked the steel of the rigger again, and I barely came away with my fingers. I was determined, one more try I could do it. I waited, and again the boat rocked and I pulled with all of my might. There it slack, so I pulled the chain around the tip of the rigger, and as the boat rolled back, the chain was clear. I had done it!

The pirate and Scott cheered from the deck. I was a hero, I thought. I shimmied my way back a lot faster than going out there, and the best feeling was the pirate's strong grip on me, pulling me over the side and back on deck. I think it was then that I finally started breathing again. "You are nuts, you know that?" said the pirate and Scott concurred. "Go below, I will take the rest of your watch," bellowed the pirate. I knew I had done well. I went below to my bunk and passed out.

It was a wonderful summer working on that lobster boat. I saw things I had never seen before. Porpoise used to swim just below the bow. They seemed to love to race the boat for a mile or two before diving back deep into the sea. The water was deep blue in the seventies at the canyon, and you could see a hundred feet down. When we pulled pots, white tip sharks used to swim beside the boat eating all the by catch. It was the hardest work I have ever done. I'm not sure my back was better for the experience of it all, but it was good for me and Scott.

The pirate was never blissful and grateful about much, and we both caught the wrath of Cong more than once. But once in a while, he was happy. Lobsters were going for $2 a pound for selects, ones over two pounds were worth $1.80 in 1974. It was a far cry from the $9 they are worth now.

We fished on the flats, and the deep lines were right on the edge of the drop-off of the Hudson Canyon or near Middle Grounds, which was halfway between the Hudson and the Fishtails. The depth varied from five hundred feet to over a thousand, so the main line would be close to half a mile long before the first pot would come up the hauler. We would coil the main line by the 15x10-foot lobster tank, which was just behind the wheelhouse. This one day, it was not too sloppy, with winds of 10–20 knots from the southwest, and the water was so clean and so blue it seemed purple. You could see four or five pots down in the deep coming up, almost two hundred feet below.

When the pirate was angry, he could curse a whole sentence of curse words, which is probably where I learned to do it. This one day, we were hauling back and the pirate was cursing away and the hauler started to ping like it did when there was a snarl coming to the surface. This sometimes happened after a storm or heavy blow, as the high fliers and large buoys would be pulled through the sea with the pots flipping around on the ocean's bottom. As he cursed, I looked down. It looked like six to eight pots were coming up in one big knot. There would also be a pile of line that the pirate would have to get the knots out of. He was the only man I had ever seen then or since who could unravel a knot three feet high and three feet wide in less than five minutes. It amazed me. It must have been all those years in the Merchant Marines.

The hauler strained from the weight, the rope pinged and sent seawater spraying into my eyes and stinging them. Then, just as the huge mess of ropes and lobster pots came close to the surface, it happened. The rope was stretching and it pinged and somehow popped off the hauler, and the thousand pounds of pots, lobster, and rope headed at incredible speed for the bottom. "Get the main line and the buoy quick!" screamed the pirate. As I ran for the three-foot coil of poly rope, I watched it disappear like a magician's act. As I grabbed the buoy, it knocked me to the floor, the tall aluminum rod and the sharp head just clearing my face and heading for the rail. The rope upended the pirate, and there he hung horizontally for what seemed like an eternity, six to seven feet off the deck. When he dropped, his head struck the steel rail with a sound like hitting a coconut with a hammer. Scott looked at me, and I looked at Scott. There lay our motionless captain, blood trickling down the deck from his head. Scott looked at me and said, "Oh shit, how the hell are we going to get home?" It was a fact, neither one of us knew how to run the boat and where to go, but now was not the time. We ran over to the pirate, and he started to come to, thank God.

We asked if he was all right, and he mumbled a handful of curse words, and after dipping his hat in the water of the lobster tank, he put his hat on and walked to the wheelhouse and closed the door.

Scott and I talked over the situation and came to the conclusion that we were going to get to go in early and with full pay. We slapped each other five. "What the fuck are you two idiots doing? Get back to work!" yelled the pirate as he busted out the wheelhouse door. He was a tough one, that pirate. He worked right through the ninety-degree heat with a welt the size of an orange on the back of his head the rest of the trip. We got to the line with the tangle, and he untangled the mess, and we pulled all seven hundred pots and headed for the dock.

If we pulled all seven hundred pots, two thousand pounds of lobster was the norm, plus a few dozen tile fish. They were worth good money back then. There were days, though, when the pirate would actually smile, and I almost felt that he liked Scott and me—although it did not happen often. When a line of pots started coming over the side full of lobster, his eyes would look like he had found buried treasure! Sometimes you would hit the right spot on the bottom of the ocean and fifteen lobsters or more would be in each trap plus a dozen crabs and maybe an eel or two and a couple tile fish. Ling and tile fish would come up so fast their eyes would be bulging from the pressure.

It was all Scott and I could do to empty the pot, rebait it, slide it down the deck, and stack it with the others to be returned to the sea. I was making good money for a nineteen-year-old in 1974. With clamming, the lobster boat, and selling a few pounds of weed on the side, I was clearing well over a thousand a week.

In the fall, there were tons of bay scallops, and in September I would dive for them when the season started. I wore a full wet suit, fins, weight belt, and snorkel and mask. On my way down to the bay, I would smoke a couple of fatties, and after diving a couple of hours, I would have my eight or ten bushels and go back to my house and open them under the apple tree. Sometimes my brother would help me after he came home from school. I sold them to restaurants and fish markets and made easy money. It was easy to make and easy to spend too.

I partied on the weekends and got twisted up from time to time, but nothing major happened for a year or two. It was in the mid '70s and there were discos, *Saturday Night Fever* came out, and the white powder was everywhere. I had snorted coke from time to time, but now everyone was doing it. I knew where to get the good shit in New York City, and as hard as I tried making money, I was my own best customer. I went through almost two ounces in four days once and did most of it myself and turned on only a few people. I always had the hot girls with me when I was holding a bag; they were safe as far as sex went. If they had Viagra back then, I would have been snorting that up one nostril and a fat line in the other, but they didn't. Once I started, I could never stop until either I ran out of money or coke…usually it was money.

Blow was magic. I could drink a couple dozen drinks, and it would not faze me. I eventually was nicknamed the Marathon Man; I liked it. I would stay up for four days and nights with no sleep and just shovel the shit in.

As I look back now, though, the highest I ever got was going to cop. I would be cranked up, and the first line would be the best and it was all downhill from there.

Between the coke and the drinking, to be honest it was all a blur for a few years. I became more and more physically and mentally dependent on the booze. I drank all night long sometimes to come down from the coke, or I would come home from a club and throw down two of my dad's tuenols, chug a half a quart of vodka straight out of the bottle, and pass out. Dad would knock on my door the next day or even the day after that to see if I was alive. There were many times I would go to sleep on Sunday night and not wake up until dusk on a Tuesday and not know what day it was, whether it was early in the morning or sunset.

I would be full of guilt and shame that I had spent all my money, sometimes three or four thousand dollars in a weekend, and I'd be full of fear, despair, and such a soul sickness that only those who have been there could relate to it.

We had a lot of guns in the house, and that was the scary part, because crashing on coke with a firearm in your hands does not usually have a happy ending. On a Sunday night in August in my mid-twenties, I had been doing coke for four days with no sleep or food. I went drinking that afternoon, and about ten at night some friends thought it would be better to bring me home. Someone drove my truck, parked it in the driveway, and left, and I came into the house. It is strange sometimes that when you are coming off a coke high like that all you want to do is eat and sleep. I had clams cooking, along with some soup and I think hot dogs. It was about a week after my dad's house had been burglarized and some things had been stolen. My father thought that either my brother or I had done it, so each of us had to take a polygraph. I think Eben owed some dealer some jing, and he knew who had done it. The cops never found out for sure.

There I was, about to have my first food in days, when I heard something outside. It was the fucking burglar coming back, I thought. All of a sudden, it was like I was in a movie. I would be a hero, I thought: "Phil catches the prowler at gunpoint and brings him to justice." I quickly loaded the Winchester shotgun, and with a pocket full of shells, I went to the front of the house to flush him out of the bushes.

I had come from the bright lights of the kitchen into complete darkness. My pupils were not adjusting to the darkness. All of a sudden a twig snapped, and I let loose with three shots. He was coming for me. I fell backward, tripping on a vine, and rolled over and quickly loaded three more into the gun and let them go as I saw something else move. "Come out of there, you fucker!" I said and loaded up again. This went on for fifteen minutes or more. My dad at that time took three three-grain tuenols to sleep and nothing would wake that man up.

Now, we lived in a residential neighborhood. There were houses directly across the street. As I learned many years later, the woman next door, who had just bought the house a few months before, was holding her children on the floor and talking to police on the phone as pellets broke her windows and sprayed her house. If you ever want to see the police in a hurry, mention gunfire!

There I was, in the pitch blackness, hallucinating with a loaded gun, and waiting for the burglar to move so I could finish him off. Then I heard a car door. I thought he had gone to his car and was going to run for it. In my head, I saw me in my truck swerving and passing him like a scene from a movie, shooting his tires out, and then he would be my prisoner. I would be famous, maybe even a hero, I thought in my twisted mind.

I ran for my truck, but as fortune would have it, whoever drove it home left the key on and the battery was dead. So I ran with the gun, confused and scared. I still could get the tires, I thought. I ran to the driveway and stopped by the edge of the road, and then it happened. I felt cold steel against the back of my neck and a voice said, "Freeze." I knew who this was, and it wasn't a burglar. I dropped the gun like it was burning my hands. "Put your hands behind your back," the Southampton town police officer said. I ranted on about how we had gotten robbed the week before and the robber had come back. I had heard him, and I was just trying to catch the thief. They did not buy it, and I spent the night in the jail... again.

One thing about snorting more than an ounce of cocaine in four days is that psychotic episodes seem like reality, including the tree police. You believe it all. Tree police were when you were out of it, and at night, you could see police up in the damn trees, watching and coming to get you. At times, I would close myself in my room and get ready to go out to a club—at least I thought I was doing that. After a few hours of getting ready, snorting pile after pile, I would be on my hands and knees looking under the door to see if there was somebody waiting for me. My pupils would be completely dilated and solid black and I would chew my lip or grit my teeth for hours at a time.

My drinking and drug abuse in my mid-twenties got really get out of control, mostly accelerated by the abuse of cocaine. It got ugly. From ages twenty-two to twenty-seven, I got three more DWIs and should have gotten three hundred more. I was lucky I never hurt someone or myself, at least not too badly. Traffic violations were dealt with once a year. Sometimes I would plead guilty to three and they would drop six or seven others. My uncle was now the town attorney, and his influence kept me from going to jail.

I became a periodic drinker and would not drink for months sometimes and tell myself I had it under control. The courts or the detox units would want me to go to Twelve Step meetings, but I would not stay long and tell myself I was too young or that I did not drink every day. I would always find an excuse, and slowly I began a cycle of obsession, compulsion, and total disregard for all family, friends, and most of all myself.

I crashed and totaled a dozen cars and trucks, hitting trees at over 70 mph and walking away, snapping telephone poles, falling asleep while driving only to be awakened by the crash of hitting a mailbox at 50 mph, on and on.

I was the last one to know I was an alcoholic, it seemed, as I denied my problem like any good alky. "If everyone would just leave me alone," I would say often. My driving privileges were revoked or suspended several times from the age of eighteen until I was twenty-seven. I spent many nights in jails around the Hamptons, sometimes in the Village or at the state police building or in another town. They all went down the same way: you would be brought in and fingerprinted, then you would spend the night sleeping on a board, and in the morning you'd get a cold egg sandwich and cold cup of coffee.

My third DWI came one night while leaving the St. James in Bridgehampton. It was an old hotel/bar from the fifties and sixties and black people would party down there, with lots of drugs and drinking and great jazz or soul music. I had been doing coke for three days and hadn't slept, it was a Saturday around midnight when I got there. I threw down probably a dozen drinks, found a cute girl, and danced until 4:00 a.m., when I left the club. I was still really high from the coke and so the paranoia that the police were waiting for me took over. Instead of driving down the highway, I went down a side street that circled around and joined the highway again a half mile away. White knuckling it down the road, I approached the highway, and as I stopped at the stop sign, a town police car stopped alongside me facing the direction I had just come from. Alkies do one of two things when they are caught: you either make believe you are invisible or that what you see is not there. I did both. As the cop car stopped alongside me, he rolled down his window, and I looked both ways and drove down the road.

I got about half a mile down the road before the cop's lights flashed in the rearview and the siren sounded. If my heart wasn't approaching stroke level before, it was surely doing it as I pulled my truck to the side of the road. I got out of the truck, feeling that I could talk my way out of it. I recognized the cop, Bobby O. He had been after me for years and had pulled me over a lot, given me a ticket or two, but he'd never found drugs on me and never could get me for a DWI. They always asked the same question: "Have you been drinking?" I wanted to say, "No, I was watching a movie at the bar, asshole." But I gave him my normal answer, "I had two drinks a few hours ago, but that was it." Wired as I was, I did the finger-to-the-nose and walk-the-line tricks, all in coked-up time. He had seen enough. Bob cuffed me and put me in the back of his car and I was on my way to take the breathalyzer at the station. Back then, the Southampton police station was a hundred yards or so from the Shinnecock Canal that connected Peconic Bay and Shinnecock Bay.

When you are that high and paranoid, you feel that your life will come to an end if you can't get away. "I must escape," I thought. I thought out my plan. When I arrived at headquarters, Bob would come around my side of the car to get me out, and when he did I would stand up, knock him down, and run to the canal and jump in and go out with the tide. It would be morning before they found me and by then I would be sober. It was like I was watching a movie. I was the star, the hero again, the boats passing me in the darkness unable to find me. I would be invincible.

We arrived at the station, my heart pounded with anticipation. The cop opened the back door of the police car and I saw my chance. It happened just as I had envisioned. I knocked him down and took off running, my heart pounding, my lungs struggling to get air enough to continue. It was farther to the canal than I thought. One important bit of information that I had forgotten was that I was handcuffed and running even without all the coke in my system would have been difficult enough. Eventually after a hundred yards, Bob ran me down, throwing me to the ground. He punched me, swearing, gasping for air, and yelling some shit I can't remember. A couple other cops pulled him off me. As I look back today I think how insane that was. I still laugh about it, but to be real, if I had made it to the canal I would have jumped in and sank like a rock and drowned.

Word got around the station, and in the years to come, it would be called the Phil Gay Miracle Mile.

I was brought inside. I called my Uncle Ted, who at four in the morning drove to the police station. Ted witnessed the test and was a key witness to the fact that the test was given improperly at my trial. The case was dismissed, and Bob the town cop stood in the back of the court room and pointed his finger and said, "I'll get you, Gay, one day I will get you." He never did get his chance, but many of his buddies did.

After I lost my license, I would ride a bike or walk or someone would drive me from the bars at night. I never drove without my license, although there might have been a night here or there that I did.

I hated to ask for a ride home, so on many nights I stumbled home from the clubs and bars in the Hamptons. I grew up there and knew many of the neighborhoods before there were houses built there. One such night, I was leaving a club and started walking home. I was no drunker than usual and decided that instead of walking on the road to get home it would be shorter to walk straight through the woods. I did this often and would stumble and fall. My clothes would be torn up and green briars would tear my skin and leave me scratched and bleeding. I made it half a mile and came out on a driveway. I was sweating, my clothes were torn, and I started to throw up in this field. I must have passed out cold in that field.

That next hot summer morning, I heard someone yelling. It startled me, and I sat up to see a woman before me on a huge horse. I thought I was dreaming for a second, rubbing my eyes. I had passed out right in the middle of her horse pasture. She pointed her finger down at me and yelled to a farm worker, "Get that alcoholic off my property."

I sat up puzzled and looked behind me to see who she could have been talking about!

I believed that my life was not going as planned because of someone or something, but it had absolutely nothing to do with my drinking and drugging. I drank and hung out with many who felt the same way about their lives, and we were all negative and had dismal attitudes.

Although I was a periodic drinker, when I picked up that first one, I was off to the races as if I had never stopped. During those dry periods, I would work and be healthy, but there was always something missing, and I could never figure it out. Isolation was a way of life, and I spent many hours and some days alone.

There were days I would wake up and look at the clock by my bed and not know if it was dawn or dusk. My binges got worse and worse, and I had alcoholic insomnia, where I would pass out drunk and wake up in the middle of the night and need a drink to get back to sleep. Many nights I would sleep with a quart of vodka by my bed, and when I woke up, it would be empty. I would think that someone had come in during the night and drunk it. I greeted every day full of fear, guilt, shame, sickness, remorse, and self-hatred. I had people in my life and a family that tried to talk sense to me, but none seemed to understand.

One day, my father called a man from a local Twelve Step program, Pete was his name. He came to the house when I was in the middle of a full-blown, two-month binge. I was drinking two to three quarts of vodka a day, taking a handful of Quaaludes, Valium, Librium, or some of my father's sleeping pills, and smoking a dozen joints a day. I had a problem swallowing anything that was not liquid, so I might have eaten half a sandwich every three or four days if I was lucky.

I explained to Pete that I had many issues in my life that were making me drink. My girlfriend had left me, I was thousands of dollars in debt, and I had a dozen traffic violations to deal with in court, not to mention that I had not worked in weeks. He said that all my problems were because of the use and abuse of all the drugs and alcohol. He said if I did not drink, many of these problems would take care of themselves, as long as I took it "one day at a time."

He was not going to fool me, though. I knew he meant for the rest of my damn life, and I knew that he was different and that I was terminally unique. Pete assured me that all almost every alky feels that way until they got to meetings and hear others that struggle with similar issues as they. If I did not drink and get high, my life would be over. The only alcoholic I knew up until this time was a man named Freddy who had worked at my grandfather's department store when I was seventeen. He wore the same clothes sometimes two days in a row, and the smell of yesterday's booze would ooze from his pores. I liked him. He was always friendly to me, and the day he said he saw a dog and her puppies in the corner of the store basement, I laughed and thought he was joking with me. Later, after talking to my mother, I was told he was hallucinating and that he was an alcoholic and that that was what "those people" did when they drank to excess. That winter, he died, asleep in his car. He froze to death, drunk in the cold. Yes, I knew this fifty-year-old man who saw things that were not there, who lived in his car, and who was an alky—but he was much different from me.

A few weeks after meeting Pete, I detoxed myself and I was back on my feet, not drinking and feeling better, eating food, still smoking and doing coke some weekends, but not drinking. It was the summer of 1981, and although my driver's license was revoked and my truck was wrecked in the barn until I got enough money to have it fixed, I felt physically and even emotionally better.

I did not have a girl in my life and used to reminisce about hot girls I had dated, and I wondered why they had left me, why it did not work out. I remembered dating some of the hottest girls in high school and in my early twenties, sometimes sleeping with two different ones a night, sometimes three. I was at the top of my game, I thought. The four or five years that followed until I was twenty seven the progression of the disease had beat me down. Each time I binged it was worse, now I was amazed of all the negative things that followed me around like a dark cloud.

One Friday night in August, I started drinking again and had been doing coke for three days with no sleep. My sister had gotten in an argument with her boyfriend. She cried as she told me the story in the apple orchard before I went out. I went to a club near my house called Lemans; it was the one of the best clubs in the Hamptons for years. It had been a bowling alley and then some investors turned it into a disco in the late 1970s. You walked into the huge place and surrounding the dance floor on two sides were buses they had made into private cocktail lounges, with glass tables and comfortable chairs lined with striped fabric. Wednesday nights were employee nights, and the dance floor held over two hundred of the best-looking men and women the Hamptons had to offer. It was full of seventeen to thirty-year-old women, their well-tanned skin glistening with sweat. Their teeth glowed white under the black lights. Many dressed in white hot pants, tight shorts, or white mini skirts, many times with just a bikini top or halter top.

I am not sure if they had no air conditioning in the club or not, but when a thousand people filled the place, around midnight you would sweat even if you were not dancing. If I danced for a half-hour, I looked like I had been swimming. The fog would float out on the dance floor, and the smell of sex, coke, booze, and sweat was so thick it always made me high by itself. I loved that place! I would spend many a night there, until the club closed at dawn. At the end of the club, there was another small bar with two bartenders. There was a stage there where the cream of the crop would dance and be stars for the night.

Fridays were a bit slow, and fewer locals and more city people would come through the doors. It was still a great show, though. I was pretty zuted up and felt a bit better after a couple shots and a few vodkas when I met this cute girl. She and I danced and then sat down and talked. Within a few minutes, she told me she had the gift of being able to see things and know about people and their futures. I never really believed in that sort of shit, but she was cute so I heard her out. She took my hands in hers and looked into my eyes and said that she saw a white house with red barns in the back and a man walking with a cane. She began describing my Dad's place where I was living. Thinking she was DEA, I started to become more and more paranoid. She went on to tell me that she saw a young woman crying by some apple trees. The woman, she said, had had a fight with her boyfriend. This got my attention; it was my sister. I had told no one about talking with my sister. It spooked me, and then she continued.

48

"You struggle," she told me. "You have a problem, and it keeps you from being happy."

I knew she was speaking of my drinking and all the drugs I took. She said that one day soon, the struggle would be over, and I would be able to help many hundreds of people. I'm not sure what she said after that point, but I started to cry, and she held me closer and said that it would be all right and I would be set free. She told me to be patient. I remember needing a drink after this and asked if she would like one. She said no. I said that I would be right back and went to the bar for a drink. When I returned a couple minutes later, she was gone. I searched everywhere through out the club, but my angel, as I would realize later in life, had vanished.

I was shaken and left the club. It was late and I went home. I went to the apple orchard and stood there, asking God or whoever to beam me up, like it was a Star Trek episode. I fell to my knees and sobbed myself into exhaustion.

* * *

"Tumble weed Tuesday," as it is called on the east end, is the Tuesday after Labor Day. It got its name because all the vacationing people leave the Hamptons, and the streets are so vacant it looks like the old ghost towns of the West, with only the tumbleweed rolling down the streets. It gets peaceful. There are fewer sirens, less traffic, and most of all, there are fewer people. You can almost hear a sigh of relief from all who live here year-round. I love the fall today, and back then, I did too. I usually worked more, drank less, and pulled my life together. This fall would be different because I knew I had to slow down and quit drinking for a while, but try as I might, I found it really hard to stop. I blamed it on the upcoming sentencing date for my last DWI and leaving the scene of an accident, the loss of my license, and whatever else I could throw in.

49

Throughout October, I drank around the clock and could not stop. Many days, I would wake up sick inside. Some nights, I hoped I would not wake up at all. It might be nine in the morning, and I would tell myself that if I drank that day I was going to die, but I would also know that if I did not drink, I would die from withdrawal. An hour later, I would be shaking and trying to hold a glass of vodka to my mouth. Much of it would spill, and what did not spill would be swallowed. This terrible procedure of gagging and throwing up the first or second drink and finally getting one to stay down would be repeated for weeks. My stomach would burn like a hot poker was sticking me, then I would drink another four or five ounces and suddenly my hands would be steady and the tremors and sickness would stop—until tomorrow. Two quarts of vodka was the norm, and some weekends, two half-gallons would not make it until Monday morning.

On October 28, 1981, I arrived at court to be sentenced for the DWI where I had been drunk and driving home a year before and had driven up the side of a car stopped at a stop sign, probably just sightseeing in the Hamptons for the day. Thank God no one was hurt.

My lawyer stopped me in the hall and asked, "Have you been drinking?" I don't know why he even bothered asking. It was quite evident that I had thrown down at least a pint before being there that morning. When I stood before the judge, he asked me, "Weren't you here in this court on Monday?"

"No, maybe it was my brother," I said.

The judge looked back in his log and realized I had been charged with disorderly conduct on Monday. I had been drunk and a bartender cut me off, so I had stood in the doorway of the bar and would not let any customers pass through the door. "We're closed," I told the customers coming to the door.

"I am thinking the best thing for you is ninety days in Riverhead Jail, it might teach you something," the judge said. He asked if I needed to get my affairs in order or if I wanted to go right then. I said that today was not a good day, and he told me to come back on Tuesday. After all, I had so many affairs to get in order—I just needed a few drinks to figure out what they were!

I left the courtroom and walked into Southampton Village, going into bar after bar and drinking double vodkas. After three or four drinks in an hour, they would cut me off and I would go to the next place. When a bartender has a patron who orders a double at three in the afternoon, then another, he knows you are not great for business and wants to get rid of you. I went into a liquor store and bought a bottle and somehow got back home to my dad's house. I drank one after another and just could not get drunk.

As I sat at the kitchen table in my dad's kitchen, I began to tell him the sad tale of how I was going to jail, plus all the other issues I was dealing with. Dad was compassionate and said that if he had my problems, he would be drinking too. He was a hell of an enabler, my dad. He was paying my bills and providing a roof over my drunken head, plus food and you name it. Dad was an alky too, so he did not get it. When I used to see pamphlets from Twelve Step programs, I thought it was for him or my brother. Some would have printed on the cover, "Do you think that you are an alcoholic?" I would think it was so sad that my father had gotten that bad.

Dad listened that night. Wanting to help and not knowing what to do or say, he finally said, "Would you like to talk to someone?" I always thought that when these guys from the program came over, they were going to teach me how to control the intake and instead they would spout off all this shit about how long they were sober and how good their fucking lives were now that they did not drink. I mean, after all, didn't they know when they woke up in the morning that it was the best they would feel all day?

A few months before, a huge man had come to the house to talk with me. He was about my height and must have weighed 280 pounds. It seemed like he had no neck, his head was the size of a basketball, and he had huge arms. "Hi, my name is George Benedict," he said as he sat at the kitchen table. At the time, I had no license, my truck was totaled, I had no job, no money, and I was in debt over ten thousand, which was a lot of jing back then. I had not had sex with my girlfriend in weeks. I was full of fear, guilt, shame, remorse, and despair, and I probably had not had a solid bowel movement in a month.

"How are things going?" he asked.

"Good, couldn't be better, I am on a roll," I told him. I thought I looked like Clint Eastwood, was as tough as John Wayne, and as daring as Steve McQueen, with as much talent and as famous as Eric Clapton. George talked for a while. He mentioned things about his life and told me how long he had been sober. These program people all seemed to tell me that. I figured it was all lies, or at least most of it. My brother was outside talking with my father. He was in a rage that someone from the program was talking to me. I could hear him yelling. "Philip is not an alcoholic, he just drinks too much," he yelled as he kicked over the barbecue.

George and I talked—well, mostly he talked and I tried to listen. I told him of my many problems. I said the cops would not leave me alone, my father was breaking my balls, and I had no work and court issues. I said that was why I was drinking. George tried explaining that almost all of those issues were caused by my drinking. I sat puzzled as I poured another vodka with a splash of juice. They say you're not ready until you're ready, and I wasn't ready.

This October night, it was Pete who came to call on me, and I told him my sad tale. My life, my girl, my job, my license, the court, the fines and huge lawyer fees, and now jail…this was why I drank the way I did. Just like George had done months before, Pete explained that none of it would be happening if I was sober and all of it was because of my alcoholism and that I could not handle the merchandise (booze) anymore. The only thing I bought was that part. He was right—it had the best of me. Even when I did not want to drink, I would end up drunk. I could not handle the merchandise. He also said that he knew the judge and he could get me into rehab so I did not have to go to jail for three months. Pete said I needed to go to detox at the hospital and that on Tuesday, when I went to court, he would go with me.

So right there at that kitchen table in my father's kitchen on October 28, 1981, I threw down what I hoped would be my last vodka and went with Pete to the hospital. Little did I know, it was the beginning of a life I had never known.

I liked detoxing. They were a bit rough in the beginning, with the shaking and quaking, throwing up and diarrhea, and those sleepless nights— but there would come a day when I would be hungry again and be able to eat a whole meal. There were times on a binge where I could not swallow unless I had a drink in me. I could take a bite of a sandwich and chew and chew, but I could not swallow it. So to make it easy, I just would not eat for days at a time. I knew the procedure at detox and was usually pretty drunk when I came in, and this night was no exception. They had good drugs there; Librium is every alkies friend, and with a sleeping pill or two at night, I was good to go. My second night in detox, I met a nurse who was another angel in my life. Lisa was a slender and attractive woman in her late twenties with long brown hair and a warm smile that my soul needed. I told her my tale and how it seemed that everyone and everything was against me. She was a born-again, and after talking a while, she asked if I ever tried praying. Sure, I told her, lots of times I prayed in the back of the police car, in court, or after crashing from four days doing blow and thinking that my heart was going to burst out of my chest. Yeah, I prayed many times and told Lisa it did not work.

"Have you ever prayed and meant it?" she asked.

I thought a while and realized that I never had. I was always making a deal with God. "Get me out of this or that one," I used to pray to him, but I realized that maybe I had never meant it.

"Why don't you try it?" she said. "It works."

"What should I say?" I questioned.

"Ask God to remove the obsession and compulsion to drink and drug and tell him that you want to live. Say you need his help."

I asked her to leave the room and knelt down on my bed and asked God for his help. I began to cry. Such hurt, pain, and despair had been mine for so long. I asked for his love and his help. I said I was done and could not live this way any longer. I asked for the obsession to be removed, just as she instructed me to do. I meant every word I said. I burst into tears; I cried like I never have. When the sobbing subsided, I looked up, and while I tried to focus on the room, somehow it looked different. I felt different; I felt relieved. Before I prayed, the upper half of my body had been burning up and beads of sweat rolled down my forehead, yet my legs and feet ached and were cold as ice. I noticed now that my body felt warm. I felt more at peace than I had in a long time. I told myself I would be all right.

Something had happened that night in that hospital room. It was a miracle I would be grateful for the rest of my life. I felt hope. I might be okay, I thought. The biggest miracle was that from that night in October 1981 until this day, I have never felt the obsession or compulsion to get high or drink again.

This obsession was something that I had felt every waking moment from the time I was a teenager. I thought about how much I needed, and if I was going somewhere, how much should I bring with me. If I was going to a party, should I bring a stash just in case? It was with me always, that obsession.

That night, the night nurse came in to give me a sleeping pill. I said I did not want it. I denied any meds after that night, and in the morning, I ate breakfast and even hospital food tasted good. Don't get me wrong, I had some doubts and fear, but there was something inside me that was different. The feeling that I might be all right was settling deeper and deeper in my mind.

I took a shower and even shaved that day, the first time in two weeks, I think. The nurses had been suggesting it. I felt a bit stronger each day and seemed to sleep better at night. I remember a stretch where I had been going at it hard for a couple months. There was no work, just drinking, and I stopped on my own. I had a system, I would get some Librium from the doctor and use some of my dad's Tuinals to sleep. Sometimes I felt hung over for two weeks.

But this time, in that hospital, I felt no hangover and no sickness. I just felt good and rested. It was a miracle.

When I was released from the hospital, Pete accompanied me to see the judge to see if he would allow me to go to the rehab instead of jail. As I stood next to Pete in front of the judge, Pete explained to the judge that I was a sick person and would not benefit from being sent to jail. I nodded in agreement. The judge looked down at me and asked, "Are you and alcoholic, son?"

I answered the judge apparently not quite loud enough, so he asked the question again, "Are you an alcoholic, son?" The third time he asked, I said it so loud I thought the roof would come down on me: "Yes, I am an alcoholic." I cringed from the awful words. The judge gave me a speech that if I did not graduate from rehab, I would still have to go to jail for the ninety days. I told him I understood and went home to pack.

At the time, I had a footlocker under my bed that held my stash. I knew if it was there when I got back from rehab, I was done. Each time I detoxed and returned home, a week or so later the drugs were there under my bed. I knew that I did not stand a chance with them there when I came back from rehab. There was a half-pound of red Lebanese hash, two pounds of Columbian gold, and four pounds of my favorite homegrown purple sticky buds I grew that summer in the woods behind the house.

I made some calls and had a yard sale. I fronted it to some of my friends and told them to pay me when I got back from rehab.

The three of them all said that they would come and visit, which of course never happened.

It was a cool fall day when the car drove past the gate to Brunswick Hospital. There were two words that made me feel I was at the wrong hospital: "Psychiatric Hospital." I asked the driver if he was sure it was the right place, and he assured me it was. There were two floors, the alkies were on the second floor and the crazies were on the first. To be honest, they could have saved a lot of money and put us all on the first floor.

We all had stories why we were there, and never did I hear that someone was at rehab because they were an alky. One man in his forties walked the halls and always had a newspaper under his arm. He said he was writing a story for *Newsday*. Another man had a sense of humor and I liked him. His job had sent him, I guess, but I was never sure. He told me of coming home early one afternoon and finding his neighbor in bed with his wife and said he went on a binge for weeks. I said, "I am sorry. I can understand how that could have threw you for a loop, and I would have gone on a tear myself."

Then he said, "I am a jerk, my neighbor is a she and is a hot blonde. Hell, I could have jumped into bed with them both and saved a lot of problems and money." He laughed, and so did I. Well, we all had these stories. Like they say, an alky might steal your wallet, but an addict will steal it and help you try to find it. None of us were ready to tell the truth. Hell, we all had lied to ourselves and everyone else. We did not even know what the truth was.

One tall black guy named Walt intimidated everyone there, and none of the patients knew why he was there. They told me not to talk with him if I knew what was good for me. One afternoon, he sat at a bench in the courtyard, and I walked up to the tall black man and said, "Hey what's up?"

He looked at me, disgusted, and said, "You crazy white boy, talking to me."

I said, "I just wanted to meet you."

"Why would you want to meet a man like me, white boy?"

I said, "Some people are scared to talk to you, but I am not."

"Why aren't you scared" he bellowed from the bench.

"You seem like a cool guy and I wanted to get to know you, that's all."
I started to turn away.

"Why are you here, white boy?"

"I am here because of the law," I pitched at him.

"Yeah, me too, I am in trouble with the man myself. Sit down for a
minute."

I sat, and we talked for a while and as others walked by at a distance.
They glanced my way, hoping to see me being choked to death I suspect.
But Walt was a good guy. He was tough and had lots of street smarts, and
he could see that I had some street smarts myself. He was a private detective and had a license to carry a piece. He told me he liked speed balls and
bourbon. Speedballs were when you shot heroin and coke at the same time.
He told me of getting on the subway at three in the morning after doing
speedballs and drinking a lot.

"I was freakin' as it was, and then I get on the subway and all of them
white people where lookin' at me. I yelled, 'What all you white moth-
erfuckers lookin' at?' I pulled out my gun and started shooting out the
windows above their heads. I remember a lot of screaming as they all ran
to another car. I knew I fucked up and slid the gun down the floor to the
door and put my hands against the wall as I knew at the next stop the man
would be waiting."

Walt said they were there at the next stop and took him away. While
awaiting trial, his lawyer said it would look good if he sought help. He said
he needed some time away from work anyway.

Rehab is a nutty place. One day, I was upstairs in one of the hallways
reading and heard some noise. It was a man I had been talking to the day
before. Six orderlies were holding him down outside in the courtyard
and trying to put a straightjacket on him. The small man seemed to have

super-human strength as he tossed the orderlies around like paper dolls. Finally, one of them stuck a needle in his arm and he settled down and they took him away. I never saw him again, and it scared me to think what they did with him. Maybe they sent electricity through him while giving him drugs to turn him into what they wanted him to be. I vowed that would not be my fate while I was in rehab. I had made my mind up that I would tell them whatever they wanted to hear so I could get the hell out of there.

Now, mind you, I was sick and tired of living the way I was living, and part of me wanted never to drink and use drugs again. I just wanted to know how they were going to keep me from going off again: needles, straightjackets, or shock treatments? I was scared, but I would not let anyone know it. I went to meetings at night and during the day went to group therapy and counseling. I heard the same shit. You just "don't drink one day at a time." They said you could do anything for a day, just one day.

I was smarter than the others, though, and knew they weren't telling it was going to be the rest of my damn life. When I woke up in the morning, it would be the best I felt all day!

All the counselors harped on honesty and openness. Many of them were recovering themselves. I thought back to when Pete saw me in the hospital and said, "All you have to be is honest, open-minded, and willing." He might as well have said all I had to do is climb up this side of this mountain with no help. They kept saying that it was a simple program and we were complicated people. I was not sure how complicated I was, but I could see that my life sure seemed complicated. Dealing with all the car wrecks, detoxes, lawyers, bills, and getting my license back from the Commissioner of Motor Vehicles would not be an easy task. It took thousands of dollars and lots of patience, neither of which I could spare. I would bring up these things in rehab, and other patients would too; they had jobs, children, and wives to add to the never-ending list of complications, which I was glad not to have. The councilors all had the same answer that these things would all work out as long as we did not drink.

Alkies love having the answers. We were not into putting in the footwork or faith to get to that point, but we loved to talk about how we would get from here to there. I wanted to figure it all out.

One hour of my day was spent in the leather shop making wallets, key fobs, and belts. The first few days, they would not let us use the sharp tools, for good reason as we all shook so much that we might lose fingers. After we could use the tools, we cut the leather and started making leather things. It was fun and I looked forward to the class each day.

I felt so strongly that leather craft would keep me sober that when my dad picked me up from rehab, I had him stop at a leather shop and picked up $100 worth of tools and leather to start me off when I got home. I never did make one belt.

Sundays were visiting days, and my dad and once my mom came to visit me. My mom brought her new husband. We sat under one of the trees in the courtyard, and not knowing what to say, my mother talked about herself. Time went by, and I got bored and she left. They did not understand—hell, I did not understand, so how could they? They both drank a lot every day, and at the time, I did not think my mother was an alcoholic. It would take some time before I put the puzzle together. And what a puzzle it is! You come from a childhood you only can remember bits and pieces of, and then you are asked how your childhood was. You say you had a good childhood, because you do not even remember much of it anyway, and then you start getting high and drinking and it becomes a real blur. You end up in a rehab, trying to work out all the bad shit that you can't even remember.

I have read and now believe that our minds protect us from a total meltdown by not letting us feel the hurt and pain. Our memories are altered somehow. Sometimes you remember, and sometimes you don't. Many times it's better not to remember.

I had been in rehab for three weeks when my father and cousin came to visit. It was a warm afternoon in November, and we sat at a picnic table in the sun. Dad asked me how I was and how everything was going. Unlike my mother, when he said things and asked things, he looked at you with his kind, warm eyes and you knew he was interested. I had been working hard at rehab and my eyes had become more open to what alcoholism really was and I felt more confident each day.

"I think I know why I drink and drug the way I do now," I said. "I am an alcoholic, and I think if I don't drink and go to meetings, I may never have to deal with these problems ever again."

I was waiting for a supportive answer, and my dad lowered his head and said, "God, I hope so." That was all he could muster for encouragement. I was let down and almost felt that what the hell is the use of even trying at this being sober thing when they don't think I will make it? And when you really think about it, how could it be that easy? Hell, I had been trying for years to get my life in some sort of direction, be some sort of success, and I had lost the battle over and over again. Why should I think anything would be different this time? I was discouraged that afternoon when I walked back to my room. I had started to believe there was a way out, an easier answer than being a reject, being crazy, being a failure, being nothing but a drunk.

The next day at group, I cried that my dad did not support me or understand me and did not accept that I was a sick person and not a bad person. The councilor asked me if my dad drank, and I said he drank every night. Now, I drank a quart or two a day and thought you could not be an alky only drinking a few drinks a night. "It is not how much you drink, it is what it does to you when you drink," the councilor said. I was told that many people do not understand alcoholism and that I would learn how to get support from people in Twelve Step programs. I was still sad, but I tried to accept that my father and mother were incapable of giving me what I needed. It took years, maybe a decade, to come to terms with that.

I had only a few days left in rehab when a guy I knew was there one night for aftercare. He had graduated a few weeks before. I still believed I would be graduating one day myself. Everyone in town called him Bo, I never knew his real name. He liked to free-base coke. Bo wore glasses, had a pockmarked face, and was 5'9" or so. He was kind of pudgy, with pale skin. I never knew him well, but I had heard that he liked to party. That seems like a strange term to use for someone who liked to smoke a thousand or more dollars worth of a drug he did not have money to pay for and shut himself in a room with the drapes pulled, peeking out every once in a while waiting for the tree police to pop out and take him away. Some party!

I liked Bo from the first time I met him. He had an optimism and a humorous way about him. We talked for a while, and he said that when I got out, he and I would go to meetings together. He gave me his phone number. It sounded great. It was one of the things I thought about, how was I going to get to meetings and who would be there. It was good to know that I had a friend who was starting a new life like I was.

There were one or two times I almost got thrown out of rehab. There was no PC allowed, meaning no physical contact with the other sex. Now, I had not had sex for months, and I was not alone. The place was full of people like me. One day I was caught with two girls in my room. We were not having sex, but we were close when the orderly came through the door. Another time, a girl and I stopped the elevator between floors and made out like teenagers and groped each other a while. Both times, I was able to talk my way out of it and they did not report us.

Looking back, there must have been some sort of short circuit in my brain to have gambled my freedom on sex at rehab.

In a few days I would be leaving rehab. I had Bo to take me to meetings; I was going to live at my dad's; and I had some clients I would guide hunting ducks and geese. While I was in rehab, my cousin Michael and a few friends took care of my work. I brought up that I needed something to give to the judge saying I had graduated Brunswick House, and my councilor got me a letter. The letter said I had completed the twenty-eight-day program and that I had a genuine desire to stay sober. It stated that I needed to participate in meetings and aftercare.

I was scared to leave that place, I have to admit, but I could not wait to get home. One of the things I had done differently was that I had no drugs at home. There were no purple sticky buds of homegrown to fog me up again. This was different than any other time I tried to get sober.

Leaving rehab was terrifying. I did not know what to expect. I had to go back to court and be sentenced, check into probation, reapply for my driver's license, pay my lawyer's bills and other bills, and start work. And I had to make some amends, as they called it in rehab. One such amend was paying back money I owed to a man who lived down the street from my dad's. He had contracted me to paint his house the year before, but I got drunk and spent all the money, and now I owed him the $1,500.

My dad was glad to see me, and when I got into his Land Rover, he started telling me all the things I missed when I was away. I tried to listen but I could not focus. The only thing I heard was that Bo was coming to take me to a meeting at seven that night.

I got back home, and I was making myself some dinner, and out of the cabinet my father pulled a bottle of vodka and then the tray of ice cubes, as he had done every night as long as I could remember. He would make a drink every night and watch Walter Cronkite. I heard every glug as the silky clear liquid poured into the glass; I could smell it and almost taste it. I had to leave the kitchen for a minute to regroup. Dad took his drink into the den where the television was, and I went back to the kitchen to finish cooking my dinner. I could almost hear the bottle talking to me from the counter, but I tried to ignore it. I remembered that if I had a drink signal, I should drink some juice or water. I poured a glass of orange juice, and it helped a bit. I sat down and ate my dinner at the kitchen table. Dad came back into the kitchen for a refill and I said to him, "Can I ask you a favor,

Dad, do you mind if you could take the bottle with you into the den at night, at least in the beginning?"

He said with sort of a smirk, "What, does it bother you to look at it?"

I answered, "Yes, it does bother me. I am trying not to drink."

That was it, and from that night on, the vodka was taken with him into the other room and never did I have to fight off the demons while I had dinner.

It was a miracle I did not drink in those days. My brother continued where I left off, dealing drugs and drinking, and my father had his four or five drinks a night, followed by two or three three-grain Tuinals to go to sleep. I talked to him one night, and he explained that he loved when he took the sleeping pills and a warm feeling came over his head and a rush went all the way down to his toes. Shit, I thought for a minute, it's like a junkie talking about main-lining junk. I knew exactly what he felt and felt in my heart that he too was stuck in the disease. He would one day have to look at himself, but I needed to focus on my stuff as I had a full plate.

Bo was on time every night, and I was always kind of puzzled that these meetings all started and ended when they were supposed to. It was hunting season, and I was guiding clients to hunt ducks and geese as I had done since I was nineteen. Bo would call me some nights, and I would have been up since four in the morning. I would be exhausted, and I would tell him I was staying home. "Be right over in fifteen minutes, you better be ready," he would say. I would yell that I was not going, but he always had hung up by then. He kept coming, and it became easier to not argue and just get ready to go to the meeting. Every night he picked me up, seven nights a week, and we became a team.

The people at the meeting used to call us the Dynamic Duo.

Weeks went by. I got a sponsor, someone who could help me with me sobriety, like a mentor and confidant. I had one for my first few weeks, but I needed someone different, someone who was a little crazy. George, whom

I had spoken to when I was drinking and had come to my dad's house, eventually became that man. He was loud, had arms like a wrestler, and talked like he was some sort of gangster. I am not sure if he had ties with the Mob, but he spoke and told stories like he was. Part of George was all talk. Don't get me wrong, he was strong, and he told stories of taking down half a dozen guys at once in bar fights. Some of it seemed plausible, but there was a kind side to him that, even as screwed up as I was, I picked up on. He grew up in the Bronx and moved to Farmingdale when he was a young child. He had a sister and two brothers, and his father was a police officer. We shared stories about growing up in alcoholic households. The abuse, pain, and hurt had scarred him like it had me, and we made light of it, I guess to help release some of its powerful hold on our souls.

He knew about the program, and the little sayings that I hated spouted from his mouth from time to time, like "One day at a time" and "Don't drink and go to meetings." Some made sense, some didn't, but what I felt and needed so desperately was unconditional love. He was like a father and a brother rolled up into one. He listened with the patience of a saint as I ranted and raved. I was not drinking, but I still held onto the belief that if things were going wrong in my life, it was a plot. I would stay in the victim role for many years.

Alkies seem to believe they can see into the future and know when impending doom is approaching, what exactly will happen, how bad it will be, and what will be said by each person.

In the beginning, I did not trust him. It was hard to trust anyone. After all, I was lying, cheating, and untrustworthy, and I felt that everyone was like me.

Slowly, I trusted George more and more, and eventually I shared many dark secrets. He shared with me also, and mine were nothing in comparison to his. I felt better after talking with him. Unlike my father, who judged me often and felt it was his duty to point out my mistakes, George let me find my own way. Don't get me wrong, George was and still is a wild man, and in his seventies today, he still wants to get out of the car and drag some idiot out of a car for giving him the finger in traffic. Anger that borders on blind rage comes out in him from time to time, and I think we are just broken toys in the broken toy store. That is what I like to call the program sometimes.

His wife Annette is loved by all who know her. Annette is an attractive red-headed Italian who was brought up in Brooklyn. She stands a bit more than five feet tall. She loves to laugh and takes life lightly today, just as she did when I met her long ago.

I always joked with George that he was blessed to have her and that he should remember that one day when he is old and can't take care of himself, she will be there to wipe the drool from his chin. She became like a mother to me, although she was much too young to be my mother when we met. She always seemed interested in me. Like my grandmother's interest, I never doubted that Annette had genuine feelings and an interest in my life. When George was not home, I would talk to her for the longest time. She always cared and would ask many questions.

Sometimes George spoke to her in ways that would make me cringe, but it rolled off her like water on a duck's back. Civilians are just different. Annette was a civilian, as George called her. It was a given name to those who weren't alkies and were mature and balanced and almost normal, whatever the hell that is.

I went to many meetings. Like I used to hear, "go until you like to go." I did my ninety in ninety days. I was twenty-seven, and only one local guy who went was my age. Everyone else was in their fifties and older. It was a struggle listening to the old timers; it seemed like they spoke in cute slogans, like they had been brainwashed years earlier and it was all they could say. Taking on a responsibility like making coffee and setting up chairs, or being a chairperson or secretary, was suggested because this would keep me sober, they said. It took me years to figure out how making a pot of coffee kept me from getting loaded, but it did. One night, there was a meeting.

At the meeting, I was told I was the new coffee maker, and every Friday night I would make the coffee and set up the chairs. I did not drive, nor did I want to make any fucking coffee! I said, "I don't know how to make coffee and I do not drive, so I can't pick the stuff up at the store." Someone said they would pick me up and teach me how. These alkies had answers for everything. I later found that it was easier when they said I was the new whatever to just agree without comment. As I look back now, I had none of the responsibilities I do today, but I was overwhelmed some days and would say the serenity prayer over and over: "God grant me the serenity to accept the things I cannot change and the courage to change the things I can and the wisdom to know the difference."

I kept a card with the prayer in my pocket, and when something in my world was unacceptable, which was every day, I would read it.

I started to like going to meetings and heard the greatest stories. I heard a guy speak at a meeting about having the shakes in the morning. I could relate. I had them big time, and for the first drink of the day, I would have to hold the glass with two hands and I'd still spill half of it trying to bring it to my lips. This guy used to have his morning drink at a bar in the city before work. He would take off his tie and wrap it around his wrist and tie a knot in it and the other end would go around his neck. He then would hold the drink and pull the tie with the other hand and pull the glass right to his lips without spilling a drop.

Ingenious, I thought!

There was a day in December 1981 when I got a letter from the Commissioner of Motor Vehicles. My heart sank and fear struck me in the pit of my stomach, like it had done so many times before. I tried to be optimistic when I tore open that letter. I really wanted it to be good news. It had been over six months since I was arrested for a DWI and leaving the scene of the accident, and I was hoping to get my license back. I had gotten four DWIs in my drinking days. For one, I had gotten off on a technicality, but I was drunk that night as well. I had totaled six cars and been in a dozen car wrecks, and I had received over ninety traffic violations. But I had changed. I was sober and shouldn't that be taken into consideration?

The commissioner thought differently and decided I would not be able to drive until October 1984. I was crushed. How would I work and make a living, or pick up girls on a date? My dad, at the time, was waking up at 4:00 a.m. and driving me to meet my clients at the local diner to take them hunting. I felt embarrassed and humiliated, being twenty-seven years old and having my dad drive me each day. I hated it. I hated that my dad took so long to get dressed in the morning. My self-centeredness ran so deep that it makes sick to think about it. There was another reason it took my father that long to get dressed each day, but it would be years before I really understood why.

I would show up at a meeting and people would shake my hand and say they were glad to see me. I would shake their hand and try to smile, but I thought it was all an act. Sometimes I would go to a meeting and it was like someone was reading my mail. I would ask George if he called ahead and told them I was coming so they would say things I could relate to. George would say, "You're a sick one, keep coming."

I had shared about my brother one day at a meeting. I was concerned for him, although I don't remember why exactly. A man named Joe came up to me a month later and asked me about my brother. Joe was a kind and caring white-haired man in his seventies, and at first I had to think back and remember what the issue was. "Yes, things are good, and it worked out," I said. I walked away and could not believe that what I had felt or said meant anything to anyone like it had that night. I was stunned. Could these people really care? Could they really have interest in me? I started to wake up and realize that these people had a genuine interest in me and that I was important, at least a little. Growing up, when I would speak to my mother, I expected there would be some sort of comment from her or she would say, "I can't talk to you now." My Dad was a bit better, but he did it also.

When you are in rehab, they ask you to write down what you would like to accomplish in the next year. I wrote down that I wanted to stay sober, make some money, find a hot blonde and fall in love, and go to Hawaii. When I wrote it, the blonde may have come first on the list.

Today, I believe that all things happen for a reason and nothing happens by mistake—although when tragedy strikes, I have a hard time buying the second part. Through my childhood, I went to church and maybe Bible school at the Presbyterian church a few times, but I never had a real belief in a God. Back then, Dad never went to church so that was my out when my mother would say that we were going to church Sunday. She went every Sunday and had worried that if she didn't go, she would be swallowed up by demons or something. I was in touch with the sea, the sky, nature, and the beach, and I found a spiritual calmness and connection with life when I was in nature and I could clear my head and notice the beauty. I have to notice and be present even today, or even a beautiful rainbow on the hills of Oahu goes unappreciated.

I am not sure if I had spiritual signals and messages come to me when I was using. I may have been just too high to feel them, to notice. I started to notice a lot of coincidences, and I was a bit frightened at first, but I began to talk about them and appreciate them.

I began working as waterfowl guide in 1973 and made $90 a day for every group of hunters I took hunting. I had put an ad in *Field & Stream* magazine, but I only could afford two ads a season. Each one cost $60. Each year it got better and better, and now I was making and saving more money.

I wanted to go on a vacation to Hawaii after the season, and around Christmas I noticed an engagement announcement in the local paper for a friend of mine Ken. It said that he and his fiancé were working in Maui at a large hotel. I thought it was a sign. Maybe this was where I was supposed to go after the duck season ended. I called a few people and called the hotel in Maui and spoke to my friend, who told me that I could stay with him until I found a place. I did not tell him that I would not be holding a huge bag of drugs and there would be no rolling of fatties.

I made plans to go to Hawaii in February after the hunting season was over.

The protective members of my new group did not like the idea. No changes for the first year, they said, it was a dangerous place for me to go, it was a slippery slope, and on and on. I knew I had to be cautious, but I would have over ninety days by then and I would be fine by then.

New Years Eve was approaching. George, two other guys, and I were invited to a New Year's Eve party a woman in the program was having. It was my first sober party, and I was a little nervous. George drove, and we arrived a bit before 9:00 p.m. at a small house in Easthampton. She was in her sixties and a schoolteacher. As we walked in, I could smell the fire in the fireplace mixed with the scent of a perfume I was familiar with from my grandmother's house. There was a table with a punch bowl, plates of small cookies, and a platter of small sandwiches with the crusts off. It flashed into my mind that the last time I drank from a punch bowl, it was a summer party in Southampton in a house near the ocean. That night, the punch was spiked with mescaline or some shit and everyone who drank it went for a voyage.

"Great punch," someone said to our host. It brought me back. I poured myself a glass and grabbed a couple of the little sandwiches and headed over toward the fire, where everyone sat facing each other. I am not sure if everyone was as nervous as I was, but I sat down and the conversation stopped and no one said a word for what seemed like an hour, although it was probably thirty seconds in reality. My collar felt tight around my neck, sweat beaded on my upper lip, and then someone said, "Cold day today."

Oh fuck, I couldn't believe it. My life was over, talking about the weather in this ancient schoolteacher's house. What was going to happen to my life? It was New Year's Eve. I wanted to go to a club, find a woman, and have some wild sex, for God's sake. A few nights before I left for rehab, I was in detox in the hospital and imagining what my life would be like not drinking. Well, I thought that night, I would not wear blue jeans. Maybe I'd wear khaki pants and those loafers where you stick a penny in each one, yeah, that's it. And I would marry a cute little blonde girl. She would have her hair in braids, and we would make little braided girls, and our house would have a white picket fence in front. There would be no swearing. Straight people say, "No kidding" instead of "No shit," and there would be no loud music, no Stones, no Marshall Tucker, no Zeppelin, no rock 'n' roll. Maybe I'd listen to some sort of soft piano music.

And now we were talking about the weather. I knew right then and there that my life was never going to be the same!

The conversation topic changed, and later that night I watched the ball drop and realized I had never seen the ball drop on TV. I had heard about it and knew what it meant, but I was always either too high or drunk to watch it.

I was able to make it through that night because I had other plans for later that night. There was a party at a club, and I knew there would be lots of hot women there and they would be lit up and I would be sober.

It's not an easy thing to be in a club and not drink, even for an alky with years under his belt, let alone two months. It is the Lion's Den. It was recommended to me not go to those places. I was unique, I thought, and I drank soda, juice, or water the exact way I did the booze, one after another. After the schoolteacher's party, I went straight to the club and met a girl there I had known for years. I remembered her as being pretty straight and big-time boring. For some reason, she and I talked. She was easy to talk to and pretty loaded and not what I remembered. Matter of fact, now that I look back, there were many people who hung out during my drinking days that I thought were boring and straight. I was to find out that they drank more than I thought. I must have been a real mess.

The first time you meet the opposite sex sober, you are not sure what to say or do if you want to get them into bed. It gets easier, but takes some time. We talked for a while; it was past two in the morning, and she asked if I needed a ride home. There I was, sitting in my driveway in this girl's car making out like a teenager—that is what I felt like anyway. I kept asking myself what I used to do next, what did I say? I was puzzled and finally, thank God, she said, "Aren't you going to ask me in?" That was it, ask her in, stupid of me, I thought, and so I did ask her in.

Well, I have never flown to the moon or won the lottery, but the first time I had sober sex, there I was on the moon with a fist full of dollars!

January came and went, and I had ninety days clean and sober. I was still having crazy thoughts from time to time, but thank God, none of them were to get high or drunk.

George asked me if I wanted to speak for a man's anniversary, and I said sure. This happened at meetings in the program—someone would share their story and something about the person who was celebrating. I thought it would be a piece of cake.

That night, I spoke for this man in his fifties, I think, and I went on for fifteen minutes and said what it was like, what happened, and what is what like now. There were thirty to forty people in the room, and they all were at least twenty years older than me. I was nervous at first, but once I started, the words seemed to just flow. Many people from the meeting said they had never heard a story like mine, maybe because of all the drugs or maybe the way I told it, I was never sure.

When George dropped me off at home that night, we sat in his car in my father's driveway and he said, "You are going to help a lot of people one day." I smiled as I got out of his car, but I did not have a clue of what he was talking about. Help people? How and why would I help people? It would be years before I believed that what I had to offer could help anyone. They say alkies are egomaniacs with inferiority complexes—it described me perfectly, even in early sobriety.

It was mid-February when I got off the plane in Maui. The warmth and smell of the tropical air touched my inner being, and I smiled like a schoolboy leaving school for summer vacation. My friend Ken and I hooked up, and a day later I had my own condo on the beach. It was awesome. I got a deal as the manager said it needed some work, and if I agreed to have repairs done to the interior while I stayed there, it would cost me only $450 a month. Twenty-seven years old, and it was the first time I ever had my own place. I was on a pink cloud, as they say in the program. Everything just flowed. I made meetings only three miles from where I lived almost every night, and I actually met a guy who lived down the road who picked me up those nights.

I left the door to my lanai or patio open each night, and the sound of the surf rolling on the beach would put me into a deep and restful sleep. I never set an alarm and woke up when I wanted, walked out on lanai, and looked past a few palm trees to watch the deep blue sea. I would then make some fresh pineapple and maybe mango and have breakfast. I just smiled...every day, I smiled. I loved to snorkel and body surf, and it was not far to some of the most beautiful beaches I had ever seen. After a couple weeks, I was as dark as the locals. Almost every day in the late afternoon, I would run a few miles along the beach road and work out. Always I would see something new. Many of the hedges along the road were covered with large pink, yellow, or red flowers, and my sense of smell was now awake and appreciated it all.

I loved to cook and bought a tiny hibachi grill the size of a large shoebox and cooked steaks or local prawns or mahi mahi on the lanai while watching the sunset each night. Hawaii is like no other in the world, and every rainbow or sunset was magical to me that winter. I still have a large picture of a Hawaiian sunset I took one night hanging on the wall over my bath in my home.

I loved the meetings in Maui, and the people liked me, maybe it was my New York accent. I liked them too. They were relaxed and most were well-tanned and seemed more spiritual than people from New York. No one was in a hurry to do anything; they even spoke slower. The whole time I was there, I don't think I ever heard a car horn. Many nights after the meeting, I went to a club called Spats, which was located in the Hyatt Hotel about a mile from where I lived. Now, it was recommended at meetings that one who wanted to remain sober should not go into the lion's den. But I didn't want to drink. I just wanted to meet some hot beach girls and have fun, which I did. I prayed to God almost every day to have the strength not to drink or drug that day.

It was great. I was in the best shape of my life. I felt handsome, tanned, and my brown hair had blonde streaking through it from the sun. Each night, I would dress in a cool flowered Hawaiian shirt with linen shorts, and the best part of all was that I was on vacation, and when someone asked how long I was on vacation I would say a month or two. I was the man! I met girls in their twenties from all over, some worked in Vegas, some were stewardess, and all were just looking to dance the night away with a cute guy and have wild, meaningless sex all night. I was on the roll of my life! I would hook up with a hottie and then she would fly home, and then a night or two later, I would meet another and we would go nuts for another week or so. It went on and on.

I had sort of a girlfriend at home. We were both new in the program, and we were having casual sex with no commitment, so none of this gave me the "thinkies." That is what we used to call it when you got into your head with guilt, shame, or remorse—but I had none of that and just enjoyed every moment. That is how I lived, moment to moment. It is easy on vacation and much more difficult at home. I had paid my rent, had money to play with and buy myself what I wanted, and I had jing to take girls out to dinner and buy them drinks at the club. I seldom thought of home and lived like I had never lived before. I went fishing, snorkeling, and sightseeing, and I worked out or just swam for hours. I love to swim. I have heard that if you have stress or problems, water of any kind is soothing to the soul and will relax you and draw away any pain you carry from your body and your mind. I believe this to be true, and on that vacation, a little more fear, guilt, and shame left me each time I swam in that beautiful blue sea.

Six weeks later, I arrived back at JFK airport in New York. Sue, the girl I had been seeing a bit before I left, came and picked me up. I was home a day when they had a surprise birthday party for me. Sue, my brother Eben, and my dad were all there to yell, "Happy birthday!" Balloons and ribbon hung from the doorways, and the dining room table was set for lunch with party plates and fun stuff. There were presents on the chair for me to open.

I never thought much about someone having a party like that for me, as I always thought it was corny and that I would be uncomfortable. I guess it depends who is there for you. My world was small back then. My drinking and drugging buddies had slipped away, and my family and friends from the program were all I had. I enjoyed the party and we laughed and I told Dad and everyone stories about Maui and how beautiful it was there.

At the end of the party, I started to get up but Dad said, "Hold on, I have one more thing for you." He handed me an envelope. He had that sparkle in his eye. I looked around the room, and everyone seemed to know what was in the envelope. I sat back down in my chair and took the envelope. It was from the Department of Motor Vehicles. My eyes welled up with tears. Could it be? Could they have given me a chance and given my license back? I opened it, and it said that my license had been reinstated. I would have a year's probation, any tickets or accidents, and the license would be suspended or revoked.

I cried with relief. I had spent the first few months of sobriety worrying about how I would run my business and how could I be cool without a ride. I couldn't have my girlfriends pick me up to take me out forever. That was over now, except for the test. I would be able to drive again. It was a huge thing for me, but the biggest part was that I did my best not to ruin my life worrying about what I could not control. I could have worried about it while I was in Maui and ruined many a sunset or a whale jumping high in the air, but I didn't. I let it go, and it worked out better than I could have imagined.

I am not sure if civilians think like alkies do and project the outcome of lives, their future, their destiny, their fears, and doubts, but alkies are so fearful and have a huge lack of faith, mostly in themselves but also in any sort of guidance or hope from a power greater than themselves. After all, why would they? Most of us have childhoods dominated by fear and the lack of feeling accepted and loved from our parents. I had no feeling that I deserved good things, that I was handsome or smart, that I could be whatever I wanted and do whatever I dreamed.

Now my eyes began to open. Could it be possible that I had someone or something guiding me or helping me and that I would be all right? I think a lot of times in my life, I just needed to know that I would be all right.

My red 1971 Chevy Blazer was in the garage. It was still twisted up as I had not had money or the need to repair it from the last car wreck. I bought that truck when I was nineteen years old, and it had been banged up as much as me through the drunken years and all the insanity that went along with it. A few days after I got the letter, I took the truck to a body shop again. They loved drunks; we were their main business. They wanted you to keep drinking and banging up your car—it is job security. After a few thousand dollars and new fenders and quarter panels, one day I went and picked it up. I had my license back and now my truck, I was on a roll.

Bo seemed to fade away, I was not sure why. Later, I heard that while I was in Maui he started smoking weed again, but I am not sure what happened. Maybe he felt I did not need him anymore since I was driving myself to meetings now.

I owned a house painting company, and I was not sure what was happening, but I had more houses to paint than I could keep up with. I kept hiring more and more painters to help me. Maybe at one point that summer, I had four men working for me and was making over two grand net a week. For 1982, it was a lot of money.

I saved most of my money, and once in a while bought something I always wanted. I went to meetings every night, but on the weekends I liked to go to one of the hot clubs in the Hamptons, which is where I met Connie. She was twenty-one years old and had an amazing body and an ass you could bounce a quarter off of. She was drinking toasted almonds that night, and so I bought her toasted almond after toasted almond—the girl could throw them down. She tasted like a Good Humor bar when I kissed her later that night, and it made me laugh.

In the program, they say not to have relationships in your first year, but I had a problem with that one, and I loved to go out and dance until four in the morning. Hell, I was twenty-eight going on sixteen, for God's sake, and needed to have fun. As I look back, the only thing that kept me from getting high again was George, and I prayed every day that God gave me the strength not to drink or drug and thanked him every night. That, and I went to meetings every night.

Connie and I would go to dinner on the weekends and then usually go to Lemans disco and dance until it closed. I would be shirtless, sweating up a storm, sober and crazy. I loved it, what great fun. Now, dancing sober in the beginning is harder than having sex sober because everyone is watching. There were reports to George that I was dancing like a wild man, and my brother heard that I was drinking again, but they both knew I was all right and just having fun.

Connie and I dated that summer, and seeing her on a Friday for dancing and wild sex was all good. Occasionally, I had to take care of her as she would drink too much, but that was part of the deal. Eventually, it happened—she said the word that made me uneasy and edgy. The word I heard from girls I had dated as a teenager and sent me packing. "Commitment" was mentioned by Connie, and she said I was not there for her. She said she wanted to do stuff with me, more than just going out and having sex after dinner or dancing. It was always difficult to swallow after one of these conversations. It would take me years to realize that intimacy made my skin crawl. Wild and crazy sex, ass-prints-on-the-ceiling sex, was all good and right, but holding a girl's hand when she needed me emotionally made me run for the hills!

I remember she wanted me to come to her parent's beach house in Bridgehampton on Saturdays to hang out with her family. I would promise and promise, but I never could go. I made it through the summer, but when fall came, she was going to college in the city and we stopped seeing each other.

IN THE REARVIEW

I had to get used to driving sober and not worrying about the cops behind me. I had to be careful, mind you, as I was on probation. There was one cop who had given me many traffic violations and a DWI. He liked to write me tickets, and he always seemed to show up in my rearview mirror. He followed me for the first couple weeks after I got my license back. They all knew my red truck, which Dad had told me to sell. The truck was the reason I was getting into all the trouble back then, so he said. One day, that cop appeared from nowhere and followed me for a mile. For some reason, I stopped on the side of the road, shut the truck off, and got out. I was not sure exactly what I was doing when I walked up to the police car and not sure what I was going to say either. The officer had pulled over behind me and waited to see what I was doing. I walked up to his car, and he rolled down the passenger window. Nick was his name, so I said, "Hi, Nick, how are you?"

"All right," he said, puzzled and holding his gun discretely.

"You know, I have quit drinking and doing drugs, and while I was out there doing my thing, I know now you were doing your job and that I needed to be locked up. I was sick back then and needed help. I am doing the right thing now, I go to meetings and have been sober for six months, and I even got my license back. I am on driving probation now for a year, and if you keep following me around, I am sure that sooner or later you could catch me rolling a stop sign or failing to signal and I will lose my license again. If you can appreciate what I am doing and the change I am trying to make in my life, I would appreciate it if you did not follow me anymore."

Nick never said a word. He was more puzzled when I walked away than he was when I walked up to him, but that man never followed me again.

Matter of fact, almost all the cops in town were glad to see I wasn't drinking anymore. I would see them on the street from time to time. There was one cop who was always after me and had given me two DWIs. One was dismissed on a technicality. I would see him out some nights; he was a drinker and had a problem himself. He would come up and ask what was in my glass. I would tell him I was drinking juice or soda—sometimes he would even pick up my glass and smell it! If I was in a club, he would say he was glad to see that I was clean and to keep it up.

The first few months of being sober are a roller coaster ride. My body was detoxing, although it had been months. I had put myself through a lot. I remember one time when I checked myself into a hospital and the doctor asked what drugs I had taken in the last forty-eight hours. After pausing to figure out how long a period that was, I began to list them. "Mescaline, Quaaludes, Valium, cocaine, marijuana, hashish, and a lot of booze," I said with a smile, as if I was proud of my accomplishment. The doctor made some notes and left the room shaking his head. I felt that I was invincible and indestructible back then and took pride in being able to consume as much as I could and keep on going.

I recall another detox when they were checking my blood pressure, and it said 220/180. They went and got another cart and checked it again as they thought I shouldn't be alive.

Sometimes before being admitted to detox, a doctor would check how bad you were and stick a needle in your foot to see if you could feel it. My brother was in the hospital room one night with me when they did the needle stick and he almost fainted, but I felt nothing. Sometimes I would be driven from hospital to hospital as many were scared I would die in their care.

In the first few months of being clean, I think the huge mood changes were from the residue, as I used to call it. I would watch a Hallmark commercial on TV and burst into tears.

I stayed busy my first sober summer. During the weeks, I would be painting houses, and occasionally I would cater a clambake or beach party for summer residents in the Hamptons on the weekends. I had done a bit of it the summer before and I liked it and it kept me busy. I had welded some huge barbecues with my dad and bought some equipment and hired a couple people, and with a small ad in a local paper, I made some extra money. I also worked for a local seafood shop and did some of their parties as well. I named the business East End Clambakes, it seemed a fitting name. Growing up as a child, my family and aunts, uncles, and cousins would go to the beach almost every weekend in Water Mill and have a beach picnic and sometimes they would turn into an overnight camping trip, which back at that time was legal. My father had an old World War II army tent and it slept four or five of us kids. One of his friends had a camper, and he came sometimes as well. My father always did the grilling, after a few bourbons of course!

A steel rack with legs would be placed over a small fire of cherry wood, and he would grill steaks, potatoes, corn, lobster, and fish. I used to help him with the cooking, and it was from those memories that I came up with the ideas for clambakes. They are great fun, and in years to come, that business would grow beyond my wildest dreams.

The fall came, when house painting slowed and the duck and goose season started, and I was busy guiding waterfowl hunts again. My anniversary was in October, with a year of being clean and sober. When you get a year in the program, the group buys a cake. Sometimes there are flowers and cards. It is a celebration. In some parts of the country, they call that night your birthday. It was a huge accomplishment. Dad, my brother, and one of my sisters were there. I told my mom. She congratulated me, but she never came to a meeting. I think she was worried she would catch what we all had.

I was still living at my dad's, and although I was not drinking, I was angry from time to time. That's not exactly true…I was angry a lot and would explode, at times saying hurtful things to people I loved. I could not seem to help it and did not know why I acted the way I did. People who are hurting often hurt other people.

A year sober did not change a lot, and I kept things to myself often and told no one else. I was worried about money, a job, or a relationship. Sideways anger, I learned, was mostly a result of baggage, or feelings I did not share. Like a pressure cooker, the anger or old resentments exploded from me at some point. At this time, I did not know what it was. I pointed the finger a lot—I had lots of experience being a victim, but no experience talking about my feelings. You just didn't do it where I grew up. I was in fear a lot. It was me against whatever, with no higher power, no God, no one to listen, and no one to understand. At least I had George—he saved me when I was down.

COULD THERE BE A GOD?

They have little sayings in the program, including one I liked, "Coincidences are God's way of remaining anonymous."

God shots, as I like to call them, began to happen often after being sober a few months and even more after a year. They would happen like this. I would be thinking of someone, and a minute or less later the phone would ring and it would be them. Or I'd think of someone I had not seen for months or even years and I would be driving, turn a corner, and there they were, walking down the street. I am sure I was getting these coincidences when I was drinking, but I was too twisted to be aware of them. I now believe that the receptors or connectors in our minds are much better at picking up energy, signs, and coincidences once you are clean and free of drugs and the drink. Most of all, we provoke these receptors by putting energy or desires out into the universe, and they attract what we put out there. During the days of drinking and drugging, I was negative and felt always that I was a victim. I surrounded myself with people who thought and felt as I did, and guess what, I drew more negative things and whined about them more and fell into that awful pit from which the alky can find no escape.

Gratitude and hope were not in my vocabulary either. I had not a bit of hope and felt that if bad shit was going down, it was happening to me!

Now, as a sober man, I began asking for direction. I was more humble, I prayed and thanked God at night, and I would visualize things I wanted or think about people and it would happen. I began living "the secret" twenty years before I even read the book.

In the program, we don't know everyone's last name, so there was Frank the plumber or 7-11 Tom or the Golden Slipper. The Golden Slipper was a blond-haired kid about twenty-five who just could not get sober and slipped or drank every few weeks.

Anyway, one night I was home and contemplating whether to go to the meeting or not. I said to God, "If you want me to go to a meeting, have someone call and need a ride there." I swear it was three seconds before the phone rang. "Hello?" I said, laughing as I picked it up.

"Well, you are in a good mood, I was wondering if you could pick me up for the meeting?" said Crazy Janie.

Still laughing, I said, "Sure, I'll be there at 6:45."

Another time, I had been sober a year or two and needed to make a financial amend to a man who had given me a $1,500 deposit on a house painting job and I had blown it all. I thought of this man every time I passed his house, which was often as he lived only five houses away on my street! So one night I was alone, driving down the back roads to a meeting in Sag Harbor, which I had done every Sunday for months, and I think of the man and say, "God, if I am supposed to pay this man, let me see him driving down the road." I figured I would never have to pay him, right? Wrong! I came around the next corner, and there ahead of me was a gray Mercedes driving slowly down the road. "It can't be," I said out load as I raced to pass him. He was an old man of seventy-five at least, and with both hands on the wheel, he never looked up as I passed him. I looked over again, not believing my eyes. It was him...

The next morning, I was at his house with a check in my hand. I told him that I drank up all his money and I was sorry for what I did. I said that I had stopped drinking and was sorry it took me so long to pay him back. He smiled understandingly and congratulated me. The funny thing was, a year or so later, the real amend came when he called me to do some more painting on his home. I did it for half of what I normally would have charged. One morning I happened to walk through his kitchen and saw a glass he had just poured. I could smell vodka. I knew he understood me even more.

God Shots kept happening to me, and I came to believe in and understand my concept of a God. The years would go by, and that idea always would be changing. I would, in years to come, learn to roll with the change, embrace the change, and know in my heart that I would always be taken care of and learn to live life with less and less fear.

The hardest part was to truly believe there were people who cared for me and loved me.

I CAN'T SKI

That duck season was better than the year before, and I had many more clients. I saved money and went on vacation again as a reward to myself. That winter, I decided to go to New Hampshire and go snow skiing. Now, I had been skiing before, but I needed to buy some skis and ski clothes. My cousin and I went up the island to a place and I bought tons of stuff—ski outfits, skis, poles, goggles—I got it all.

My first day, I was on the lift, and as I got to the top of the mountain in Vermont, it came to me that I really did not know how to ski after all. It happens to alkies—they talk about all these things and how they have done this and that and they even believe their own lies. I had been skiing three times in reality, and now I was on the lift approaching the top of the mountain. I was scared, and as I jumped off the lift, my legs felt like rubber. I went down. I got right up before many people saw me. Another thing that bothers the shit out of alkies is to be embarrassed. The temperature was ten below zero and blowing thirty knots at least, and for a second, I thought it was a mistake. I pushed off and began to slide down the mountain. I watched other people as they snow-plowed to stop. I tried to do it, and after a lot of falls I got that part down. "At least I can stop," I thought.

I did not ski much that day as it was the worst cold I had ever felt. I skied some the day after, and then I left for home. I stayed with a distant cousin, and it was a not a good place for me as they were smoking pot all night and it was the lion's den. The poor girl had a hard time in life as years later she fell down in a drunken stupor and bruised her brain. She never recovered. Her father was the man I knew from my grandfather's department store who had frozen to death in his car. Alcoholism sometimes takes prisoners, and many times you just become a statistic. On many a death certificate, it says the cause of death is anything but what it really is: alcoholism.

I had dated a sweet girl for the last couple years of my drinking. Her name was Jane, and I would leave her at my dad's house to go buy some cigarettes on a Saturday night and not come home until Tuesday. She would always wait there until I got back, then she would call me a waste and go home. At one point, she moved to California to live with her sister to get away from me. I would call her in blackouts and plead for her to come home. One such time in a blackout, I was crying to her on the phone at 4:00 a.m. I said I could not live without her and that I wanted to her to come home so we could get married.

Now, the only person sicker than the alky is the person who is in love with him or her. A few days later, I got the phone call from Jane. She said she was home in Sag Harbor, but I did not give her the feeling of hugs and kisses. Then she asked, "Don't you remember what you told me the other night? You wanted to marry me."

"Of course I remember," I said, but I sure didn't. Now I would have to play the game, and in the end I hurt her again. It was sad what I did to that poor girl. It was sad what I did to a lot of girls. I would get suffocated and feel trapped and put on my running shoes. She was as sweet as could be and would do anything for me. She loved me. But when the issue of commitment came up, I would feel like I had to run, and that is what I did.

When I got clean, I got a phone call from Jane, maybe a month or two into it. She had moved back to California and was moving on with her life. She congratulated me, and we talked for a while. I wanted to say how sorry I was, I just could not find the right words.

One of the important steps in the program is making amends to people you have harmed, but it did not seem like the right time that day. A few months later, still bothered, I asked a guy at a meeting, "When do you know when to make an amend to someone?"

"The opportunity will just present itself," he said.

I thought, "Cool. Hell, she lives in California. I may never see her."

The very next day, I came home from work and there she was, sitting in my father's kitchen at the table and talking to my dad. I am not sure what God is, but I was sure of one thing, the opportunity was right there in my dad's kitchen and I knew it was my time to ante up. Jane and I talked for a while, not too much was said about the past, just what was going on. She must have told me four or five times how good I looked. We ended up going out to dinner and we talked. I found the words. I told her how sick I was, how I must have hurt her with all the drunken promises, the cheating, the lying, all of it. She had tears in her eyes. She accepted my amends, and we talked like we never had before. Jane told me about her life and asked me some questions about being in recovery and what it was like. I answered what I could. I had learned a lot about the disease in a short amount of time. We hugged and said we would be friends.

So when I came back from skiing in New Hampshire, I remembered that she did some skiing in California and had told me to call her. I called her, and she was glad to hear from me and happy I was still sober and doing well.

I spoke of my desire to take a ski vacation, and she said there was a place called Big Bear Mountain that would be perfect for me. It was a few hours drive from LA and she offered to drive me. I bought a ticket and flew out with all my ski stuff the next week.

Jane was great and helped me get set up and found me a log cabin for $650 for a month and left me at Big Bear. Big Bear Lake is a small mountain. I am not certain, but I don't think it was much over seven thousand feet. It was a small town back in 1982, and the best part was that it was warm and some days you could ski with just a T-shirt. My first day going up the lift, I had a smile from ear to ear. A mile or so behind me was the deep blue Big Bear Lake; it was some pretty for a boy from New York who had never seen such a place.

There is something to be said for learning to ski a year sober...no fear! Maybe it was because of the residue in my system from my drinking and drugging days, or maybe because I felt like I was twelve again, or maybe just cause I felt more alive and real than I ever had my entire life. I was like the children I saw on the mountains: doing jumps, bombing down the double black diamonds out of control. It was a blast; I was invincible again. I skied almost every day, and at night I would eat dinner in my little cabin and go to meetings that were a mile away. I rented a four-wheel drive and had a blast skiing and living the good life. As days went by, I felt more in control and more confident and thought I was a star! I went to Mammoth one week and skied there a few days while I was in California. It was a bigger mountain with tons of snow. I skied some days in powder there, which I loved. Even if I crashed and burned a lot, the fluffy snow was forgiving and soft.

Near the end of my stay, I spoke to my older sister. She and her husband lived in Snowmass, Colorado, just outside Aspen each winter. She wanted me to come out and visit for a week. My money was running low, but she convinced me to come out for a week. At the time, my sister was married to a very wealthy man. He did a fair amount of drinking and would ski with us once in a while, but he paid for a private ski instructor each day to keep my sister out on the slopes so he could hit the bars of Aspen with his drinking buddies. They were business lunches, as he always called them, but I wasn't buyin' it, and I didn't care. My sister was a beautiful skier then—all those private lessons worked magic. Even I got some help to become a great skier. I skied every day and must have changed my return flight date three or four times before I left Aspen a month later. I remember the first day I was there, my sister asked, "We are going to a party tonight. Do you have any cowboy boots?"

"No," I said.

"Well, I will buy some for your birthday present," she said.

At the Western store, I saw the price tags. Some of the boots were over a thousand dollars. I picked the cheapest ones I saw; they were $350. My sister said, "Those won't do. You need these, these are Lucchese and the best."

I didn't argue and tried them on. The price tag was $750.

"They are too expensive," I said.

"Don't worry about it," she told me, and I was soon ready with my new boots. My sister was full of piss and vinegar back then, full of optimism and joy, and after skiing at night she was full of vodka most of the time. She didn't work and had plenty of her husband's money to keep her in furs and new powder suits—it was the land of make-believe.

Unlike today, Aspen was a quiet small town with a wonderful history. It had some great restaurants and clubs where we would go for dinner or dancing. There were some of the most beautiful women I had ever seen. They had tanned faces from the warm sun reflecting off the snow, and everyone was fit. In the day, they showed off their hard bodies in thousand-dollar powder suits, and at night they walked into the restaurants and clubs wearing ten thousand dollar mink coats and enough jewelry around to feed a family for five years. But at the same time, these wealthy and beautiful people were mostly down to earth and pretty cool, unlike many of the WASP beach club types I had known growing up. I would be at clubs at night and I could smell the cocaine; it was in people's pockets, up their noses, and coming out of their pores. Coke was huge in the '80s, and all I could think of was what it would have been like if I was still getting high. I could only imagine.

There were tests from time to time. The drinking did not seem to get to me much, but sometimes in the club I would see someone doing coke in the bathroom or chewing the side of their lip off and I would have to get out of there and head home. One test came when I was skiing under the lift and found a sunglasses case. I put it in my pocket and skied down to the chair to come back up. My sister and I were in the chair, and I opened it to find a fat Thai stick wrapped in plastic and at least a couple grams of coke. My eyes popped open. "Why the fuck could I not have found shit like this in the old days?" I asked my sister.

My sister and I decided to give it our skiing instructor as a tip. He loved it.

Meetings were great, and there was good sobriety in Aspen. I went several times a week and would take a bus from Snowmass or borrow my sister's car. It was a wonderful feeling being accepted. No matter where I traveled to, I found I could walk into a meeting and it would happen: that magic of belonging, being accepted. People liked me, and I made friends quickly no matter where I was. I loved to ski and went every day. Skiing powder was my favorite. When we had fresh powder, I was at the lift when it opened and would ski until the lift closed. I got better and better at powder skiing. I would giggle like a young boy when I skied in the trees—it was a rush. Skiing while the fresh snow was falling was awesome, each turn whooshing as the powder kicked up in my face. If the weather was sunny and warm, the following day I would go to the lift later so the hard pack had softened. Many days, I wore a Hawaiian shirt, and even with the SPF thirty sunblock, I browned up like a native.

After skiing for two months, I was broke. When I got home, I started looking for painting work. I had some builders and some real estate people, and word of mouth was all I needed to get rolling again. Being a compulsive man, I focused on what was in front of me and what I needed to do and the best way to get to the finish line quickly and still do a good job. Being a son of a perfectionist has many advantages as well as many faults. I was a perfectionist and struggled with it for many years and still to this day. It has taken me years to tell my staff they did a good job, that I was proud of them, or maybe even give them a bonus from time to time for a job well done. My father tried teaching me what his father probably taught him: do it right or don't bother. All the years growing up, I would do something and it was never good enough. When I was drinking, I did not care. I never followed through with many projects and ideas, so in that way, no one could tell me it was not done right. But now I was sober and took pride in what I did. The more work I had, the more money I was making and the better I felt about who I was. It was the beginning of being a workaholic. It would take many years and a strong lesson to teach me that who I was as a man had nothing to do with how much money I had.

My house painting business took off in April. I would hire as much help as I could, and by mid-May, I'd be working seven days a week and sometimes twelve hours a day. It was hard to find time to go to meetings, but I always found the time somehow. Memorial Day weekend in the vacation area of the rich and famous has never changed. The summer residents came out in late April or May and realized the paint was peeling, the patio needed mason work, and the deck needed to be replaced—and it had to be done by Memorial Day weekend.

I don't know why, because it was not like the world would end, but to them it was most important thing in the world, and all the trade people filled their books with work and tried to get it all done. Of course, you never got it all done, but when you did get it done, you were still a hero. After Memorial Day, it was still busy, and the next push was the Fourth of July. Then many years, it would just die, as all the summer residents were there and wanted to enjoy their houses.

I remember after being sober a year or so and working on Memorial Day, I had to bring some porch furniture back to a client's house after painting it. I approached Bobby Vans, a well-known restaurant in Bridgehampton. A couple had just gotten out of a red Porsche and crossed the street in front of me hand in hand. The girl was hot, with long blonde hair, and the guy looked like something out of some commercial. Both were either high or drunk—I could tell by the way they crossed the street. I had an instant resentment for the dude with his hot car, hot lady, and lots of jing. I was sweating and delivering furniture on a holiday. I had it all going on. When I got home, I called George and told him about these assholes who were pretending to be having a good time. George said, "They were probably having a good time, because they can when they drink, but you can't have a good time anymore when you drink."

Now, I am not sure if I was more pissed off my seeing the two cross the street or hearing what George had to say, but it was true. I couldn't have fun when I drank anymore. It was over, and maybe that was what I was pissed more about. My days of having fun while taking in a few drinks was done. I was done.

GONE FISHING

The summer of '83, I had a couple workers painting two houses on South Main Street in Southampton for a builder. I had bought my cousin's twenty-foot Sea Craft that spring, and I wanted to do a lot of fishing. I got a new motor, fishing rods, gaffes, LORAN, and tons of new lures. I had a fair amount of time fishing on boats, including a few trips to the Hudson Canyon and my season on the lobster boat with the pirate, but mostly we would just go shark fishing maybe thirty fathoms south of Shinnecock Inlet. The inlet had been formed by the 1938 hurricane and its 150 mph winds, which cut through the beachfront. Dad said that before the hurricane, there was a dirt road and you could drive from Southampton to Hampton Bays along the dunes.

The summer before, I had borrowed the boat a few times and caught some sharks and a couple tuna. I loved it out there on the sea. It was quiet and peaceful, and every trip was full of adventure. Friends would pay me some gas and bait money, and when we came back to the dock they would take a fillet or two and I would sell the rest to local restaurants and fish markets. It didn't take me long to figure out to cut out the fish markets and deal direct to the restaurants so I could make more jing. I fished at least four days a week that summer. I went where the fish were, the Canyon was seventy miles offshore and no place for a twenty-foot boat, but forty fathoms was an hour and twenty minutes if it was flat and I could run thirty knots. That summer, I caught fourteen mako sharks, a couple threshers, dozens of blue and brown sharks, a couple hundred Mahi, and over two hundred tuna, mostly yellow fin. I caught more fish that summer than many of the forty-foot sport fishing boats. I loved it, and although it was tough in the ninety-degree sun all day, I was fishing and making $400 to $600 a day. There were days when a blow would come up and I couldn't leave the dock, so I would go clamming. I catered a few clambakes that summer and sometimes only had to buy a few lobsters and some corn. I always joked back then that they could drop the bomb and 95 percent of the people would starve to death in the first month, but I could live on what I could hunt or fish forever.

Shark fishing, although boring sometimes, had its wild moments. I remember one day fishing with a friend around thirty fathoms and about twenty miles offshore. It was late June and hot, close to ninety degrees, and there were no boats in sight. The wind was calm, and we had been chumming for five hours at least with only a couple blue sharks. Blue sharks were more of a pest; they were worthless at market and they used to steal the bait. The chum or ground fish, usually bunker, is either mixed with water and ladled over the side or a block is dropped over the side in a net bag. The bag works well, and you don't have to smell the rotten stench of the bunker, which would always have someone on board throwing up as soon as the aroma hit their nose. I seemed to be immune from that. The problem was that you had to keep your eye on the bag as a large shark could swallow it in one gulp, tearing it from the cleat of the boat. That day, the slick looked like a shiny river cutting through the rolling sea, and it went for a mile at least. At times, I looked back a quarter mile and saw a fin coming up the slick. Along the slick, little dark sea birds called stormy petrels danced like little ballerinas picking up bits of the floating fish. Sharks smell the blood and swim up the slick toward the boat, where you have an assortment of baits at various depths waiting for them. You pay out some line off the reel to the depth you want the bait to drift and then tie on a balloon. Then you pay out more line until the bait is anywhere from twenty feet to a hundred yards behind the boat, and then you wait. We would leave the reel on free spool with the clicker on so the shark would run with the bait for a few seconds. We'd let it eat the bait, put the reel in gear, and then set the hook. Then all hell would break loose. The fillet of bluefish was the mako shark's favorite, but mackerel or whole squid also worked well. For hours, you watch the slick and the balloons as the seabirds coasted back and forth over the boat, occasionally a shearwater would glide into the line and the reel would scream for a second and your heart would skip a beat until you saw the bird caught in the line. When the wind was calm, the boat's drift was minimal, and less drift meant less chances of hooking a mako.

This day, I was on the verge of falling asleep when I heard the reel click once or twice. I opened one eye, and the reel started to scream. Line was coming off the reel so fast it almost had backlashed by the time I got to the rod. I put my thumb on the reel so it would slow the line, but it was burning my thumb. At the same moment, I heard my friend let out a scream. I looked up to see a huge mako shark eighteen feet in the air about twenty feet behind the boat. He had taken the close bait and he was going nuts. The fish was a beautiful dark blue and gray with a snow-white belly. Time seemed to stand still as it reached the top of the jump. It hung motionless in the air for what seemed to be minutes, but in reality was only a second. When he fell back into the water, a geyser of water soaked us in the boat as the shark was so close.

The mako spiraled on some of the jumps, and others he went end over end. A second seemed like minutes, and after seven huge jumps, the fish fell back into the sea at least two hundred yards from the boat and he was gone, free at last. The line had broken from either chafing on the sandpaper-like skin of the fish or because it was nicked. My friend and I did not say a word for a couple minutes, we just sat there stunned. We later estimated the size of the fish at close to four hundred pounds—it is something I will never forget.

Tuna fishing was different, with much more action than fishing for sharks, and pound for pound, they give a stronger fight. I have fought giant tuna that weighed over five hundred pounds on stand-up tackle, but I have never boated one. It was like doing battle. It was usually on fifty-pound tackle, and the line would eventually part or the hook would straighten. That summer, most of the fish I caught were yellowfin tuna, with a few bluefin tuna in the late summer and fall, and some long fin albacore. Trolling plastic lures at speeds of seven knots seemed to bring them up from the depths. It was a combination of the noise the lures make slipping through the water and the instinct the fish had, like a dog chasing a thrown stick. They couldn't help themselves. I had a small boat with no outriggers and could troll only five rods.

At times, tuna would hit with just a splash, but other times it would look an explosion had gone off behind the boat, leaving a hole in the ocean the size of a garbage can. After the knockdown, line went screaming off the reel and the rod would bend so the tip of the rod would almost touch the gunnel. I still love that sound. My boat had no fighting chair, and the battle on a stand-up rod could last an hour with a fish over a hundred pounds. Most of the tuna I caught on my boat that summer were between forty-five and a hundred pounds. We would release any tuna smaller than forty-five pounds to catch another day. This is something most boats do not do anymore, which is one of the reasons there are less and less tuna.

Chunking for tuna in late summer and into fall was red hot sometimes. There was a hole twelve miles southeast of Shinnecock Inlet where I was fishing with my cousin one day for sharks. Everyone on the boat was smoking herb but me, and most of them were asleep. The drift was poor as we had no wind, and the sea calm, with less than three feet of chop.

I caught something passing under the boat out of the corner of my eye. I was unsure if I really saw it or if my eyes were playing tricks on me. I was throwing chunks of bait over the side when I saw it again zigzag under the stern. "Yo, we got a fish in the slick, a big one, not sure what it is," I said.

Everyone jumped up just in time to catch the fish dart by and pass off the stern again. There were four of us on the boat besides me. "It's a sword, no, it's a mako, no, it's a marlin," they all said.

"I saw a flash of gold, I think it is a huge yellowfin," I said.

The fish disappeared for two minutes while the debate went back and forth. Then it took the closest bait. It was half a mackerel on just a thirty-pound rod. The reel screamed, and my cousin grabbed it to prevent a back-lash. It took line so fast it amazed us. My cousin locked the reel in gear, set the hook, and it was like it was still in free spool. It did not slow the fish down in the least.

My cousin weighed in at close to 650 pounds. Everyone called him The Whopper. He walked to the bow, put his back into it, and yelled to me, "Start it up! I am running out of line!"

Whopper was standing on the bow, and I could see the reel over his shoulder. It was down almost to the backing and still line was screaming off the reel of the gold International thirty. Now I started the boat and we ran toward the fish. The boat had almost planed, and yet the line was still peeling off the reel. With one arm, my cousin motioned to go faster, which I did. Finally, we hit almost 2500 RPM and he began to get line back on the reel. Everyone in the boat knew how close we had just come to losing all the line.

Then, slowly, Whopper started reeling in. I had cut back the throttle, steering the boat toward the angle of the line in the water.

As usually happens, the fish got his second wind and the reel screamed again. The fish sounded toward the bottom. We were in 120 feet of water, so he couldn't go far. Then it stopped taking line. I slowed the boat, and my cousin took back more and more line. Sweat poured down his face like someone was holding a hose over him. Words of encouragement came, "You got 'em, Whop. Hang on, he's yours."

I was quiet, focused on running the boat. I knew that no fish was yours until it was in the boat. Lots of things seemed to happen when the fish was alongside the boat at the end of the fight. I had seen it too many times: the angler for some reason tightens the drag at the last minute, the mate grabs the leader and pulls too hard so it snaps, losing the fish, the knot breaks from the stress, the knot pulls, or the hook breaks or bends. I slowed the boat. I could see the line coming to the surface. "He's coming up!" I yelled.

I put the boat in neutral. Sixty yards off the port bow, I saw the fish surface, its huge head bobbed like a barrel floating to the surface. I put the boat in gear, line was coming in faster and faster as we approached the fish. "Get the gaff!" I screamed. Some asshole grabbed a tuna gaff that was five feet long. "Not that gaff! The flying gaff!"

A flying gaff is a long pole with a hook almost ten inches across and a half-inch nylon line shackled to the hook, which is tied to the cleat of the boat. The gaff hook should be struck into the side of head or close to it. You pull the sharp hook into the fish with all your strength, sinking it deep into the flesh, then you twist and hope the hook releases from the pole. Whopper reeled in the line, the leader approached, I pulled the boat alongside the huge fish, and bang, the flying gaff was set. We all stood there in awe. The fish was huge. Another line was looped around the tail, and at just that moment he came back to life. The fish went crazy, thrashing and banging the hull of the boat with its tail, and water was everywhere. It took a couple minutes before the fish settled down. At times, I thought the huge tail would crack the hull. Then we all tried to figure out how to get him into the boat. It took all four of us to bring him aboard, and when we finally had him on the deck, it was the first time we realized the size of this huge tuna. We all cheered and high-fived each other. I think it might have been a world record being that it was caught on thirty-pound line. My feeling was the tuna sounded and was swimming at a fast pace until his head hit the bottom. He was stunned. That was when he bobbed to the surface. If we had not gotten a gaff in him right away and the fish had regained his senses, it might have been several hours of fighting the fish before we had the chance of gaffing him again—if we were that lucky. It was a giant bluefin tuna and weighed over seven hundred pounds when it was weighed back at the dock. I had my picture taken next to the fish. Although I did not catch it, I felt that by running the boat I had a shared in the feat.

The fish was sold and headed for Japan. Whopper gave us all a cut of the money later.

In the '70s and early '80s, the fishing off Long Island for tuna, marlin, and mahi reached its peak. Boats that did overnight trips to the Canyons over eighty miles from the inlet would catch dozens of tuna per trip. Inshore, I would catch five to ten a day, several days a week. I loved the excitement. It would not take but a year or two before the inshore fishing for tuna would die almost completely, and today it is rare to catch tuna inside the Canyon. The price reflects that. I was getting three dollars a pound for tuna loin back then, and now it runs twelve dollars. I sold my boat, *Blue Runner*, that next fall.

NEVER TOO OLD

By the time I was two years sober, I would come into the kitchen some days and see my dad reading one of my self-help books. Dad used to spend most of his time in that kitchen, it seemed, more than any room in the house. Breakfast was two hours, lunch was another two hours, and then came his tea each day at four thirty. It was not that he ate much—he just liked sitting is his chair and looking out the big picture window. I loved that view too, the big red barn, the apple orchard, and the huge vegetable garden beyond. I used to leave the books around the house on purpose, hoping my brother would pick one up. Now my dad seemed to be drinking more than he did when I was drinking. But then again, what did I know? I was so twisted then that I could not have known for sure.

The day came when he asked George and me many questions about alcoholism and meetings and the possibility that he might be an alky. George and I took my dad at seventy-two years old to his first meeting, and he liked them, and like me, he enjoyed the stories. He felt accepted also. I did not think about whether he was going because he was lonely. He liked it there, and slowly he became happier about life and made some new friends, so that was all that really mattered.

There is something else that comes with the gift of being in recovery. It seems that for once in your life, you fit, you belong, and there may be a purpose for your life. Growing up, there was something missing. I could not figure it out, so I did more drinking, more drugs, and had wild sex with more women. I felt I had something coming, something that was going to change who I was, a purpose and a meaning, if you will. It is a gift some people get only to a small degree, and I am not sure if it has to do with how much pain you put yourself through, that soul sickness and the depression that borders on suicide. It is a miracle and nothing else, of this I am sure.

In the weeks that followed, my father went to meetings, asked more questions, and even though he took his sleeping pills at night, he was not drinking. I was not sure if he was an alky when he first started coming, but he liked it. I liked that he wasn't drinking, so it didn't matter. I had the problem many do when starting sobriety—I was a volume drinker, drinking quarts at a time. When some said twenty or thirty quick ones, that was me. In my twenties, having a dozen shots and a dozen rums or vodkas was an every-Saturday-night thing, plus all the dry goods added to the mix. So my dad only drinking a third of a bottle seemed like a light hitter to me.

Later that changed, when I heard a woman at a meeting tell the story of only drinking two beers a night. She was a five-foot-tall woman who would obsess about drinking the two beers every day until she quit and went to the program. Her husband worked late. When he got home, he would ration her beer to her, one before dinner and one during, and that was it. She wanted more, but that was all she was allowed, and at times she wanted to commit homicide to get a third! Many of us at the meeting felt her anger and wanted to kill the husband too, for the torture she went through.

She loved the taste and the feeling it gave her, the time spent thinking about when she would have the drink and how she would feel. It was the same as me. It made sense: "It doesn't matter how much you drink, it is what it does to you."

My dad liked his new friends, and many nights there was a newcomer at the kitchen table he had invited back for coffee.

There was a skinny man in his sixties named Harry. He was there often. Harry had some sort of trust fund, I think, and he didn't work. He was just a drunk and never did drugs. One night, after a Friday night meeting, my dad and he were at the kitchen table talking. I came home and joined in, and then a while later, my brother sat down. Harry asked us both questions about what coke was like and pot and hash, etc., and my brother, who was still using, had firsthand knowledge, maybe from the night before. Harry brought up opium. What was that like? he asked. Eben and I agreed that it was the best high there was. Harry asked where a lot of it came from, and we told him that in Thailand it was everywhere and cheap. We laughed for a while longer and the night ended. A few months went by, and I realized I had not seen Harry at meetings. I asked my Dad, and he said he had not seen him. Then, sometime later, he was at my father's kitchen when I came home one night. He told of great stories of Thailand!

There was soon a time when my younger brother Eben went to meetings also, for a year off and on, and many nights, all of us would be together in a meeting. Maybe it was such a miracle what had happened in my life that they wanted to try it. I was no saint by any means. I wasn't drinking, but I'm not really sure I could say I was sober either—I mean really sober. The nutty thoughts and angry outbursts were frequent, and mood swings happened every day.

I think the way the program teaches people how to live could benefit any human being. It teaches you to help others and be there for others, to better yourself so you are content, to connect spiritually with a power greater than yourself and be grateful, and to begin to accept yourself. It is huge.

George told me often that I would help many people, and some of those people were my family, thank God. Some things change quickly when you get sober. Physically, you feel and look better. You are not thinking of killing yourself on a daily basis. You are not isolated as much. You are surrounded by people who are concerned about you, and slowly you begin to learn how to do the right thing.

It reminds me of a funny but not-so-funny story. It was early in my sobriety, maybe two years. I had given my mom a ride to JFK that day when my sponsor George called. I told him what I had done, and he said, "What a nice thing that you did for your mother."

"Yeah, and I only charged her fifty dollars," I said proudly.

"What?" George said.

I could hear from his tone that he thought the charge was unfair, so I said, "I usually charge her one hundred."

I could not get that charging my own mother for a ride was sick. He called me a sick fuck and hung up the phone. It took me years before I realized how twisted I really was.

I look back and realize what a sick relationship I had with my mother. Through my childhood, she was inconsistent, lacked support, and unavailable. Later, she waved her money like a carrot before a horse. I hated that about her. She had left us when I was nineteen years old, but I think that emotionally she had left ten years before that. There was also a guy she was dating, and all of us kids knew but never told Dad.

Once, I went to her house for dinner a few months after she left my dad. I would always be the bartender and pour two for me, one for her. I was asked by dad on my way there to make her see the light that the six acres of land she wanted for the divorce settlement should really belong to us kids. We kids were always told we would never have to worry and that one day we would be worth millions. We would sit in the den smoking Thai sticks or homegrown, waiting for our ship to sail while watching *General Hospital*. In some ways, it was humorous, and in other ways it was kind of sad. We wasted years waiting for it to happen.

So I was to be the spokesman for my brother and sisters. Already loaded with huge resentment when I walked to her door, it only got worse after half a dozen vodkas. I talked it over with Mom at cocktails, as she called it, but it never ended well, and many nights I said something in anger. Or worse, I stuffed my feelings inside and did not say anything. I would then head to the bar and try and drink the anger away.

She eventually got her settlement and the six acres of land in Water Mill. I suggested she invest some money and subdivide it so she would make more money. She told me she did not want to spend the ten thousand to do that and sold the six acres for $230,000 to a man who lived down the road from us who came out on weekends a month later. In a year, he had subdivided the land and sold it all for $560,000. My mom would never take suggestions. This was one of the many stupid financial blunders she made in her life.

The way we lived growing up was not as bad as some and worse than others, I guess, but there was always the sense of not having enough money to buy certain things. We always had clothes and food on the table, thank God, but there was always a struggle. I knew as a young child that I wanted to live without the fear of not being able to make it. I wanted to be different. Maybe I did sit with my brother smoking a bong and waiting to be discovered or waiting for someone to arrive with a million dollars, but when I got sober, I knew that if I wanted to be a success and have nice things, I would have to work hard and earn them. My father tried to manipulate us by saying he'd leave us land, and years later, my mother tried the same thing with money. They wanted us to stay around and not abandon them; it was their way of controlling us.

When I was two years sober, my dad said he wanted to give me two acres of land. He wanted me to build a house next to his to keep me close. It scared me at first. The responsibility of it seemed overwhelming, and the taxes would be a few hundred dollars a year too. I told him thanks, but I declined the offer. It makes me laugh to think about it now.

A year or two later, I took my father up on the offer and the land was put in my name for a dollar. I think my sister and brother resented it. Dad did not say so in words, but I figured he was leaving me the land, and the balance of his estate was to be split between my brother and sister. My oldest sister barely ever visited my dad, like it was too dingy and it smelled like dogs at his house. Also, I think she and my mother were closer than she was to my dad.

FALL APPROACHES

I love the fall. The beaches are beautiful on the east end, the ocean still warm enough to swim in until late October, and best of all, many of the people are gone. When I was a teenager, I remembered it would be a ghost town after Labor Day weekend. Some of the stores would close, and it became peaceful. From the time I was a young boy, I always knew when the summer was coming to an end. I would drive on Meadow Lane toward the inlet, and swallows would swarm over the dunes and the marsh. The small, dark birds would dart and pitch, catching small bugs and prepare for their migration south. I would be sad and happy at the same time.

In the fall, I put away the paintbrushes and brought out the hunting equipment. As the years went by, I would guide more groups of hunters for waterfowl, and more clients heard about me. I was interviewed by Nelson Bryant, an outdoor writer from the *New York Times*. He wrote an article about me, and for years I had clients who read it call me. My success continued, and each winter I would have saved money enough to go on extended vacations. I loved to ski and would rent a house in Aspen and have a blast. I would buy a season's pass and ski a lot; one year, I skied fifty-six days in a row.

Some days I would ski with my sister, and others alone or with friends I had met in the meetings.

I would meet women here and there, skiing or out at night and sometimes even in meetings. One such woman was a cute little blonde named

Mary, who approached me a couple times after the meeting and wanted to get coffee with me and talk. She usually wore sweat pants, big glasses, a huge sweatshirt, and had her hair tied up in a bun—I guess she was just coming from the gym. There is a suggestion in the program: no thirteenth stepping, or having sex with the newcomers. I had broken that a few times in my first five years, but I was getting better with. At least that is what I thought. I knew Mary was only sober a few months, so I made an excuse the first time she asked me to coffee and told her I had plans, which I didn't. After the second time, I agreed to meet Mary for coffee before the meeting for an hour, then we would go to the meeting. I had no intention in getting wild with her. I thought we would have coffee and conversation and that would be that.

Friday night came, and I went to a place called Bentleys in Aspen to meet her. I walked past the bar looking for Mary and walked past a couple booths, and then I heard my name. I had walked right by her. She wore no glasses, and her hair was not in a bun. It hung on her shoulders in wavy blonde curls. A tight red sweater brought her nice breasts to my attention, and a pair of black leather pants showed me she had been hiding a lot behind those sweats. I said to myself right there, probably out loud that George was going to kill me. As we talked, I looked into her light blue eyes, and to this day I could not even tell you what was said. We talked for an hour or so and then lost track of time and raced to the meeting. Her middle name was Theresa; I called her Mary T from the beginning.

I waited a few minutes after she went into the meeting so people would not think we arrived together. What a joke. They all knew what was up from that night on. After the meeting, we went to the Chart House for dinner. I think we were making out at the table before dinner even came—neither one of us could eat. I was infatuated with this Mary T, I know that now, but I was thirty-two going on fourteen emotionally. After dinner, we walked around Aspen. We would stop and kiss like schoolchildren, the snowflakes floated down and touched our hot faces and lips and melted instantly. Aspen is beautiful when it snows, and that night it seemed so quiet. The streetlights flickered, and it was like we were there alone. We talked and walked for a while, and then I dropped her off home and we made a date to see each other two nights later. Something about her made me weak in the knees and sick to my stomach. I think it is normal to think of the type of girl you want to marry or fall in love with–all men do it—but this was so far past obsession that it was out of control. I thought of her meeting my parents. My father would love her smile, her beauty, her laugh, and her intelligence—and all those things would make my mother hate her. Yes, she was the perfect girl for me!

I knew the French restaurant where she worked in downtown Aspen. The next night I had to see her, so around eleven I walked into the place and asked for her. She was a bit stunned to see me, but she smiled and I smiled back. I wanted to grab her and hug her to death right there. Mary told me to come back a while later, which I did. Years later, Mary told me that the night I came to find her at work scared her and she was going to tell me she could not see me, but something happened that night to change her mind. To this day, she does not know exactly why she changed her mind, but she did, and from that night on, we could not stay away from each other.

She had a young daughter, maybe fourteen years old or so. Mary told me about her, but all I could think of was the two of us walking into the sunset. Mary T and I fell as deep into infatuation, lust, and desire as one could get in the short two weeks we were together. Mary later said that by the second night, I was telling her I would send for her, fly her to my home in the summer so she could be with me, and in the winter I would be back with her in Aspen. We skied together some days, but most of the time we shacked up at my rented house at the foot of Aspen Highlands. One time she said she had a cold and was not feeling well, so I drove to her apartment and brought her to my place and took care of her. Maybe that is what changed her mind about me.

While all this was taking place, I had let my walls down, the walls that had been protecting me from the kind of injury that hurts more than physical pain. I built huge walls to protect myself and keep the abandonment, rejection, and loss at bay. I am not sure why I let Mary in, why the walls came down and why I became more vulnerable. It snuck up on me. I had sex and needed reassurance—I could not help it. I would tell Mary that we would do this together and that together, and then I would ask, "You want to do that right?" Constantly, I needed to be reassured, and if I had not gotten it from Mary over and over again, I would have panicked for sure. But she told me what I needed to hear, that we would be together and she wanted me. I wanted to believe it.

Most alcoholics suffer deep wounds from abandonment and rejection. Hell, most of the fucking human race is wounded, but the difference is that alkies stop themselves from killing themselves from their wounds by numbing the pain with drugs and booze, at least this one did. Sometimes we dabble in gambling, sex, and food too, but getting twisted makes it go away, at least for a time. Becoming an addict and an alcoholic saved my life. It took years for me to know that and thousands of dollars at the shrink shop, but it positively saved my life.

For me, entering a relationship was ten times more fearful than sliding out on that outrigger on the lobster boat tripping on mescaline, I can tell you. I could do the casual dating thing easy, wild sex was right up my alley, and I could even hold hands a bit, but when it came time to sleep, I had to be alone. Once I started to feel vulnerable, all bets were off and I went running. My mind would play tricks on me, though. I would find fault with the person. She slurped her soup, her legs were too short, her legs were too long, she was too into me, too controlling, and it went on and on, then I would say, "It's not you, it's me." Most of the time, it was intimacy that scared the shit out of me.

I remember a August summer night in my second year of sobriety when, after a meeting, I was eating an ice cream cone on a bench on main street in Southampton with Jack, a newcomer in the program. Jack was trying to get sober, but he could not quit smoking dope. He used to come to meetings stoned a lot. We all knew it. He didn't think we did, nor did we really care. Years before, there was a story of how Jack was stoned coming back from New York City, driving thirty-five on the Long Island Expressway and bringing back a half-pound of Columbian weed when he got pulled over by the cops. He slowed down and pulled over, but he would not unlock the doors and sat in the cab of the truck trying to eat the half-pound!

Jack and I were talking and laughing on the bench when a girl walked up to me, looking at my ice cream, and said, "That looks good."

"It is, why don't you get one?" I told her. I was in one of those relaxed moods, and it did not really even register that she thought maybe I looked good as well and was sweet for me.

She came out of the ice cream store and sat down between us and introduced herself. What a brave move, I thought. Her name was Barbara, and she was out for part of the summer from the city. She was about five-foot-six with long brown hair, a tight body, a nice tan, dark brown eyes, and beautiful. She was easy to talk to and confident. After our ice cream, I asked for her number and she gave it to me. I told her I would call her the next day, and she walked down the sidewalk. Jack was quiet the whole time, and after she left he said, "Unbelievable. She is hot, and she just walked up to you." He was stunned, and he walked toward his truck shaking his head.

I had a smile on my face and a sparkle in my eye. I had it going on, I thought as I started up the truck and headed out for a ride by the beach. I stared at the stars and listened to the sweet sound of waves as they rolled on the beach. The stars were brilliant and I thanked God for my sober life. I am a miracle, I thought.

Barbara and I dated for the rest of the summer. Went to the beach, had dinner and lots of sex, but I always headed home late at night when she fell asleep. Her summer lease ended in town, and one weekend in early September, we made plans for her to come out for the weekend at my place. I had rented a small house in Southampton that summer from a friend. I picked her up on a Saturday. There was a storm that night so we stayed in. The power went out, and we had candles lit all over the house and had incredible sex for the whole night in every room, including the bathroom I think. I tried to sleep, but it was difficult as her arms kept winding around my neck. I felt that I was choking as it was. Sex I could do—well, in fact—but the intimacy of hugging each other while we slept was not easy for me, and of course I could not talk about it. I knew there was something wrong with me, but if I said anything, there would be dialogue of some sort that would make me sweat and want to run for cover.

The next morning, I stood in the kitchen cooking breakfast when Barbara came up behind me and kissed my neck, then she slipped her hand in my sweatpants and grabbed my Johnson. Now, today I would handle this situation in a much different way, but that day it was too much for me. I couldn't breathe, I felt trapped, and I had to push her away. I said in an impatient tone, "I am trying to cook breakfast."

She was hurt and now the dialogue I hated would begin, talking about feelings. It was more scary than anything I could ever imagine. "What's the matter?" she asked, her eyes filling with tears. I was sweating, and my throat went dry. Terrified, I wanted to run. Change the subject, I thought, about anything. "What is the matter?" she asked again.

Run, run for cover, breathe, breathe, answer her, for God's sake I said to myself. "Nothing is the matter," I said sharply.

She wasn't buying it. "I know there is something wrong. What is it? Tell me."

Of course there was something wrong. I had entered into a place where no man like me should ever go, a place I was ill-equipped to handle. I couldn't even come close to pulling off a bluff. In fact, I was scared shitless of intimacy. The touching, the fondling, the closeness of it all, and talking about it was the end of life as I knew it. This conversation could never happen, ever, ever. Most of all, I wasn't sure what the hell intimacy really was anyway, at least back in those days. Christ, I was thirty years old and emotionally going on fifteen. How could I possibly understand what I was feeling? In fact, I used to have to call George after many meetings and tell him I felt like shit.

"Well, Phil, shit is not a feeling," was always his answer. I had to explain what happened and what was said at the meeting. "Phil, I think what you are feeling is shame. Did you do something like that years ago, maybe never dealt with it and it now has come back to you?" It would come back, and we would talk about it. I was reassured it was shame and that it was a legitimate feeling for me to have and that it was normal. I would feel better. I would hang up the phone, thinking I was normal.

At that moment, being in that kitchen that morning with Barbara, being asked what was the matter, how could I explain it to her? I was not even aware of anything other than my skin was crawling, I could not breathe, and I needed to run. Fuck talking about my feelings, I said to myself.

"I am worried about work," I said. "I just had a client call and I have to work today."

"I didn't hear the phone ring. Why work? It is Sunday, aren't we going to the beach?" Barbara pleaded.

If a conversation was not going the way I wanted, I would let my anger shut it down. I could yell louder than anyone I had ever known, and that is what I did. It was ugly. Barbara cried and ran for the other room. I let her go and ate my breakfast like it never happened.

Now, she had come out on the train from Manhattan to see me. The guilt and shame of it all was overshadowed by anxiety and panic. I knew how bad it was, but she had to go and quickly.

"Where would you like to go?" I said as I walked into the bedroom, where she lay on the bed weeping. The beach was her answer, and she got up and started to pack her bag with her clothes. The drive to the beach was absolutely silent on that warm summer morning. She was in tears as I drove away from the beach. She walked up to the beach carrying her bag, and that was the last I ever saw or heard from Barbara. I was sick inside and relieved at the same time. I talked about it with George later in the day. He had no answer, no one did, and I did not know why I had done that until many years later.

A few years ago, while I was looking for something in a drawer, I found an old address book from those days. There were lots of names of women, and then I came across Barbara's name and I remembered. I still had guilt about the day I had dropped her off at the beach; I could see the tears roll down her sweet face as I drove away. I called the number in the book, but the call would not go through, so I sat down and wrote her a long letter. I told her how sorry I was and what a hurtful thing I had done by abandoning her at the beach that day. I explained the fears I was feeling that morning, and I mentioned the struggle I had with intimacy and the urgency I had to be alone. I mailed the letter to the address in the book, but a few weeks later it was in my mailbox. "Return to sender" was stamped on it.

It seems that many times we hurt people before they can hurt us.

COMING HOME

It was a warm June day when I picked up Mary T at the airport. I had been writing many letters to her since I left Aspen a few months before. She looked beautiful, and we talked to each other and told stories of what we had been doing since we had been apart. Arriving at home, I introduced her to my father. His eyes sparkled as they always did when he admired a beautiful woman. He loved talking to her, and it was hard to pull her away sometimes. Dad accepted her right away, and they would become great friends in the years to come. It made me happy to know she was accepted by him. My brother and sister liked her too, and it was fun when all of us were together. Many times I was the scapegoat, and they all enjoyed teasing me, but it was all in fun—at least most of it was.

I showed her the beach and the town. I told her stories of growing up and many things about nature my father had taught me. We enjoyed each other. I was still living at my dad's then. I would help out with expenses a bit, and I did some work around the place from time to time, but with my brother, sister, Mary T, myself, and Dad under one roof, it was a bit tight. It worked out, though, as Mary would only come for a week at a time back then.

A day or two later, I took her to meet my mother. I had a devilish sparkle in my eye as Mary and I drove into the driveway of Mom's house. It was really her new husband's Paul's house, but we always called it her house. Mom had married Paul about the time I got sober. He was a good man and put up with her, which gave him a VIP pass when he reached the pearly gates in my book.

To say the least, my mom knew how to manipulate me and my siblings, and each one of us held underlying resentments toward this woman, each one of us had our own issue. So that is where the devilish twinkle came from—I knew Mom would probably worry about Mary not being good enough. Not being good enough for me was not the biggest issue—it was that Mary would not possibly embarrass her. That would be the real issue. Mary was the first woman I had brought to see my mother since I had been sober. Mom's name was Eunice, which always reminded me of someone in the fucking circus. You know, "Eunice the Great." Anyway, there she was at the front door to greet Mary T and me. She wore one of the thirty cashmere sweaters she owned, a thick gold necklace that must have weighed a pound, Lily Pulitzer green flowered pants, and shoes that cost enough to put new tires on my truck.

"You must be Mary," Mom said. "I have heard so much about you."

I always choked when she said things like that. I gave Mom a test once. I said three sentences to her and then asked her what I had just said. She failed miserably. If she was lucky, she could get one. She was one of those people you could tell was giving you that look, like, "I am listening to every word," yet her eyes would wander and you could just tell she heard nothing you said and did not care either. Talking to Mom was like doing your time. You needed to do it, it was your duty, but you hated it and wanted to be somewhere else. When you left, you knew it would be a long time before you were to return.

Eunice had on her happy face. She was in her "I love my life so much" mood. It was an act. I saw right through it and wondered if Mary did too. I did not have to say a word when we left. Mary said, "Your mom is quite something" on the ride home, and we laughed about Mom. It was all good. I saw a movie called *The Three Faces of Eve* once. It was an old movie depicting a woman who was a schizophrenic. I think she might have been played by Bette Davis. That was Mom…one minute she was friendly and happy to see everyone, and then she would flick a switch and call someone a goddamn asshole or something else derogatory. "They are all morons," she would say about the plumber, the auto mechanic, her doctor, and anyone else who pissed her off. She always wanted you to know that she was right, and I hated when she would point her finger a foot from my face and say, "You will listen to me now." When I was drinking I used to put up with it, but after a couple years sober, I started to tell her to treat me with respect and stop talking to me like a second-class citizen or a child. I was over thirty by then. It took a long time to put a stop to the insanity. It took my sisters and brother years to take back their power.

Mary and I went to meetings together. She liked many of my friends, and they liked her as well. George and Annette went to dinner with us some nights, and we had a lot of laughs. Finally, the time came and Mary flew back home to Aspen. I was sad to see her go. Lots of phone calls and letters kept us in touch with each other. She told me years later that she kept all the wonderful letters I wrote from my heart. Writing was good for me.

In the spring of 1988, I took Mary to Kauai. I wanted to propose to her and have her come and live with me in New York. I had decided after meeting Mary that it was time to build a house on the two acres in Water Mill. It would be our home, next door to my dad's house. That June she packed all her stuff and her little MG sports car in a moving truck and flew out to live with me. Her daughter Jaime Sue came also. She was almost seventeen by then, and she brought two of her girlfriends from Aspen—all three were cute as could be. My dad was a bit shocked, as was I, when they all showed up. He thought it would be a good idea to put up the tent so the young girls could sleep in the apple orchard for a while. Now, my brother was twenty-four or so and when these cute little Colorado girls showed up at the house. I knew I would have to keep on eye on him. It was probably not long before they were all getting high out there in the tent. I had a talk with him, but it didn't help. A few days later, the moving truck showed up, and I could not believe all the stuff Mary had packed up and brought to New York. My dad's barns were filled with Mary's belongings.

My house was being built and would be finished by October. Mary and I would walk next door while it was being built from time to time. The driveway and the house were exactly as I envisioned it years before.

I used to throw parties at my father's house in the back field when I was in my twenties, and I would take a girl back to smoke a joint or do a line in the woods. There among the white pines, which were twenty feet tall then, we would sit in a grassy meadow and I would take a toke and speak about how this would be where I would build my house one day. "The driveway will come down from the road, circle around these trees, and my house will be right there," I would tell them. The strange thing is, the driveway and the house are exactly where I dreamed they would be fifteen years before I had the property and had the house built.

The white pines gave us privacy, and I loved to tell Mary the story of how my dad and others had planted them all. Even to this day, it puts a smile on my face.

I borrowed $155,000, and the house cost $152,500. I was told to borrow $20,000 more than I needed, but the thought of having to borrow more money scared me. I would have financial fear for some years like I had never felt in my life.

I painted the house inside and out; all the wood trim got four coats of paint. I got contractors to do the lawn and irrigation system, and I bought rugs at a discount from my grandfather's store at cost plus a third. It was better than a stick in the eye, I guess.

Even though all my needs had been taken care of since I had been sober and always had enough work and enough money, I had never had the responsibility of a mortgage. Then, a year later, there was a home equity loan for another $35,000. I was full of fear, and like any good alky came the anger—they went hand in hand back then.

They say if you want to look at your character defects, get into a relationship, and if you want even more problems, get involved with someone with less than a year of sobriety. And if that is not enough, what the hell, just marry them and really torture yourself!

Living together was a huge adjustment for both of us, but Mary T had been married before—I had never even lived with a woman. She was a good woman, though, and my friend, and we did have many fun times living in our new house. Jami Sue, Mary's daughter, got a job working for a family not far from where we lived and moved in with them.

Mary was full of spirit and had a great sense of humor—even to this day, she makes me laugh. It was not long before she too was working, but her money was her money and my money was my money.

We planned our wedding and set a date of June 3, 1989. Mary's parents and she did not talk, so there would be no money coming from them, and my mother chipped in and gave us five hundred dollars as she had invited six of her friends. The rest was up to me. The restaurant where we had the wedding in Southampton gave us a deal—that was $11,000—and then another $4,000 for flowers, the church, the minister, and on and on. You get an education in the costs of getting married quickly, but somehow I came up with the money.

Mom said she would give us a rehearsal dinner at her house, which was nice of her, and after church one Friday evening in June, we arrived to a party of forty or so people. There was a large table set up on the deck for her and her guests, and the wedding party sat at a large round table on the lawn. George, Annette, my sister, and my brother Eben were at our table. Just before dinner, my mom came up and said she wanted to talk to me about wedding etiquette.

"Now, tomorrow when I arrive at the church, you will escort me down to the front of the church to my seat, and after the service is over you will leave Mary at the altar and escort me out of the church," mother dearest instructed.

"But that is not what we rehearsed, and I am not sure about leaving Mary at the altar, this does not sound right," I said to her.

This angered her. She looked at me with her cold eyes and pointed that finger a foot from my face like she used to enjoy doing and said, "This is the proper thing to do, and you will do it."

My mom had her way of pushing my buttons, and she made me feel inadequate and angry with her condescending and demeaning tone. She took control. I let her have it and did not stand up for myself, even when I knew what she was saying was off the wall. I was mad at myself for letting her get over again. I felt like stupid young boy who had just been scolded.

As I sat down at the table, the veins in my thick neck bulged as I approached stroke level. My face was tight and I was gritting my teeth a bit when George asked, "Are you okay?"

I told him I was fine, you know, fucked up, insecure, neurotic, and emotional. Then after he asked the second time, I explained what had just happened and said I had to escort Mom after the ceremony and leave Mary at the altar.

"Leave me at the altar, I don't think so," Mary said in an angry tone.

George said, "Phil, your mom is very confused. That is not proper etiquette, and she is mistaken." He then told me to just do what was rehearsed and not to worry about it.

I was lucky if I could stay conscious in the church because I was so nervous, let alone walk my mom down any isle.

June 3, 1989, was a beautiful hot sunny day, and I prayed to God to give me the courage go through with the wedding.

It was a beautiful wedding with maybe eighty people. Mary T and I were glad when it was over. The reception was a lot of fun, lots of dancing and not too much drinking as almost half the people were in recovery.

During the next few months, Mary and I went to meetings together sometimes, but I seemed to go to many more than she. At times I think she was intimidated by my sobriety of eight years, but we worked and life was good.

My waterfowl guiding business had really taken off, and I had five guides working with me through the early nineties. It paid the mortgage and then some. I grossed over $80,000 in three months annually and started to get more and more press. I was written up in *Outdoor Life*, *Field & Stream*, *Newsday*, *New York Post*, *Sporting Classics*, *Wildfowl*, and I was even on TV a couple times and did a commercial with my dog once for the Outdoor Life Network. In the spring, I would start looking for house painting work. I hated it by then, but it paid the bills. And in the summer, I did clambakes for the summer residents. Mary T helped me cater the parties, although we decided it would be better if we did not work the same events; I had several each Saturday night and some during the week.

So even as life was full of stress and lots of debt, we lived a good life and didn't fight a lot. When we did fight it was ugly, and I would say things that hurt her, and she learned how to push my buttons as well as my mother.

Mary did not communicate well, I thought, and she would say that I did not care. If I did ask what was the matter, she would say I only asked once and then walked away and that I needed to ask her more than one time. When you argue with someone you love, the wounds take longer to heal. I thought eventually the time would come when we needed help.

"I think you are crazy," I said one day. It came easily—hell, my dad used to tell my mother she was always crazy. It was what you did as a man when you could make no sense of the ranting and raving from your woman.

"I'm crazy? You're fucking crazy." This was her response when she had no idea how you could be so stupid, insensitive, or uncaring. I worked well with facts, numbers, and situations I could see and observe, but with feelings I had not a clue.

"Don't you know how this makes me feel?"

This was another good one. Christ, I don't know many times I had no idea what the hell I was feeling, and now I had to figure out what someone else was feeling. One day there was an argument, probably about sex, money, or control, and Mary always liked having the last word. Hell, I liked it too and was better at getting it. She screamed something and then locked herself in the bathroom and muttered expletives through the door. I hated that, the shutting of the door. It enraged me, and she did it often. I felt like what I had to say didn't matter. I kicked the door, but she was right behind it. It hit Mary T. There was blood, and in an instant I realized I had done the unthinkable: I had hurt a woman, especially my wife. We cried and cried, huddled on the floor and holding each other, and I said, "I am sorry, I did not mean to hurt you." I must have said it a dozen times. I took her to the doctor, who gave her four stitches on her forehead. I think she made up an excuse at work that the dog had knocked her down.

My anger made me sick inside, and I felt ashamed for weeks.

The only good thing to come out of it was that it started us in therapy. We saw a woman together, and then Mary would see her therapist and I would go to mine. It was good for me, as I was not aware of what was triggering the anger, fear, and resentment.

The most powerful thing I did in my first year of sobriety was go to the Caron Foundation in Pennsylvania. It was called the family program, but I'm not sure what they call it today. George recommended it. It was a week-long program. You stayed there, had a roommate, and it was intensive. There were ten in my group the first time I went, three men and seven women, and after a day of hearing how the men had been physically abused by their alcoholic parents and the women had been physically and sexually abused, I told the group that I really did not think I belonged there. That is where I learned how much denial I was carrying around. In my childhood home, our family did not even talk to each other at times. I found out this was called silence abuse. Sometimes I thought my mother had a hearing problem. I learned a lot there, and I started to recognize how damaged I was. I could not remember a lot from my childhood, so it was difficult to get a handle on my fears, anger, and insecurities.

One time, the counselor put all of us in group in some sort of trance. They called it guided imagery. I thought it would never work, but I was in for a huge surprise.

Soft piano music played in the background. It was relaxing, like the sound of water flowing over rocks in a small stream. The instructor would say things like, "Now you are a small child. You are five years old and you are at a small pond and you kneel down and look at the reflection of yourself in the water."

In an instant, I was at a pond near my house, where I spent many afternoons catching frogs, and saw my reflection in the water. The instructor continued, "Now you are going into the house where you lived, you sit down for dinner, take notice of everyone at the table." At my table, I saw my mom, dad, brother, and one of my sisters—but it was weird, I could see the lime green linoleum kitchen table, the ugly green kitchen cabinets, but when I looked around at everyone at my table, no one had a mouth.

"Now go to your parents bedroom, visualize what it was like there," said the woman. I opened the door and my parent's beds were almost ten feet apart. They slept in different beds and hardly ever touched; I don't think I saw them kiss each other twice in my life.

"Go to that special place, that place safe place where no one would find you," said the instructor. There was a tree house I had built in a huge willow tree that had blown partially over in a hurricane. It was close to the house, and I could sit up there fifteen or twenty feet from the ground and no one ever knew I was there. I visualized the floorboards just as they were over twenty years before. Some were gray and weathered, and others had blistered white paint on them; some were wide and some were narrow. It was where I would run and hide from the world.

After this I sat up, tasting the salty tears as they ran down my cheeks onto my lips. The whole group was sobbing. We each talked about our imagery and discussed it with the group; it was one of the most powerful experiences that I've ever had.

When I was asked to walk around my house, I went into every room looking for someone. They were all empty. It was explained to me that no one was there emotionally for me, thus the empty house. The part where no one had mouths was strange, but it was to signify how no one talked. Silence abuse began to make sense to me. These safe places I went to in the imagery gave me instant relief; I felt safe in my mind, as I had almost thirty years before. I actually started to smile as I lay on the floor of the room remembering these places.

When we left Caron, we promised we would keep in touch. I spoke to a couple of them over the next year or two, but I lost touch like you do often in life.

I look back and realize how much courage it took to go through the self-realization, the long hours of tiring work involved there. It was like they stripped me down to nothing, like a child, and then tried to put me back together again. I left Caron on that Saturday feeling like I had been through major surgery. It took me weeks to feel like my old self, but really I would never be the same. Not that it all goes away, because it doesn't. Some scars heal and disappear, and some just don't—you have them until you die.

Life went on next door at my dad's. The dysfunction ran rampant, and my brother was still going wild drinking and drugging, and my sister was almost forty now and living there too. Hell, I was thirty-four when I moved into my new home. Living with Dad was easy and cost less. I would buy my own food and help out once in a while around the house, but I knew about the resentments I began to have living home. In my heart, I knew it wasn't right and felt that I was taking advantage of my father's easygoing nature. It would come out as anger toward my dad from time to time. When I left, I could see it in my sister and brother and the way they disrespected him and took advantage. My sister rarely had a job, and my brother did not pay rent. I think my sister and brother resented themselves for living there, and it came out sideways at my dad.

I felt bad for Dad and talked to Mary about it. She told me that until my Dad had been through enough, he would continue to put up with it.

One afternoon I stopped over, and Dad was having tea. He was alone, and we talked about things, the program, life—it didn't matter, there was always something to talk about. In his eyes I saw sadness and asked, "What's the matter? Is something going on? Is your health okay?"

He had lost his hair many years before and shaved his head. He was thin, maybe weighing 130 lbs. But the man had All his teeth in his seventies and girls still brought a twinkle to his eye. This day, the sparkle had faded, and I knew there was something he wasn't telling me. He looked up at me. His eyes filled with tears and his voice trembled as he said, "I am so sad, I can't do this anymore, I don't deserve it."

I got out of my chair and held him as he cried. It broke my heart. "What don't you deserve? What has happened?" I said.

Dad said that since I had moved out, things had gotten ugly at the house. He said my sister and brother were mean to him and said hurtful things. I felt anger toward my siblings and shame for things that I had said to my dad in the past. My dad looked up at me and said, "What should I do? I can't live like this."

"I think you should throw them out on their asses, that is what I think you should do," I told him.

We discussed it more, and I knew he was friendly with a counselor at Seafield, George's rehab, and I suggested that Dad call him and ask to meet. Dad called and asked me to accompany him. I agreed, and the next day we drove to Westhampton. Dad's friend was Stu, he was six-foot tall, with a full head of silver hair, and he spoke in a gentle manner. He greeted me with his firm handshake and a smile. "Good to see you," he said. I had known Stu for many years; he never seemed to age and had wonderful sobriety and many words of wisdom.

"Hi, Philip, how are you doing?" he said as shook my father's hand.

"Not too well," said my father as he sat in a chair facing Stu.

"Tell me what is going on, how can I help?" Stu said with a smile.

Dad looked down and told many stories of the disrespect that had been taking place in his home for many months. Stu said nothing for five minutes, and when my father paused he said, "What do you want to do, Philip?"

"I am not sure what I can do, they scare me," he said.

Stu then looked toward me and said, "Phil, will you help your father, make sure that no harm comes to him?"

"Absolutely, whatever he wants to do, I will help him," I said.

"You know what I would do if my children were talking to me and treating me that way?" Stu asked.

"What?" my father questioned.

"I would kick their asses out on the street," Stu said sternly.

My father laughed and sighed at the same time. "But how would I tell them? I can't do that alone," Dad said fearfully.

Stu asked me, "Would you be present when your father talks to your sister and brother?"

"Yes, and if you want them out of your house, I will see to it," I told Dad. My father smiled for the first time in days. He had a tear in his eye as he thanked me.

The day came, and I sat next to my father in his house as my sister and brother were told they had to pack up and leave. Neither argued, and a date was set, and when that day came they were gone.

I am not sure how long after my siblings had left the roost, but a thirty-year-old girl from the program moved into my sister's room in Dad's house. Roxy seemed harmless enough, and I actually never asked my dad if she was paying rent or not. He had made it clear when he bought a used Volvo. My sister wanted me to talk to him as she thought he was going to spend all of "our" money before he left this earth.

"So you bought a new Volvo?" I said to Dad.

"It is not new, but a great car," he said.

"What did you pay for it?" I questioned.

"None of your damn business," Dad said with that sparkle in his eye. I felt like saying good for you, but I laughed and changed the subject and never brought up his business and his money again. So Roxy may have done some cleaning, some cooking, and who cared what the hell she was doing? The man was seventy-six years old and happier than I had ever seen him.

My dad had a routine of getting up around nine or so. He would take a shower, turn on a radio, and shave. It used to drive me crazy when I lived there, as there was only one bathroom downstairs, and he could be in there for an hour. As a young boy, I can remember sitting next to him in the bathroom and watching him shave. Back then, there was a long procedure of mixing soap in a small cup. With a small brown bristle brush, he would whip it around and around until a thick white lather appeared. With the brush, he would fluff it on his whiskers. The bathroom would be so fogged up he would wipe some soap on the mirror with a washcloth so he could see to shave. He would hold his face taught with fingers from one hand and slowly pull down the razor with precision. Then he would swish the razor in the sink, which was full of hot water, to clean it off and make another pass on his face.

"You will be doing this one day soon, you know," Dad would say with a twinkle in his eye. I was five. I wanted to know if I should start soon, just so I could practice. It made my dad chuckle.

So one day, I wanted to ask my Dad if I could borrow a tool from his shop and walked into the house. I never knocked, I just walked in like I always did. Walking through the kitchen, I heard this strange sound. I stopped and listened. I continued into the hallway, and when I got to the bathroom door I realized Dad was singing along with the radio. In all my life I had never heard my father sing, ever. I knocked on the door and my father said, "Come in."

I was laughing when I said, "What the hell is going on in here?"

My father devilishly said, "I am shaving."

"No, I mean the singing, what's up with the singing?" I said.

"I am in a good mood, something wrong with that?" he laughed. I said something and shook my head and closed the door. I had forgotten what I wanted to ask him and laughed the whole way home. I spoke to Mary about what had happened. We both laughed, wondering if Roxy was doing more than a little cleaning around the house. I never asked him, though, it was none of my business.

EYES WIDE OPEN

Mary T was not great managing money and somehow needed money a lot. By the early '90s, she had filed for bankruptcy twice. Angrily, I found out she had opened credit card accounts in my name, and it would take years to get back my good credit. I never understood what she was spending money on, and when I asked questions about details, we would get into huge arguments, so I left it alone and hoped she would find her way. I put a five thousand dollar down payment on a brand new car for her. She was to pay me back over time, but it got lost in the shuffle. In the winter, we would leave for a couple of weeks, although we really didn't have the money. Usually we went back to Aspen and went skiing—at least I went skiing. Mary would either go shopping or out with friends. I skied alone or with my oldest sister, who lived there.

Before long, Mary and I had been together for four years. Many nights, we ate dinner in the living room while watching television. This one night while talking, Mary slurred her words, and when she looked at me her eyes almost crossed.

"Fuck, Mary, you're toasted, aren't you?" I said.

She denied it and we argued, and then she broke down and cried. Christ, she had been going to meetings for years. She had a sponsor, a therapist, and a sober husband who loved her. Maybe he didn't say it very often, but he did love her. How could this have happened? I panicked and picked up the phone and called George; he would know what to do. He was shocked.

For years, we had spent time with he and Annette, and never once did he suspect anything. "Phil, if I had noticed I would have said something," he said.

It has always stunned me. I mean, how it could have happened without me picking up on it? The only thing I could ever come up with is that, until that night when she appeared high and slurring words, Mary took prescribed medication and just maintained a subtle buzz. I was a garbage head and took huge amounts of drugs, pills, and booze. She was an LPN, and being a nurse, Mary knew how to get the right pills by telling doctors false symptoms. Meds were not my deal—I knew lots of people who abused Valium, Quaaludes, codeine, and many more, but none of them were in control like Mary was, at least until that night.

George pulled some strings and got her into a rehab he owned in Pennsylvania, and I drove her down. Looking back, I knew things had gotten rough at home. I felt overwhelmed a lot, I had my financial fears, and Mary and I fought a lot. She had moved into the guest bedroom months before. I looked through her room when she was away and found all sorts of unopened boxes and pill bottles in drawers, and it started to make sense. I felt sad for Mary and guilty that I should have known. I had been in recovery for almost ten years. I should have known and done something. I felt helpless and confused for weeks, even after she came home. I wondered what was in the unopened boxes, so I started opening them. Earrings, shoes, necklaces...all from *Home Shopping Network*. Finally, I figured it out. Mary was glued to the television many nights and on her days off, toasted, and would see some $39.00 diamond earrings and have to get them. This is a sickness that is probably shared by millions all over the world.

Mary returned from rehab a few weeks later. She and I had many trust issues and a tough road ahead of us. She was different and more real with me. "Maybe it will work out," I would think. I try now to remember if she moved back into our bedroom, but I can't recall. I sadly think that, like my parents, we were living the further and further apart.

I think that maybe we were just supposed to be friends, not husband and wife. Maybe we should have met each other at another time. And other times, I reflect and feel that it went exactly as it was supposed to go. I learned from her and she from me; we worked out a lot of issues and fears.

I have to say, she was there for me probably more than I was there for her. I had many times when my brother would call from jail through our marriage and plead with me to come and bail him out. "Please help me, don't let me sit here," he would cry out on the other end of the phone. There were many nights when she held me as I cried myself to sleep. When I returned from boarding school, I was fourteen and my brother was eight years old. He wanted to be friends and do things together, but I had started doing a lot of drugs and did not want him to get hung up in it and all I thought of was myself. I think he had done some drugs and drinking before my mom left, but when she left, he and I went wild and sometimes we would go out together and wreak havoc. We were buddies, and although we used to fight from time to time, we had fun together.

When I reached my bottom in '81, he lost me. I could not hang with him. He was caught up in addiction, and it was dangerous for me—I had to be selfish. I would later realize that it hurt him a lot. Many holidays, he would arrive at my mom's house coked up, and when Mary T and I had the holidays at our house, many a Christmas did I open the door and there he would be, stoned to the bone on blow, his eyes popping from their sockets and pupils so dilated that he resembled Charlie Manson. Standing there chewing his lip, his face gaunt and his body thin from lack of food, his skin so pale, and he would ask, "Can I come in?" I knew from past problems that he would ruin everyone's Christmas, and I would have to tell him, "You cannot come in here high like you are." I would close the door and stand with my back against the door, my head lowered in sadness. I felt like I had betrayed my brother, my own blood. I was crushed.

The experts in the field of alcoholism are not therapists, not counselors, not CSWs. The experts in alcoholism are in the rooms of Twelve Step programs. I heard George say this and I still hear it from time to time and it is gospel to me. Years of abuse, years of sobriety, working steps, attending meetings, hundreds of hours talking to my therapist, and most of all, being there for the sick and suffering made me very educated in this damn disease. When I closed that door, hung up the phone, or didn't pay his bail, I always prayed to God for him to ask for help, to want to live a better way. He was in my prayers always.

FORGIVENESS

Sometimes when you look back through your life, you remember bits and pieces. The hurtful times stand out along with a few fond memories of when things were good. I am not sure if it is living in New York or what, but sometimes I feel like life goes by in blur and it's a waste if you don't enjoy it while it's happening. I am guilty of wasting some parts of my time on this earth: wondering, thinking about the past, wanting things to have happened differently, maybe wishing I had a great woman who loved me, success and lots of money, and wishing things had been different between my parents and me growing up.

One spring day, I arrived back home. Mary T and I had gone on a vacation skiing out west and had been married a couple years. I said, "Mary, I am going next door to see Dad." It was what I always did when I came home from being away. I walked through the back field to his house; it was tea time. Around four thirty every day, my dad could be found in his kitchen having his cup of tea. Sitting next to him in a chair at the table was his dear friend, Jake. Jake was a 120-pound Chesapeake Bay retriever who thought he was a person—actually, so did Dad. The huge dog sat in a chair with a small plate in front of him, his yellow eyes glued to my father's cinnamon raisin toast. He barely looked up at me. I gave Dad a hug and said hello to Jake. He looked back at the toast on my father's plate. "He really missed me huh?" I said. Dad wore an old tan shirt that had a couple holes in it, khaki pants, and work boots. I never saw him in a pair of blue jeans his whole life.

His left boot had a shaft through it where his brace attached to keep the man upright. "How was your trip, did you ski a lot?" he asked as he sipped his tea.

"It was fun, I skied almost every day. They had lots of snow," I said as I looked out at the lawn. We talked for a while, and I am not sure why this was the time, but it was, and I asked if we could take a drive. You see, resentments are poison, especially to alcoholics. Resentment will make many a man pick up the bottle.

We arrived at the bay. We had a common bond there—the clamming, the hunting, and fishing we had done for years there. I don't know, the truck just drove us there. I didn't even think about it. I shut the car off and did not know where to begin. I said, "Now please hear me out and do not interrupt me." Looking for the right words was so hard, part of me didn't want to hurt this man of seventy-four years and part of me wanted to punch him in the face. "I have to tell you about some things that have bothered me for years, and they are getting in the way of me being happy, me being happy with myself, being happy with my life, being happy with you." I then said, "I am just angry with you, really fucking angry at what you did, what you and Mom did. How you treated me, or mistreated me is probably better name for it, the disinterest from Mom in me growing up. There were many times you didn't stand up for yourself and let Mom degrade you and humiliate you. Christ, abandoning me and sending me to boarding school when I was thirteen. Shit, I did not even know how to make my bed, had never been away from home. You know how that made me feel? Hurt, that's what. It fucking hurt. I cried myself to sleep every night for weeks. And you know why I am really angry? Because you didn't stand up to Mom and let me stay home. All the times I tried to do things well, it was never good enough for you. You always criticized me and made me feel stupid, like a failure that would never amount to anything. Christ, you both used to tell me that. I thought I was stupid until I got sober. I am angry for all the times I needed you to be on my side, the times I needed your encouragement, just a hug for God's sake, would it have fucking killed you?"

My dad's big brown eyes were filled with tears as he listened. Those eyes that looked toward me when I was young, the eyes that hurt me, the eyes that sparkled at times when he inflicted pain on me, now those eyes now were full of sadness, shame, and hurt. He had grown old now. No longer did he have power over me. His hair was gone, his body was thin and frail, and his skin was wrinkled and dotted with brown spots from years of being in the sun.

He looked out the window and started to speak. "You know, it was not easy raising you kids. There were no books. We always had money problems. Hell, we just didn't talk about what was happening, it was what we did in my house when I grew up." He looked back at me, the tears rolling down his reddish cheeks. "I am sorry what happened to you. I am sorry that you didn't get the love that you deserved. I am not sure even why I did the things I did and said the things I said, but I did all that I knew. I did my best, and if my best was not good enough, I am sorry for that."

My eyes started to fill with tears. I sobbed and did what came naturally: I reached for him, and my strong arms hugged his thin frame, and I told him I loved him.

Miracles do happen, and the miracle was not that I could love a man who hurt me, not that I could love a man who abandoned me, who struck me with canes and paddles and told me I was useless and never would amount to anything. No, that was not the miracle. The miracle was that I could speak out, verbalize my feelings, be angry, let it go, and then forgive him. Yes, this was a huge miracle indeed, and I never looked at him the same way after that afternoon.

Many times, life goes by and you never get the chance to say what you need to, to bring up old pain, to make an amend and free yourself from years of self-hatred, or in my case with Dad, let him know that what happened to me was hurtful. Years went by, and I am not sure if it was the tears we shared by the bay that day, but my father and I became closer. It happened slowly; I let him in, and he let me in too. The resentments finally and slowly began to melt away.

That spring and summer passed quickly, and I was always busy. I worked a lot and catered a fair amount of clambakes and dinner parties for the summer people, and then it was fall again. I think all people are affected by the change of seasons. There is an adjustment to be made. In the fall, the days start to shorten, and it gets colder. Many people have different interests and hobbies, but most people have the same job—they do what they do regardless of the season. When the summer ended, catering events stopped. I would have to adjust to less pressure, less hours working. The phone calls would slow down, and I would feel relieved on one hand and unneeded on the other. Meeting with clients about parties they wanted me to cater, coordinating the tents, the party rentals, the food, the staff for each event—it took sometimes over eighty hours a week, and in the fall, I had lots of time. I would start up the house painting business, as the fall is the best time to paint exteriors because the air is dry and temperatures are still warm.

I was not fond of painting, but I was good at it and it paid the mortgage. When October came, the phone would start to ring and hunters would call to reserve their dates for the season, which started in early November then. In the early '90s, the business of guiding waterfowl hunts was reaching its peak. I would employ five guides, and some weekends we were taking dozens of clients hunting. I leased several hundred acres through Southampton, Bridgehampton, and Water Mill. I took a lot of famous baseball players, football players, some of Wall Street's most successful stock brokers, just people from all walks of life, and I would get phone calls from as far away as Hong Kong from clients wanting to book a duck or goose hunt. I saw it all back then and heard lots of wild stories. Every day was an adventure. It was hard work and long hours getting up at 4:00 a.m. every day, but I loved it.

My dad loved to watch me and would drive down and park on the edge of the field and talk to the clients when they came in. Although he never really said the words, I knew he was proud of me. I owned thousands of goose and duck decoys and had invested thousands of dollars into equipment. With all the press in magazines and television, I was turning people away. I worked every day but Christmas. Sometimes I would take a group of hunters in the morning and another group in the afternoon. There were over forty thousand ducks and geese here in late December…more waterfowl than people.

GOD'S ANGELS

On Christmas Eve 1991, there was a knock at the door. It was my father, holding a Chesapeake Bay retriever in his arms. She was six weeks old and chocolate brown, with blue eyes, and her feet were yellowish brown. I named her Boots because on each of her feet, her fur was light yellow. She was a tiny brown bear, but I knew from the huge paws that one day she would become a powerful, big dog. She would, of course, have to wait until the next season before she could hunt. I brought her up to my face and gave her a kiss.

My whole life we had dogs. My dad was partial to Chessies—they were top dog in his book. We had one dog, Gunner, that was mentioned in the book *The Complete Chesapeake Bay Retriever* by Eloise Cherry. The beach club made a special exemption in their rules for Gunner, and he was the only dog ever allowed at the club. He was a huge dog of over 120 pounds and had the head of a lion. There were heavy ropes tied on the beach in front of the club that extended out a hundred yards to the barrels, where you could swim out and rest and swim back to shore. My father told me that on many days, Gunner would swim out to the barrels with the bathers from the beach club, and if a swimmer was ever in trouble, Gunner would swim out to help them.

People remember dogs, better than some family members sometimes, and stories about great hunting dogs are told for a lifetime. One such memory was a Chesapeake I had named Abe. He lived with me years before at Dads house.

Abe and I were hunting with clients in a storm in the '80s in heavy, 30 mph winds and rain. The ducks were flying bees that day. We shot a duck. It just had a broken wing, and Abe swam to retrieve it. Abe swam through the white caps from the two-foot waves, and at times they washed over his head. Each time he would come close, the duck would try to fly and skip ahead of him, then fall back into the water. Chessies do not give up the hunt. Matter of fact, years before I had to take a boat and retrieve the retriever, as Abe swam after a duck and went almost out of sight in the middle of the bay. This day, I had no boat and could only watch him through binoculars as he pounded through the waves in pursuit of our duck. The duck crossed the creek over three hundred yards away and ran up on the beach and then downwind twenty yards and straight into the brush and weeds. Abe was still fifty yards from the shore. The powerful dog got up on the shore, shook himself off, and started to hunt. Abe searched around the beach and finally picked up the duck's scent and ran downwind and disappeared in the brush for a minute or two and then appeared back on the beach with the bird and just stood there looking back at us. I thought to myself, "Hell, he is over a quarter of a mile away, he does not know where we are." I got out of the duck blind and walked into the water and yelled and waved my arms. Abe started running upwind. "Where the hell is he going?" I thought. "Dumb fucking dog," I said and walked back to the blind. I had another duck blind on the other side of the creek several hundred yards upwind and that is where he ran to. Now Abe was over a half mile away. We watched as he got to the point of land where the blind was anchored, walked out on the sandbar, and swam with the current all the way back to where we were hunting so he could ride the current. My clients were amazed and asked, "How did you teach your dog how to do that?"

I laughed and said, "He is smart and figured that all out on his own." I laughed with tears in my eyes when he arrived at the shoreline in front of our blind, holding his duck, almost making a thousand-yard retrieve. I remember it like it was yesterday. Abe was out of breath for a few minutes, then he was ready to go again.

I have been blessed with many wonderful dogs in my life, and each one would do anything for me. A retriever's job is just that: they are born to hunt, retrieve, swim, and run. Abe retrieved thousands of ducks, pheasants, and geese in his life. He lived the dream.

I was on my first sober vacation in Hawaii when Dad called me with sad news. Abe had gotten old, his hearing was not good, and whether a friend of Eben's was not careful or he did not hear the truck start that day or not, he was killed when the truck backed over him. I broke down and sobbed for hours, feeling guilty because I was not there to protect him. It was my job to protect him as he had done for me; I felt I had failed him. It was one of the only times in my sober life that I wanted to drink the gut-wrenching pain away.

IT WOULD ALL CHANGE

Mary T and I were doing life. It was hard sometimes, and I know now there were some trust issues that needed mending between us. Something was about to happen that would change my life forever, and she and I would become closer than we had been in some time.

We returned from vacation, either Florida or somewhere warm, and I went to my dad's to see how he was. As usual, he was sitting at the kitchen table; I think he was having lunch. I gave him a hug and sat down to catch up on things. He seemed kind of tired and his skin had a pale, yellow tint to it. He was glad to see me, but when I asked him how he had been he said, I have not been feeling well, I think I had a bad clam."

I asked him if he had been to the doctor, and he said he hadn't, so we called right then and made an appointment. He went through some tests over the next couple of days, and then the doctor called and wanted to see him. My sister and I went with him to the doctor's. We sat in the waiting room, and when his name was called, he wanted me to come with him. My sister waited. Dad had not been eating much and was unsteady on his feet as I helped him to the chair. The doctor entered the room and said hello and sat down and said, "There is no way to say this easily, Mr. Gay. You have cancer in your liver. It is difficult to say how long the tumor has been there."

Dad grabbed my hand and started to cry. I lost it. I wanted to be strong for him, but I fell apart. We held each other for a couple minutes, and the doctor waited to continue. We looked up, and the doctor continued, "We could try chemo. It could give you a bit more time, if you are up to it, it is your choice."

Dad thought for less than a few seconds and said, "I do not want to do chemo. How much time do I have doctor?"

"Could be six months, it could be less, it is hard to say."

There was more sobbing, and then my father said an amazing thing I will never forget: "You know, I have lived a long life. I have done everything I wanted to do, and if it is God's will that my time is up, I will accept that."

I fell apart again and tears' bitter taste hit my lips. The doctor said he was sorry, and Dad and I hugged each other for a few minutes and then we went outside and told my sister. She broke down; it was the heaviest and saddest news we would hear ever. She and I both loved my dad and he loved us, I knew that now.

I will remember that day for the rest of my life, every word and every detail. I'd seen it in movies and on television shows for years and heard about other people going through it, but you never think it can happen to you.

My dad was a trooper that winter afternoon. He asked if we could get some ice cream. We did, and then he wanted to take a drive to the ocean. Driving toward the beach, I can still hear him say, "Well, I will get to see Billy and Sophie, and father and mother, it won't be so bad."

I could barely keep the car on the road, then we stopped at the beach and looked over the ocean. It was his love—the sea, the bays, the marshes—all of nature he loved.

"This will be the last time I get to see the ocean," my father said. It was like getting punched in the stomach. I was in so much pain, crying and sick to my stomach, that I wanted to run. But I didn't run. I just sobbed and opened my window and smelled the salt in the air and watched gulls slide back and forth effortlessly in the southwest wind over the waves breaking on the beach. "No, Dad, that's not true. We will bring you down anytime you want, we will take you," my sister and I both said.

We drove back home. The car was silent. No one could find words to speak, and I don't know how he knew, but that was the last time he would ever see the ocean again.

BEGINNING OF THE END

We sat down with Dad when we got back to his home and discussed what he wanted. He told us he did not want to go to a hospital and wanted to die in his own home—not that he ever used the word "die," but we knew what he wanted. My sister and I talked and made some calls. With Mary T and her nursing, we could do this. Death still scares me. It is complete abandonment, and even with spiritual faith and a belief in the afterlife, it is a fear I talk about with my therapist and friends. No one can prepare you for losing someone you love. Sometimes you deny, bargain, shut down, and get angry. You say things like, "This isn't fair. Why him? Why now? Just why?" Then you wonder why God does this and you become angry at God, even though you don't have a clue who God really is. I heard once that everything happens for a reason, but I feel some things just happen for no reason.

My mother's father and mother both died when I was a teenager. I went to the funeral. As with most traumatic things, I could not recall even being there when they were buried. I always wanted to go like my grandmother— she died in her sleep. She loved to eat the crisp fat on top of the rib roast. I think it did her in, who knows. My father's parents died before I was born.

I was eleven years sober now and responsible. I would do what was needed. So did my sisters and brother—we all did what we could. We had a nurse come to watch him at night. My sister would come around nine or ten in the morning, and I would come over around then too. She would feed him when he was hungry, and she would have to change him as his bowels began to fail with time. One day I walked in while she was cleaning him up and he said in a pathetic tone, "It is so sad that you have to clean up the old man like this." She was wonderful with him and said, "Oh no, Dad, after all, you did it for me when I was young, and now I am doing it for you." He was helpless and allowed his children to take care of him. There was magic happening. There was healing and dying taking place all at the same time.

Some days I would have to bathe him because my sister was not strong enough to carry him to the bathroom. I had to learn how to carry him so as not to hurt him. I would wash him and dry him and carry him back to his room and put on his pajamas. One day, I had to dress my father to take him to a doctor's appointment and realized something that brought shame and disgust to me. You see, through my lifetime, there were many times when I would be waiting for my dad to get dressed and take me somewhere. Impatient, I would yell at him to hurry or I would be late, and when I was late, I would yell at him in anger. I never knew why he took so long until that moment.

After helping him with his underwear and socks, he needed to rub a powder on his knee so his brace would not chafe the skin, and then the brace had to be tightened, each strap like a small belt that was pulled and cinched up snug. I realized something else at that moment: I hated that brace, I hated that my father had polio, I hated that he could never run with me. I wanted to take the brace off his leg and crush it with a hammer. My mind was filled with so many thoughts and feelings that I could barely concentrate on the duty at hand. I felt a lump in my throat and my eyes filled up with tears. "I am dressing my father," I had to say to myself over and over again to bring me back. With the brace tightened, the pants went on and then his shirt. Next was the shoe for his left foot; it had a hole through the heel where the bolt went through to hold the bottom of the brace secure to his shoe. Then the bolt went through the shoe and a pin clipped onto it to secure it. His other shoe went one, and then they were laced. I helped him up, and I tightened his belt. It took almost thirty minutes. I was so uncomfortable and sad while doing this but I could not figure out why.

I realized how self-centered I had been. My father had accepted his disease and went through his whole life and barely ever complained. I never heard him ever say a word about the brace. I am sure he hated it too, yet never did he complain. I spent many hours of wasted time being angry with a father because it took him too long to get dressed and it made me wait. I was sick with disgust and shame, and it still bothers me at times even today.

My sister would leave late in the afternoon, and Mary T and I would be with him until nine o'clock, when the evening nurse came to take over. Mary got off work and we would hang out with my dad. She had a great way with sick people and especially loved my dad. At night, we would sit on his bed, and Dad would tell us the best of stories. Mary T and I were like children listening intently to stories of his life growing up, sailing on his father's huge boat up from the Bahamas, or the story of meeting my mom. He would tell them in such detail that you felt like you were there.

He told of one night he and my mother had been at a cocktail party and Dad had gotten a bit smashed. They had an eighteen-year-old babysitter for us kids, and I assumed from the story she was pretty cute. Well, Mom caught my father trying to chase down the babysitter in the bedroom, and the news of it was all over the beach club.

"Your mother was so embarrassed, what was everyone to think?" Dad said with a smile. His stories were the highlight of my day, that's for sure.

We kept Dad comfortable, and one day he was feeling pretty chipper and mentioned that he would like to have a Twelve Step meeting right there in his bedroom. I was always responsible for writing the list of attendees. "Let's have Freddie, Jennifer, Joan, Barbara…" Dad paused.

I asked, "But don't you think we should have some men at the meeting?"

"You and I will be there, that's enough," he said, chuckling. He loved beautiful women, and he was charming, so the women loved him.

I would act as the chairperson and read the preamble. The meeting always started with my father, and we would not close it until everyone had shared. I look back, and now I have been to thousands of meetings, and none have ever been as powerful and full of emotion as the ones we held in my father's bedroom.

The women would come into his room and hug his head and give him a kiss, many with a tear in their eye. Dad would light up when they walked in. The sparkle in his eye returned. He loved the attention, and the love was felt at every meeting. Dad would talk about drinking sometimes, but many days it would be acceptance that we would talk about, that of approaching death. Dad would talk about how he accepted that his life was coming to its conclusion and how the last few years sober were the happiest of his life. Whatever he said touched us all. People who came were able to let go of pain there. It was safe. They released hurt from the past that had been haunting them.

At the end of the meeting, we would all hold hands and say the Lord's Prayer, and many days I could feel electricity flowing through my hands.

Dad loved the meetings and seeing people. Sometimes people would hesitate at entering through the door—the smell of the cancer permeated the room and scared them. We who were there every day got used to the awful smell of the human body breaking down. You never forget that smell.

Dad's doctor's name was Blake. He was young and kind to my father. We all liked him. Blake would come to the house from time to time to check up on him. My father slept well and didn't need any painkillers until the end. He was alert, and although his appetite was small, we would cook him whatever he wanted for his meals.

My older sister flew out from Colorado. She stayed at my mother's house and would come over for a week or two while he was sick and then she flew back home. We prepared my father for her arrival. She did not know Dad as well as we did; she and my mom had become best buddies after my parents split up. Sometime they would even dress in the same outfits, it was weird to say the least. Many times, my sister would visit my mom and go back to where she lived out west without even stopping by and saying hello to Dad. He would hear about it and he tried not to show that it hurt him, but we all knew it made him sad. My dad's house had that smell of dogs and old furniture, and many of the chairs would have torn fabric. The rugs showed signs of wear, the paint had some chips, and some rooms had wallpaper from the '60s. On many walls, the glue had separated and a corner of the paper hung down. Dad couldn't afford a weekly maid. He had retired and lived on Social Security and money that his wealthy sister was generous enough to give him. Dad carried resentment toward my oldest sister for years for not caring enough to call and come to visit him when she was in town.

My sister helped with the cooking and she cleaned the house or made runs to the village for supplies.

Eben would occasionally stop by and see Dad, but it was hard for him. Many times it would be late afternoon, and he was high or drinking. He would talk to my father for a while, but he would have to leave after a short time. He just couldn't deal with it. I talked to him a couple times about what was happening and I knew my brother just could not handle it emotionally. I understood. I knew I could only do what I was able to do because I was sober.

Everyone in the family had a purpose, a job they were good at, which would help my father. There was paperwork and nurses that needed attending to, bills and loans that needing paying, and I did most of that. My father at seventy-nine was sharp as a tack and knew where I could find what I needed and helped me with his loan amounts and many other questions I had. He understood I was trying to help him.

After a couple weeks, my father's appetite waned and he seemed to sleep more. More and more blood was showing up in his stool. There were times I would help my sister and then have to go outside and regroup. I would either throw up or have the dry heaves and cry for a while and then go back in the room. I wanted to be strong and not breakdown in front of Dad. I felt he wanted me to be strong, but there were times I found myself bawling with my head on his chest, and he would stroke my hair and tell me it would be all right.

One day out of the blue, he looked up at me with those big brown eyes and said, "You know I am proud of you, Philip." I had heard him say it more since he had gotten sober, but knowing this might be the last time I heard these words from him, my eyes welled up with tears and I hugged him, saying, "I know, Dad, and I am lucky to have such a wonderful dad."

Through the sickness came healing. It was happening to me, Mary T... hell, all of us every day. We heard affirmations we had waited for years to hear. Did it heal all the deep wounds we carried? It never does, but it opened the door for forgiveness, and that was what we all were able to do, forgive that man.

I have to say those weeks we stayed by my father's side, I felt more emotions than I ever thought I was capable of and released much of the hurt I carried for my father and from him at the same time. It happened somehow. As my father lying there, helpless, needing each one of us, he would say, "It is so nice of you to help me" or "I love you."

I realized later that the other gift was that we were all preparing for the day when he would pass. We all knew it would come, and I allowed my feelings to come up and I allowed myself to cry and hold him, tell him I loved him, and tell him he had done a great job in being my dad. Hell, I know today that I am the wonderful man I am because of who he was. It could have been different. It was shitty growing up, but I was thirty-eight years old now, and in the years to come, I would come to realize that I was like my father in many ways and would thank him many times over.

He amazed me many times. We had to talk about what he wanted when he passed to the other side, including where the funeral was to be held, what hymns and prayers he wanted, and anything special we had not thought of. He knew exactly what hymns and prayers, and I would take notes as he spoke and never would he break down. One day near the end, Eben and my sister left the room and Dad whispered to me, "Make sure that you look after them." I would never forget that, especially where my brother was concerned.

When death is close, many people did not come to visit much. Maybe it was too painful for them. They looked at their own mortality and death frightened them, so rather than see what was in the cards, they stayed away. They sent flowers or food. It was okay, it was all they could do. By now the smell of death, that awful smell of the cancer, filled the room even more. Flowers arrived many days, and the dresser in front of his bed was covered with flowers near the end. My dad's nephew, John, came to visit from Virginia. He was close with my dad and had come to visit me in rehab when I got sober. He actually paid three thousand for my rehab. I tried to pay him back, but he said to just stay sober. He was a nice enough man, kind of strange sometimes, but my dad loved him.

John was probably ten years older than me and had thick glasses and was not as deaf as a post, but pretty close and always spoke in a loud voice. My dad was pretty deaf too, so it got loud in that bedroom.

"Hi, Uncle Philip, how are you feeling today?" John asked my dad in his booming voice.

"Good as I can be, I guess, considering things," my father answered as I helped him sit up in bed.

"Boy, Uncle Philip, you sure have a lot of admirers. Just look at all those beautiful flowers," John said with a smile.

"Who are they from?" Dad asked.

John walked over to the dresser where the flowers in their vases sat and started to read the cards. "This one is from George & Annette, this one from Jennifer," he paused for a second, and then said, "and this beautiful vase of orchids is from your daughter."

My father looked at each vase, then looked back at the flowers she had sent before she came from Colorado and said in an angry voice, "I don't like them. I don't think there is enough oxygen in here for me and those flowers, take them out."

It was all I could do not to laugh.

John said, "Well, Uncle Philip, she may be here later to visit, and it would hurt her feelings."

"I don't care, I want them out," Dad repeated.

John thought for a second. "How about if we put them out in the living room now, and would it be all right if she comes to visit, we bring them back while she is here?"

Dad reluctantly agreed, and from then on, we would switch the flowers from the living room to the bedroom when my sister showed up.

There was a night near the end when Mary T and I asked him if he was scared of dying. He told us he was not and said he looked forward to going to the other side. I asked him just one thing: "Dad, please send me a sign when you get to the other side and let me know you are okay."

"Sure, no problem. I will let you know. Don't worry."

In the days and years to come, there would be many signs that would come from my father. He watches over me to this day.

The meetings became less frequent as Dad did not have the strength, and he began to have more pain, so Mary T would inject him with the morphine the doctor had left. Sometimes he would sigh in relief when the liquid hit his bloodstream, and I felt almost jealous that he was escaping it all. I had done the drug and knew the taste you got in the back of your throat when it hit you, the warm feeling from the top of your head to the tips of your toes.

I did my best. It was the hardest time of my life watching him fade away over those weeks, but looking back, I am so glad to have been there for him. For me, it was huge and healing. There would come times near the end that hit me hard. He would get this look of panic and he would be choking from fluids in his lungs. It happens near the end sometimes.

156

I have come close to drowning a few times when I was a teenager, surfing after a storm or hurricane in ten- to fifteen-foot waves. I would lose my board and have to swim to shore, the waves pounding my body and rolling me around like a dishrag. I would come up and gasp for air, only to look up at the next wave crashing down. Each time I'd get less air into my lungs and more water. I would gasp, choking, and it terrified me.

Father had that look, choking in his hospital bed. His thin, bony arms would flail about. It was pathetic to witness. I would panic and say, "Do something, for God's sake, give him something, he is choking." I had to run from the bedroom and head to the apple orchard, screaming. Finally, after more morphine, he would settle down and fall asleep.

PEACE

Dad died on Good Friday, April 24, 1992, around two in the afternoon. My sister was with him when he passed. I was in the living room when she told me and walked into his bedroom. The smell of death was overwhelming. Walking to his bed, I sobbed uncontrollably. I sat beside him and held him and said good-bye. The room was different. It seemed empty. His powerful spirit had gone, and just his body remained. There, in that empty room, I knew he was at peace and not suffering as he had been the last few days. I felt sick inside and relieved at the same time. Dr. Kerr pronounced him dead, and an hour or so later, they rolled my father out of the house where he had lived for over forty years and took him to the funeral home. My oldest sister had gone back the week before to Colorado.

Mary T and I were quiet, and there were not be many words said as we locked the door to his house and went home.

I stopped by the next day and walked through Dad's house. It was never as empty and quiet as it was that day. My mind recalled his words, his smile, his touch, and the sparkle in his eye. I sobbed. I would miss him for years to come and think of him often.

There were plans made. We called the minister at the church where we would hold the funeral and made arrangements; the day was a blur. I broke down in tears many times. Mary was great and held me close as I sobbed like a young boy.

While my dad was sick and dying, any differences between my family and Mary disappeared—we were all at peace. It was peaceful those days. Very sad, but peaceful. This, however, would be short lived.

Mary T and I came down for breakfast on that Easter Sunday morning, and there in the living room, we noticed our first sign. We had a Christmas cactus sitting near the fireplace and it was in bloom. Mary said, smiling, "It's a sign from your dad. Look, four blooms, one for each of us." This Christmas cactus was supposed to bloom at Christmas, and it had not bloomed in two years. When we went to bed the night before, there were no buds and no sign it was about to bloom. I had tears streaming down my cheeks as I smiled, knowing Dad was okay.

The funeral was on a Tuesday, and my oldest sister did not make the trip back from Colorado. It was sad that she didn't come. My brother Eben and Mary were at the church an hour or so before the funeral. I had written a eulogy, and a friend of my Dad's was also going to say a few words. The front of the church was filled with flowers. We read the cards; one vase was from my Colorado sister and sat on the altar with many others. The church was filled to capacity and the crowd overflowed onto the steps and the sidewalk outside. I was overwhelmed.

Dad had picked out some hymns weeks before he died, including "Onward Christian Soldiers," "Amazing Grace," and the "Battle Hymn of the Republic." Tears rolled down my cheeks as I sang that day. While Dad's friend gave his eulogy, a strange thing happened. The flowers and vase that my sister had sent flew off the altar and fell to the floor. No one was near them; they just fell over. I looked over at Mary T and she raised her eyebrows. I gave my eulogy next, and I began to speak. I had thought I could do it without falling apart and crying, but that is not what happened, and I really did not care if I fell apart. I was a grown man and I was crying and talking about how much my father was loved. I told some stories about him. There wasn't a dry eye in that church.

After the funeral, family and friends came up to us and paid their respects. I thought about it later, how many people came to me with tears in their eyes, smiling in a sad way. Many people did not even know Dad all that well, and some had not seen him in years. Many were touched by the feelings I was able to express.

It was a few days later when George, cousin John, the reverend, Mary T, and my sister and brother went to spread my father's ashes. It was at Lane's Island in Hampton Bays, a marsh west of the Shinnecock inlet where my father went duck hunting for over thirty years. It was his request. The afternoon was somewhat gray and cool and a light wind blew from the west as we walked the marsh toward the channel that led out to where my father hunted and where I had hunted as a young boy. I held the urn; it was all that was left of Dad. It seemed sad to live such a good life and end up in a can. After the reverend said some words, we took turns throwing the gray ash that was once my father into the bay. We then stood with bowed heads for a minute and prayed. When we looked up, there was a flock of geese flying high over the marsh in front of us. One of the birds flew from the back of the V formation and flew up and became their new leader. He led them into the horizon, and it was another one of many wonderful signs we were given. We smiled, and we all knew he was all right, wherever he was.

It probably would have been better if we took time to work through what we needed to let him go, but sometimes it happens so fast and you are left with a huge amount of decisions that have to be made quickly.

I was thinking of buying the estate after he died, but I decided my family would have resentment toward me for years and any chance of my brother getting sober would be squashed.

"THE WOOD PUSSY"

After the sale of the house, there were a lot of things to clean up. After forty years working in his shop out back, there were plenty of toasters, radios, and lots of other projects that my dad had just never got to.

I thought about Dad almost every day, especially when I was working next door on his house. I would be cleaning up either part of the house or the shop and come across something that would trigger a memory. There was a sailboat my dad called "The Wood Pussy." I am not exactly why it got that name and never really got a straight answer from my father, but that boat needed to go some place now that the house was sold. The eighteen-foot wooden sailboat had been lying in the weather for many years. I did not want it, and my brother told me in an angry way to take a chainsaw to it.

At this time, maybe a year after he died, I had a wild dream. The dream was in color, and in the dream I was up on a ladder painting a house out west, maybe in Montana. The house was huge, and there were many people working on it. The dream was beautiful. Dark green hills rolled on and on as far as the eye could see, and there were no other houses but the one we all were working on. It seemed like almost everyone there was in the program. Dick the carpenter was cutting boards with a saw, Frank the plumber was carrying copper pipes downstairs to the basement, and 7-11 Tom handed out cups of coffee. Someone on the ground yelled up to me, "Phil, you got a phone call!"

"Okay," I said and climbed down the ladder and walked into the large living room and picked up the phone.

"Hello?" I said.

"Philip?" I heard my name on the phone and started to cry. It was my dad.

I cried and asked, "Dad, are you all right? Where are you? I miss you, Dad."

"I miss you too, son. I am well. Things are good. I can walk now, I don't need a cane anymore, you know."

I started talking again, but he interrupted and asked, "Philip, what are you going to do about that boat? You, know you should keep her she is a sound boat, a good boat, you would enjoy sailing her."

Dad used to take me sailing when I was young on a lightning sailboat. There were races on Saturday at the yacht club he belonged to. My uncles also sailed, but I never really got into it and I knew he wanted me to. Feeling a bit guilty, I said, "Dad, you know, I don't think I would ever sail it. I am not really into sailing like you and—"

"Well then, Tom would like the boat. He loves to sail. Call him and give the boat to him, he will take her."

"Okay, Dad, I will call him tomorrow and ask him. Dad, I really miss you so. I am so sad you had to leave us."

"I will be watching you, don't worry. I am fine and happy."

That is when I woke up. Mary T asked what happened and if was I all right. I cried as I told her the story. It is one of the few dreams I have had in my life where I remember every detail to this day.

I called Tom the next day and told him of the dream. Tom was a gray-haired man in his seventies. Dad and he had met many years before in a meeting and become friends. He missed my dad, and we talked while he looked over the boat the next day. He liked the boat and came a couple days later and I helped him load it on his trailer.

It was not be long after when the will was be read and the settlement were checks cut to each of us.

There were items each of us bought from the estate; they had been appraised just after my father passed. The appraised cost of the items was deducted from our checks. I bought the most: some guns, artwork, and a canon that was over one hundred years old that had been on my grandfather's yacht. The story my dad used to tell us as children was how his father used to sail into Boston Harbor when he was courting my grandmother and fire the cannon to let her know he was sailing into port. It was a romantic story, and I had the old cannon reconditioned and it remains in my living room to this day.

There was some finality to it when the checks were handed to us that day in the lawyer's office. My brother, sister, and I seemed to go our separate ways after that for many years. I lost contact with Eben and spoke very seldom to my sister. Dad was generous with me, and it probably bothered both of them. My brother and sister used to sit getting high, imagining that one day we would all be millionaires and why bother working or getting a job. Living in dead man's shoes is what we did.

I am not sure what happens when a son loses his father. That aloneness I felt for the first time in my life was overwhelming sometimes. I counted on Dad a lot. I counted on him to listen, and even though I had become a man and was more successful in business than he ever was, I could always count on him to be there. My mother could never listen. She cared about nothing but herself. I remember telling my mom when I became a millionaire. It was a big deal to me. Her response was to change the subject and speak of a cocktail party at a woman's house who I had spent maybe fifteen minutes talking to my whole life.

I am glad he was there just to listen and not judge or criticize, even if it was later in my life. Since my dad had gotten sober, he learned how to just listen and be there and not feel that he had to solve all my problems. He didn't have to always try to protect me from the world.

His success was that he was an honorable man who always spoke his mind, helped many people and expected nothing in return, and raised a family. He lived his entire life with an awful disease of polio and never he wanted people's sorrow, never complained. When Dad died, I saw many things from his shoes. It opened my eyes, and at times I wanted to apologize for not knowing what he lived through and what he kept from us.

I must have caught myself a hundred times the year after he passed wanting to either stop by or call him with good news. It made him smile, he loved the good things that were happening in my life since I was sober. He was proud.

A STORM APPROACHES

It was fall before I knew it, and I was consumed with work in preparation for the hunting season. I loved that time of year, and although I did not know it at the time, it would be the last time I would hang up the ladders and paintbrushes. I began guiding hunters again. I had several farms planted in corn and rye from Southampton to Bridgehampton representing hundreds of acres of crops where geese and ducks would flock by the thousands all fall and winter. Also, I had six duck blinds on ponds, creeks, and marshes. I was fully booked for the season, and many other hunts had booked already for the guides who worked for me. I counted on it each year as it paid a large part of my mortgage for the year and kept food on the table.

In 1992, the season started on November 3 and ended on January 31. As usual, I worked every day except Christmas.

One day in November, just before Thanksgiving, I had a hunting party from New Hampshire, Craig and Jim. I met them around five in the morning at the local dinner and headed to the field. I had taken them goose hunting the season before on a cold January day, and now they returned. It was raining and blowing over 40 mph from the north. The roads were flooded as we drove to the corn field to hunt. It was the first time in my life I hunted in a lightning storm, even to this day. We arrived at the field, and I was a bit concerned walking in the open field carrying guns made of steel with all the flashes of lighting above us, but we ventured out anyway.

As the three of us walked out, the heavens lit up, and the darkness disappeared for a second or two and it was like daylight, then complete darkness fell upon us again. This happened several times before we reached the pit blind we were to hunt. I figured we would be safer below ground in the pit than standing around up here. The temperature was warm, maybe close to sixty, the wind blew, and the fat raindrops hit my hood with authority and stung my face. I looked up in the sky for the first ducks of the morning. Ducks that feed in corn fields come heavy in rainy conditions, and I knew it would be a good morning. Shooting time is a half-hour before sunrise, and it was just about that time when it was light enough to see. Flocks of ducks would struggle in the heavy wind toward us and then the flash of lighting bolts would zigzag across the sky, followed a split second later by a crash of thunder that sounded like a cannon, and they would peel out in the wind and leave us. It was something I had never witnessed before.

Finally, a bunch of mallards were close to gun range, and I instructed my clients to be ready and we threw back the pit doors and fired. Three ducks hit the mud in front of us, just outside our decoys. As I stood up to retrieve the downed birds, my clients yelled, "On the right, a bunch on the right comin' right in!" I dropped back in the pit, and the birds came close on their side and two more went down on the next volley. My clients wanted to keep shooting, but I finally got out with the dog and retrieved our birds. I told them we could shoot only mallards, as we had our one-bird limit on black ducks. A few minutes later, a group of ducks came and we had our limit of three ducks per man.

The ducks kept coming, and my clients offered me more money so they could keep shooting. It was against the federal law, and I said no. Although over the years I had been offered money before, something cautioned me with these men. For some reason, I knew they were feds. As a guide, it was my job not to let these men shoot over their limit nor let them shoot my limit; it was a strict federal and state law. It was not long after that I ended the hunt. The rain had stopped and the storm had passed—at least I thought it had.

The rest of the season went well until mid-December, when two federal agents came to check us at our blind. We had a slow morning and had only bagged a couple of ducks. The agents checked us, and then one of them said he found corn in front of the blind in the water. It is against the law to bait or corn waterfowl, and he looked down in the water and found a kernel of corn. I knew it was a set-up and walked out in the water as it looked like, while bending over, the agent was pulling the kernels out of his shirt pocket.

"Go back to the blind," he said, pointing toward the shore. I had been searching the bottom—the water was clear, about two feet deep, and there was no sign of corn.

"Show me one of these kernels," I said.

"If you do not go back to shore with the others, I will arrest you for interfering in a governmental investigation," the agent barked. I walked back to the blind with my clients. It was total bullshit, and my guys knew it. The feds left, and we picked up and went in.

I would later have to hire an attorney, as in a few weeks I received the letter from the feds that charged me with a tagging violation, baiting, wanton waste and several other charges.

In mid-January '93, I was hunting with a client named Walter. He booked me several weekends a season. He mentioned he was bringing a guest, Bill James, to hunt in the morning. The name sounded familiar, and then he reminded me that back in the late '70s and early '80s, he hunted had with me and Bill had actually introduced Walter and me. He just bought an island not far away for around twelve million dollars. The island was a 465-acre island that had not been inhabited for years.

They were amazed that I had not heard he was big and that he managed money, I think over three billion at that time. Money and fame never really made the impression on me it did on other people. I judged people for who they were as people.

Walter had a gift in that, if he booked three weekends a season, it would either rain or snow five days out of the six, which is perfect weather for waterfowl hunting. This Sunday was no exception. The wind was northeast, the temperature around thirty, and we had sleet and rain mixed. "You guys have a perfect day," I told my clients as I sat down for breakfast.

"You remember Bill James, don't you, Phil?" Walter said.

"Sure, been a long time, Bill," I said as I shook his hand. The diner was packed with hunters and guides that Sunday morning. My five guides and over twenty hunters sat eating breakfast before heading out to the blinds and pits. We loaded up on greasy eggs, bacon, French toast, and lots of coffee, and then I looked at my watch and said, "Hey, guys, we better pack up and get out there. We're running late."

After a short drive, we arrived at a cornfield where a thousand ducks had been feeding at dusk the night before. We put on our rain gear and began our walk to the pit in the field. We walked leaning into the thirty-knot northeaster carrying all our gear and the sleet stung my face and now I was assuredly awake. We set up a huge spread of duck and goose decoys, and after making some last-minute adjustments as I did every hunt, I headed back to the pit to join my hunters. The clients loaded their guns and organized thermos bottles, bags, and lots of shells.

"We've got five minutes," I barked at them.

I saw the first bunch of ducks in the darkness swinging high over the spread. They went past us, but I thought they'd be back. Another bunch screamed by low to the ground, teal I suspected, as they disappeared into the blackness. We were set. Shooting time was only minutes away. "Okay, now don't move, a bunch of ten on the right, swinging downwind, and they are comin' in front, all right take 'em!" I yelled.

Four ducks fell, I ran out to get them. When I returned, I said, "They are all black ducks. We can only take one more." The limit was one black duck per day per man. A single swung over the box and one of the hunters on the end of the box made a great shot in the heavy wind and it went down. It turned out to be another black duck. "No more black ducks," I said. We must have had ten bunches of ducks come the next thirty minutes, but it was difficult for me to tell what species they were. It was sleeting, and dark and heavy low clouds kept it from getting light. Finally, I was able to determine the species, and in an hour and a half, we had bagged ten geese and a dozen ducks.

Bill said, "Today must be the best day this season."

"No, actually two days ago, I had some doctors out, and in the snow we bagged fifteen geese and twelve ducks and we were done in two hours," I spouted off proudly. I knew my job. I was a great caller and knew the birds, and I watched them day in and day out. Don't get me wrong, I was tough and was the farthest thing from being mild-mannered and polite with the clients at times. It was hard, you had to keep an eye on them; some of them could shoot each other or the dog or me if I wasn't careful. Others, like these men, were experienced hunters, but I kept an eye on them just the same. I have a constant ringing in my left ear. I've had it since I was twenty-five, when a hunter discharged his gun by accident while he was loading it. The muzzle was inches from my head when the gun went off. Another day, an asshole shot at a goose while I was standing twenty feet in front of the pit blind. The shot missed my knee by inches as I felt the wind go by my leg. I lost it screaming at him, and he was lucky I did not crack him over the head with his own gun. I never saw him again after that hunt. It was for the best because he was a moron.

"So are we the only hunters you are guiding today?" Bill asked.

"Phil has five guides, all those hunters in the diner are out with his guides in different fields right now," Walter piped up. I told Bill about all the fields, the thousands of decoys I owned, all the equipment, and how we each had radios and were in contact with each other. If a field was hot, we would call each other and bring another group in when we had shot our limit, and then another, so I could try to get birds for everyone.

Bill said, "I just bought this island, and I would like to have you come over and take a look around. Do you have any time next week?"

"No, I can't. I am booked every day and can't go until after the season in two weeks," I told him. I guess when you have a lot of money, the one word you don't like to hear is no. He said he could have his seaplane pick me up at East Hampton airport and fly me to the island any day next week. I think in the next week Bill called me two or three times, and finally I agreed to go and see the island. I have to be honest, I never felt it was anything more than a plane ride to explore an island that many people had never set foot on. I knew the island, and I called it Fantasy Island from the beginning as many fantasies became reality there.

Fantasy Island was only a ten-minute plane ride from Easthampton. It was awesome looking down over the island, and a man met me with the caretaker as I got off the plane. I soon met a man, Jack, who was an architect and worked for Bill. The caretaker was an old man who had a fake ear, I learned later he'd had cancer. His skin was wrinkled from years of being in the sun and the weather. He greeted us, but I got the impression he wasn't that pleased to see us there, especially stepping off the noisy seaplane. The island had been abandoned over twenty years before. Many trees had gone down in hurricanes and storms, I suspected, and the buildings were old and needed lots of work. I loved the place. We drove around in an old army jeep, and I could just feel there had been some magic that had taken place there. Fields were overgrown, and it was like the land that time forgot. The next time I came to the island it was by helicopter. I had never been in a helicopter or a seaplane. It was a different world for me. I felt kind of important. I came home, and that evening I told George about what had been going on and how this wealthy man was trying to pick my brain. George said, "I think he wants you to work for him."

"Doing what?" I asked, still in the dark.

"Why don't you put together a resume and plans for hunting on the island and have a meeting with Bill and see what happens. What have you got to lose?" said George. I didn't argue with George; he always was able to see what I could not. I put together ideas and plans and a resume and into the city I went. I waited for a while, then a cute girl introduced herself and said she would be back for me as Bill was on a call.

Now, I was a country boy, and the only thing I knew about Wall Street was what I saw on TV. At that time, I had no money in the market and liked it that way. A few minutes later, I was escorted to his office through a large room with dozens of desks and men in shirts and ties yelling in their phones. It was noisy. Then I entered his office.

"Hi, Bill, how are you?" I said as I shook his hand.

"Pretty good, how did you like the island?" he asked.

I sat down across from his desk and began telling him what I saw on the island and the potential. While I was talking, Bill kept his eye on the six screens on the wall behind me, stock prices, I assumed, and he was able to have a conversation with me and then stop to buy thousands of shares of this or sell thousands of shares of that. I was amazed he could focus on so many things at once. I went over maps, and I went over plans for shooting ducks, geese, and even organizing pheasant drives on the island. I stayed with him for close to an hour. He said he would get in touch with me and I left the city, not exactly knowing what would be next.

Days later, I got a call. They were to pick me up at the airport; it would be another seaplane. I landed and met Jack, who would be in charge of much that would go on there in the next few years. Jack had a thin frame, about six feet tall, a chiseled jaw with a well-trimmed silver beard, and silver hair to match. He seemed like a nice enough man, and we walked down one of the dirt roads that divided the center of the island.

"So what did Bill say?" I asked.

He hesitated for a few seconds, then said, "Bill is offering you $50,000, a new four-wheel-drive truck and a new boat to come and go from the south fork, a cell phone, and an expense account, and we will set you up with a fax machine if you don't have one."

I walked a few steps and Jack said, grinning in a pleased way, "Well, what do you think?"

I showed little emotion and said seriously, "Well, I considered a different number."

"What number were you thinking about?" Jack questioned.

"One hundred thousand is what I want to be here full time," I said.

He was set back for a second and didn't know what to say. We continued walking up the road. "That is a lot of money, I will have to talk to Bill about it and get back to you," Jack said. I was a bit taken aback. That wasn't that much money…hell, my mortgage and taxes were close to fifty thousand. We walked for a while longer, and eventually we ended up back on the beach at the seaplane. We shook hands, and all I had to do was wait for the call. I did not want to give up my three businesses for fifty thousand dollars; that have been would be crazy. I wanted to stop painting houses. I had been doing it for over twenty years; it was twenty too many in my book. I wished I could talk to my father about it. Mary T was great and listened and let me talk it out, over and over again, for a week. I heard nothing from Bill. A few more days went by, and I caved. I wanted to do it.

I would eventually write a contract where I would only work April through November, five days a week, forty hours a week, and no weekends. November through April, I would work only ten days a month. I felt that would give me time on the weekends to do clambakes in the summer and run my waterfowl business in the winter. They would give me health insurance and 50K. They agreed to the terms, and I was scheduled to start in April. I was honest and told Bill about the trial and the charges the feds had against me. It was not spoken, but both of us knew that for me to be in charge of this program for the island, I could not be convicted on all of those charges.

APPROACHING MELT DOWN

It was a cold and lonely day when I opened the envelope and read that I was being indicted by US Fish and Wildlife—it happened that February. According to the letter, they had eleven counts or violations of the Federal Migratory Bird Act against me, and I had to appear at the Federal Building with my attorney to discuss them. I went with my uncle, who was still the town attorney, and another lawyer. When we walked into the building, I had a huge knot in my stomach. We were directed to a room where three men waited. They introduced themselves, and we sat down as they went through the indictment. This is when I realized the two men posing as clients during that November lightning storm were in fact undercover agents working for the US Fish and Wildlife Service.

Certain violations of the Migratory Bird Act can carry not only fines but also jail time. After the feds went through the charges, they said if I would plead guilty to some of the eleven counts, they would take my hunting license for three years and I could not run my guiding business for five years and would pay a five thousand dollar fine.

Upon hearing this, I snapped. I jumped up from the table and said, "Why don't you just cut my nuts off, you cocksuckers?"

My lawyers grabbed me and my uncle scolded me, "Phil, now goddamn it, calm down, get a hold of yourself."

"We need to have some time with our client," the lawyers told the feds, and they left us alone to talk it all over. I told them what had happened the day when I thought the one fed was pulling kernels of corn from his pocket. The other day hunting with the two undercover agents, I could remember nothing went wrong. "We shot our limit that day, and that was it," I told my uncle. "I did not do what they say I did. It is bullshit."

The feds came back into the room and sat down. We told them there would be no deal, and they said they would set a date for trial and that I would be notified. We walked out of the Federal Building, and I could hardly imagine such a nightmare.

In the weeks that followed, I researched and found an attorney. He did not want to take the case at first, but after talking a while on the phone, he agreed to defend me. The cost was huge to me at the time: he wanted $25,000. I met with my new attorney Ken a few days later. It was difficult to remember many things as they happened months or even a year before. I would have to get a list of witnesses who could testify. Proving my credibility was paramount, according to my lawyer.

There were only a couple weeks before the trial so we did not have much time.

The stress got to me, with sleepless nights no appetite. I became so full of fear and stress that I would eventually develop sores in my throat and inside my mouth and I could barely swallow or eat. I lost weight, and although I went to meetings and spoke often to George, the fear consumed me. I prayed every night and asked God to take care of me. I asked others to also pray for me.

When one reflects back on their life, there are times life is a struggle. Everyone's struggle is different. Mine was a huge amount of fear about my marriage not working out, fear of being alone and solving many things without my dad, and fear of losing my business, my job on the island, and the court case.

Mary T was great then, and I am sure she got tired of hearing me go over and over this case and how I felt I was being set up by the feds, but she always helped me by listening and giving me her support.

A few days before the trial, I found myself at Lane's Island, where my father's ashes had been spread almost a year before. I walked out on the marsh. The March day was damp, many gray clouds hung low in the sky, and a southwest wind chilled me to the bone. I continued walking and reached the edge of the bay. Bursting into tears, I fell to my knees, and as I cried I called out to my father to help me: "Dad, please, I am sick inside with fear that I am going to lose everything. Please, please just send me a sign that it will be all right."

I am not sure how long I kneeled there on that marsh, my head hanging in despair and sobbing, but slowly I felt something was behind me. It felt warm on my neck, like there was someone there breathing on the back of my neck. It startled me, and I spun around. But there was no one there. Then I noticed the light; there was a ray of sun beaming through the dark clouds and surrounding me. I looked in disbelief for a second. I looked as far as I could see to the west up the marsh and as far as I could see to the east, but only where I knelt was there a single beam of sun. Then, seconds later, it was gone. I knew that was it. The sun was the sign. I cried, "Thank you, thank you, God, for that sign."

I ran back to the truck, laughing and crying like a crazy man. I wanted to tell all who cared about me that I was going to make it. I drove over the bridge, past the Coast Guard station, and my doubt started to come back. I made a couple turns, and now three miles from the bridge, I said, "God, if that was the sign, give a sign that was the sign."

Some people just need to be hit in the head when they are so surrounded in self-doubt and fear, like I was that day. When I told my story to people who loved me, they told me I was a nut job and it was definitely "the sign."

Dressed in my new suit, I drove up to Uniondale that rainy day in April to meet my attorney at the federal courthouse. It was the first day of the trial. We had worked weeks on testimony and lining up witnesses. I had some great witnesses. Jim was an army major who had been awarded the bronze star in Vietnam; George was a colonel in the army; John was a colonel in the reserves; we had a firearms expert from Nassau County Police; our local meteorologist, Mr. Hendrickson; plus Uncle Ted and two others. Outside, the prosecutor wanted to talk to my lawyer and me. We went into a room, where he said, "We are willing to have your client plea down to pleading guilty to three counts." I wondered what had happened to the other eight counts.

My lawyer pulled me aside and said, "It's a good deal and you should think about it."

The fear had me by the throat and I began to sweat. I had only minutes to make my decision. Something about it did not make sense. Why would they want to make a deal now? Maybe they did not have a strong case, maybe something was wrong. My mind was spinning. "You want me to plead guilty for something I didn't do? I can't do that, no way, I won't do it," I said. "Let's go, let's go all the way."

The prosecutor, Mr. Roberts, was brought up from Washington DC for the case. He had a pompous smirk on his face. I wanted to bitch-slap him every day, and he knew it.

It would be a jury trial that would last two weeks. I had never been in such a place of fear.

The first morning, we waited from nine until eleven-thirty as the feds waited for the paperwork to arrive for the other seven charges. It was coming from Brooklyn, they told the judge. The judge said that if the paperwork did not arrive by noon, he was throwing out the other charges. Now, I could probably have ridden a bike from Brooklyn to Uniondale in that amount of time. Noon came, and the judge dismissed the other charges. I don't think there were any other fucking charges. I think the feds thought I would take the deal of pleading guilty to three and had made them up.

After lunch, the feds presented their case. One witness for the prosecution was the undercover agent who had come hunting with me that November day during the thunderstorm; he took the stand first. He drew a diagram on a board showing who shot which duck, where they fell in the field, and what species it was and what sex. I was shaking my head. How the fuck could this guy have remembered all of this in a violent thunderstorm with 50 mph winds? I asked my lawyer to ask him what the weather was like that day. The agent said he thought it was raining, he was not sure how hard, nor could he remember if it was windy, nor could he remember the lightning and the thunder, and yet he could recall where each duck fell and who shot it. The feds brought up a biologist and the fed who had planted the two kernels of corn and then it was time to present our case.

My lawyer had tried to keep me off the stand, but I wanted to be up there. I felt strongly in my heart that the jury would see my innocence, and against my attorney's advise I took the stand. I did well. My lawyer asked me questions about the day we hunted in the thunderstorm, about the diagram the fed had drawn, and what I thought about it. I said on the stand that it was a wild day, with the wind blowing, bolts of lightning, torrential rains, and it was over six months ago and impossible to remember who shot what duck, which species each of us shot, and especially where they fell in the field. I said I knew that we did not shoot over the limit, even though the feds offered me money to do so. I looked in the eyes of the jury after. They believed me; it made sense.

Cross-examination did not go as well, and Mr. Roberts knew he could get under my skin. After an hour of questions, it was getting late in the day and I needed to piss in the worse way. I thought I could stick it out, but finally I snapped. He had asked the same question over and over again, but each time while I was answering it he would butt in and ask me something else, trying to confuse me. I told him I could not remember.

"Did you or did you not give two geese to the agent without placing a tag on them?" Roberts repeated. It is a state and federal law that waterfowl must be tagged with your name, address, phone number, species, and date if what you shoot is given to another person. I knew that I had not done it. It was one of those laws many hunters did not even know about, but it was a law and I had fucked up. I finally barked at him, "The state DEC don't even enforce that law!"

There was silence in the courtroom. I knew I had blown it by losing my temper, and when I looked at the jury many of them just looked down. There are times in all our lives when you want a replay, and this was a big one and I knew it. "No further questions for this witness," Roberts said as he spun around, proud of himself, and walked back to his seat.

"I am sorry," I told Ken as I sat down next to him.

"It's okay, don't worry, you did fine," he reassured me.

I respected Ken. He knew a lot of my history, he trusted me, and he was doing a great job. Court was adjourned until the following week. Ken told me to try to relax and have a good weekend. I said the same to him as I walked to my truck and was relieved that I would not have to testify again. It is a long drive from Uniondale back to Water Mill, and I had plenty of time to think. It was hard not to beat up on myself for mistakes I had made. Christ, all for a fucking duck—I would have been better off if I had held up the fucking 7-11.

Mary T and I were having problems again. I couldn't remember the last time we had sex; she had moved back into the guest room, and that part of our life was on hold. She gave me support, though. I needed her, and if it was not for her and George, I do not know what I would have done. I sat down and told her about the trial, what had taken place that day. I asked people to pray for me. I told them I was scared and needed their help.

The weekend dragged on, and finally it was time to drive back up to the federal courthouse. I was hoping it would wrap up this week. Strange, but it seemed that almost every day I went to court it was raining. It was perfect duck weather; they love it when it rains. Ducks never get wet, they have an oil duct near their tails and they rub the oil all over their feathers with their bill and it keeps them waterproof. It's amazing how they would sink without it.

I arrived and went through security and upstairs to the courtroom to meet Ken. We presented my witnesses, and some of them were there already and Ken was briefing them. I was nervous and went outside and stood in the hall. Each witness called testified to my integrity, and many of them had hunted with me for over seven years, some longer. The army colonel said that I had a type-A personality and was tough and could have used some time in the military...the jury laughed.

The best part was when Mr. Hendrickson took the stand. He had been recording the weather for NOAA for over fifty years. Richard was a tall, thin man with a large handlebar moustache. I had known since I was ten years old. He knew my father well, and looking at him, you wouldn't know he had a mind like a steel trap. Roberts had a smirk on his face as Dick took the stand, and he asked Mr. Hendrickson his name and how long he had been recording the weather.

"How old are you?" Roberts asked.

"Seventy-five," Dick said proudly.

"Now, I am sure you cannot remember what the weather was on the date in question, could you Mr. Hendrickson?" said Roberts, thinking he had him as he smiled a half-ass grin at the jury.

"No, I sure couldn't," Dick said as he reached into his pocket. "That's why I brought this little book."

The smirk on Roberts's face was gone, as he panicked and said, "What book is that?"

"I record the weather every day in this book, every hour, I record temperature, barometer, wind, rainfall, and conditions. I brought it and thought it would come in handy," Dick said with a twinkle in his eye. There were a couple chuckles coming from the jury. They loved him, and who wouldn't? I spent hours and hours listening to his stories of him growing up, the Depression, his years working on his father's farm, and the '38 hurricane. He was fascinating, and now he was fascinating the jury. It was the best!

"Yep, it is all right here, a lot of wind that day, up to fifty, and we got two to three inches of rain between four and eight thirty that morning, plus lightning and heavy thunder. Yep, it is all right here, big storm that day," Dick reported.

Roberts was so rattled, all he could do was get Dick off the stand. He had confirmed my story.

That moment, when I looked at the jury and a couple of them smiled slightly, a bit of hope came into my heart. "Maybe I will make it, maybe just maybe."

It was our last witness. The prosecution gave its closing arguments and then Ken gave ours. The judge gave the jury instructions for their deliberation. He instructed them to find me guilty or not guilty in each count and also to consider if I has been entrapped by the federal government on each count as well. There were some instructions Mr. Roberts objected to, but the judge told him to sit down or be in contempt. The jury left, and Ken told me, "Phil, go relax, get something to eat at the restaurant across the street." I got up from the chair, my legs stiff from sitting so long and I was drained.

My mind thought back, wishing I had done things differently. Why the hell didn't I tag the geese? What a stupid mistake! So what if it was twenty degrees with a thirty-knot wind and I was freezing. The agents told me that day they had a cousin who lived in Connecticut who loved geese. They asked if they could they have the two I had shot. Cousin, my ass. I wanted to beat them both senseless.

THE MAN IN THE BLUE JACKET

I walked toward the stairway and looked out the huge second-floor courthouse windows; the rain pelted against them. Almost at the stairs, I looked out into the parking lot and there was man walking with a cane. He limped like Dad, and he wore khaki pants, a blue jacket, and a white hat. The same clothes my father wore almost every day of his life. I was stunned for a second. My heart pounded. I ran down the flight of stairs, almost knocking over the guard by the door, and ran outside. It had taken me less than thirty seconds. There were no cars leaving the parking lot, no cars driving down the road, and then I ran and checked each car where I had seen the man. No sign of anyone. Drenched from the rain, I went inside the restaurant and ordered a sandwich and questioned my sanity. He was there, I saw him, dressed exactly as my dad dressed, with the same color jacket he had worn for years, the LL Bean white sailing hat, same height as Dad, the same limp. I would later realize it was another sign to let me know that, no matter what, I will always be taken care of when I pray and mean it.

It took two hours for the jury to reach a verdict. I sat next to Ken as they walked into the courtroom, and I could see no expression from them. I thought the worse. "On count one of the indictment tagging violation, how do you find?" asked the judge.

The first juror said, "I find the defendant guilty as charged."

My heart sank as I put my head in my hands.

"Count two, baiting, how do you find?" said the judge.

"I find the defendant not guilty," the juror instructed, "and also I find that the defendant was entrapped by the federal government."

I began sobbing uncontrollably as I listened to each count from the first juror and the eleven other jurors that would follow, each one would find me guilty of not tagging the two geese I gave to the undercover agents after the hunt, but I was found not guilty on all the remaining four charges and two of them also said I had been entrapped by the federal government. My lawyer had his arm around me as I cried and asked if I was all right. I was, but I could barely speak, and by the time the last juror spoke, the tears of joy slowed and I smiled toward the jury, thanking them. I had so much on the line—my business, my honor, my reputation, and most of all, whatever faith I had lost sight of had returned. The man in the blue jacket was my visual sign, and I felt better than I had felt in years. Tears rolled down my cheeks that day listening to each juror, and I was overwhelmed with sadness for the loss of my dad, joy of being free, joy of someone caring for me, those twelve jurors, my eight witnesses, and Ken, who had fought for my way of life, my dignity, my honor, and my innocence. I felt so blessed.

It was not over. The judge gave me a $500 fine, I had to do a hundred hours of community service, and I was given a year of federal probation for those two geese with no tags. Trust me, it has been a lot of years since that day, and I have given ducks and geese to friends and people a few times, but never have I given any without tagging them first!

I walked into federal probation the first time, and there were three men waiting to see the officer. A couple guys looked like they were made men, who knows. One guy was there for embezzling money from his clients in business, a banker of some sort.

When one of the tough-looking guys asked me why I was there and I told him it was a migratory bird charge for giving a goose to someone, he thought I was caught having sex with the goose I think, because he gave me a weird look and never really said much to me after that. My probation officer said that in fifteen years he had never heard this. I had to explain the law to him. "What should we do with your one hundred hours of community service?" he asked. I thought for a second and said, "Well, I am a recovering alcoholic and could volunteer my time in the detox unit of the hospital."

"Perfect, have them sign something that says you were there each month and bring it in to me when it is complete," he said.

It was funny, I had been going to visit patients in detox units for over ten years. I liked to do it, and putting in one hundred hours would be perfect. He was right.

ANOTHER PAGE

They say there are times in your life when you end a struggle and begin another, like turning a page in a book. The months of fear and worry about the federal case were over, and it was great news to Bill, as he could not have a convicted game violator as his new gamekeeper on the island. I could have used a vacation on a tropical island, but instead I jumped into my new career, gave up my house painting business, and began taking a boat to work in the morning. It wasn't a bad way to go, I would say to myself, and my Chesapeake Boots would accompany me each day to the island. She would stand with her feet on the rail, her ears blowing back from the breeze as we crossed the bay each morning. I loved it, it was an adventure. I would wonder how many people were going to work by boat.

Stress seemed to be part of life back then. I was always busy and never sat still for long. Mary T and I saw each other at night, and once in a while we would go out for dinner and maybe do something together, but for the most part our relationship was superficial. She was happy I had given up the painting—she said the chemicals made me crazy.

My contract said I was to work forty hours weeks, but my job description never included many of the tasks and jobs I did there. Many times I would get a phone call from Bill's assistant Betty at seven on a Sunday morning saying that Bill was coming to the island or a friend of his or for some reason and he wanted me there. Mary hated that I would leave on a

Sunday, and although many days I did not want to go on Sunday, I would go. I never denied being there for him.

Going to work every day was an adventure, and I loved it. There was stress and schedules I needed to meet, but I did my best. Many times I felt that I was doing the job of several people the first few months, and in fact I was. A twenty-acre field on the north side had overgrown with trees over the years. Hurricanes Gloria and Hugo had knocked them down like they were toothpicks. They all needed to be cut up and the stumps pulled and roots excavated so we could till the field and plant corn there for waterfowl, and it had to be done in less than sixty days. A World War II landing craft was leased, and all the trucks and equipment had to be brought to the island by this manner. There were two bucket trucks from a local tree company that I hired, plus bulldozers, and later would come a huge tub grinder that cost over $150,000 to shred all the wood and stumps. It was amazing. In the midst of all this, I had hired a man from the south side who would help with the farming, and he and I went to Pennsylvania and bought a tractor, corn planter, a disc, and some other equipment we would need. We placed an ad in the paper for labor. Starting pay was $8.00 per hour, but it didn't deter people from applying. I hired fifteen or so people in less than two weeks. They earned every dollar. There would be temperatures in the nineties that June, when all of us were pulling the final roots from the dirt. You would sink halfway to your knees in the dry soil that was like flour from the lack of rain. I always worked with the laborers. I always felt that employees gave more when they saw their boss out there, and many times I was with them choking on the dust and pulling up those roots.

Many days I would eat lunch with the workers, and we would talk. It was late May, a beautiful day, and I saw a dozen of the guys taking herbal things, and I asked, "Why do you guys take that stuff?" A couple of the black guys looked over and said, "We are on probation and we have to take a piss test tomorrow." When I had hired many of these guys I knew they were not saints, but hell, neither was I years ago, and in years of being sober I had given many people jobs who were trying to get their lives back in order. It is what I did. "It cleans out your system so probation won't give me a dirty urine," the young man told me.

"So why don't you just not drink or drug until you get off probation?" I asked with a smile. It was a stupid question to ask an addict or alky, and I sort of laughed to myself when the words left my lips and he looked at me and said, "Why would you want to do that?"

Laughing, I thought I would have answered the question the same way years ago. Not get high? Why would you want to go through life like that?

We cleared the north field and another on the south side, and by mid-June they were planted. I had high hopes that a corn field on an island in the middle of bay would be a home run as far as providing food for ducks and geese. The field was limed, fertilized, and planted, and finally it rained and a few days later the corn came up. We had put up an electric fence around the field to keep the herd of two hundred deer from eating it all, but within days, they either jumped over it or jumped between the wires, and in a matter of days it was eaten to the dirt. It was beyond my control, but I felt as though all of our hard work was for naught. From the time I had started in early April, I had been working over eighty hours a week, doing many tasks that were not in my contract, and I began to get resentful and angry. I told my supervisor that he needed to get someone to take the load off quickly. After a month, he finally hired a young kid who said he had been building houses for ten years and picked up some of the burden. He was twenty-six, so that meant he had either started building houses when he was sixteen or he was full of shit. I chose the latter.

During late June and early July, my laborers and I started building pens for the pheasants for the shoots we were planning for the fall and winter. Driving pheasants had originated in England and Scotland, and it is what Bill wanted. Jack, a gamekeeper from a preserve called Port of Missing

Men on the south side, gave me some help and advice and even came to the island to look it over once with me. I had also worked on pheasant drives when I was twelve once in a while on weekends. I did it for fun mostly. They paid the leaders thirty dollars a day and fed us a couple of hot dogs, a Coke, and a jelly donut. When I started there a year before, the pay was seven dollars a day.

In the late eighties, I had been a guest there shooting. Clients of mine would invite me when one of their group could not make it, so I was pretty familiar with what went on behind the scenes of the shoots held at that preserve.

The pheasant drives were one part of my job as gamekeeper that I didn't feel as confident about, but I had faith through practice that I could pull it together. By November, we had over three thousand pheasants on that island, and each hunt would be an experience that all who were involved would never forget. At least that is what I hoped.

The summer was a blur. I would get home after eight at night most of the time, and my catering business suffered as I was too exhausted to return phone calls.

I catered what I could, and I had a dozen people working for me, but I just could not do it all.

I went to meetings when I could, but I only could make two or three a week instead of five or six. My new career was a huge undertaking. My supervisor said to me one day that, after a couple years, it would be easier and I would have to work less and get the same pay. I envisioned that one day I would retire there, maybe even live there and spend my free time fishing from the dock.

In the late spring, I leased a farm on the north fork from a local farmer, and I installed a pit blind there for shooting. We would have the two blinds on the island on two ponds, a steel pit blind on the sand spit on the south side, and the farm on the north fork.

In the late spring, I was given a cell phone. It was the first cell phone I had ever had and it took me a while to figure it out. Then came a fax machine, a pager, a new F-250 pickup truck, a twenty-six-foot Parker boat, and an expense account. The expense account gave me $500 a month, and I would sometimes spend $2,000, then I would have to wait over a month to be reimbursed. I was resentful about spending my money for a man who made millions each month, but I did it anyway.

I had been working on the island for a few months when many people who barely ever talked to me began being more friendly, asking me questions about how it was going and how I was. I began getting recognition I had never felt before. My ego loved it, of course. Hell, who wouldn't? It was exciting.

It was the beginning of losing who I really was and letting my self-esteem get wrapped up in what I did: I was the gamekeeper of Fantasy Island. I remember ordering over a hundred thousand dollars worth of hunting equipment one time. I was a kid in a candy store!

The idea was that we would have guns, clothing, ammunition, and equipment so that a friend or client of Bill's could fly in by seaplane and we would have everything he needed to hunt pheasant, waterfowl, or deer.

When the summer was almost over, I heard news that changed everything in my world. The US Fish and Wildlife service closed the Canada goose season on the entire Atlantic flyway, from Maine to the Carolinas. I was devastated. I had some farms with three-year leases that had just been renewed that winter—ten thousand dollars worth of land leases. Some I negotiated down, some I let go of, and others I had to pay.

It takes time before you really see how lucky you are sometimes. If I had not been hired as the gamekeeper, this closure of the goose season could have crushed me. My waterfowl guiding business provided me with over 60 percent of my income for the year. I would have lost a lot, I am sure.

My guiding business grossed less than $25,000 that first season of the closure of the goose season, and after paying leases, I made about $15 an hour for over three hundred hours of work.

The reason for the closure was that a population of a subspecies of Canada goose that nested in the Ungava Peninsula in northern Quebec had decreased for several consecutive years. It would take three years before we were allowed to hunt geese again, and the crazy part was that Fish and Wildlife finally discovered that the birds they were trying to save wintered in Delaware and Maryland and did not even fly to Long Island.

In November, we had our first pheasant drive and after one or two, I became more confident. On a shoot, there would be no less than fifty people to work the shoot. There would be twenty-five beaters who would walk through the woods and push the pheasant toward a desired location where the shooters would line up fifty yards apart, and when the pheasants would flush, they would fly over the shooters, who would shoot what they could. Then seven or eight dog handlers would be stationed near the shooters to retrieve the game. There were also boat captains who would ferry workers and dog handlers back and forth, a catering staff to feed everyone, and assorted other staff. Most of the shooters would arrive by seaplane or helicopter. I estimated that each shoot, not counting the birds, cost over a hundred grand. It amazed me.

I had read the old books about the island and the hunts they used to do back in the sixties. One hunt I read about was done on the meadow on the northwest point. The point reached out into the Bay and at its widest point was four hundred yards wide. The narrowest point was twenty yards. The meadow had waist-high grass in some places, and the birds liked to go there in the late morning when the sun was higher and it would warm them. Many days in the fall, there would be a cold front coming through, and a stiff northwest wind of twenty-five knots was not uncommon. I remember one such day. I blanked the birds with beaters, pushed hundreds out onto the meadow, and then brought the shooters in and positioned them in a line from beach to beach. The pheasants would flush one or two at a time, lift up in the wind, climb to fifty yards or sixty yards, then curl back and head back to the island. They had no choice; it was a half-mile for them to reach land to the north, which is far too long a flight for a pheasant. The closer the beaters got to the end of the drive, the more birds were flushing. At times, dozens would come high over the guns. Then there would be an explosion of pheasants, a hundred or more, and the shooters could not load their guns fast enough. Eight guns shot close to five hundred rounds in less than thirty minutes, but the dog handlers collected only nine pheasants! Bill was beside himself. He slapped me on the back and said, "Great drive, that was unreal!" All the shooters were cheering as they were shooting at an almost impossible bird. Hell, they were flying seventy miles an hour with the wind and over fifty yards up in the air.

After a few hunts, I got better at it. There were some days when the driven hunts produced over four hundred pheasants. Nothing went to waste, and the birds were cleaned. Some were given to the guests and the dog handlers and the rest would go to feed the homeless.

They were long days, though. I would arrive on the island some days at four in the morning if I was guiding a waterfowl hunt for guests. We would start the drives at eight thirty, and I wouldn't get back home until well after dark. My relationship with my wife suffered, and we fought sometimes about the long hours I worked. Many times I would get home and have to cook my own dinner and go to bed.

The farm we leased had twenty acres or so of corn, and a few weeks after harvest, close to a thousand ducks would feed there each night after dark. When it rained, you couldn't keep the ducks out of the lot. One such day it was raining hard all day and blowing east at twenty-five knots, which was perfect duck hunting weather. Bill had some guests who were arriving by helicopter to hunt. The weather was so bad that he had to drive and pick them up at the airport as the helicopter would not fly. I waited at the farm and watched hundreds of ducks swirl around the corn lot for over two hours before my shooters arrived. When they arrived, I suited three of the guests up with camo, guns, and ammo. They followed me in their Range Rover down a muddy farm road a few hundred yards where we parked and walked the rest of the way.

We walked through a foot of mud, and after a two hundred–yard walk, we arrived at the pit blind, jumped in, and got ready. On the walk out to the blind, hundreds of ducks jumped and flew off, but I knew it would not be long before they would return. My three shooters were European and had never shot an automatic gun, so I had to load each gun, go through how to shoot it and so forth. I thought that hitting a duck in that wind and rain would not be an easy task. It wasn't ten minutes before the ducks started coming back to the muddy corn lot and our spread of decoys. My guys shot well, and within thirty minutes, we had taken our limit of twelve ducks. I had wanted my boss to wait at the barn with the other three guests, but he went to shoot on the island. They killed one duck.

I worked mostly weekends on the island and guided some hunts on my farms and blinds on the south fork when I was off. The season was fair, but because of no goose hunting it was quiet as far as bookings went.

I went to some meetings, saw my friends once in a while, and Mary T and I would join George and Annette for dinner, but mostly I was consumed with work.

Boots, my Chesapeake, had fallen out of a pickup truck on the island that fall and torn the tendons in her rear ankle. I had taken her to different vets. They all said the same thing, that she would never retrieve or run again. I beat myself up a lot for letting her ride in the bed of the pickup on that bumpy road the day she got hurt. After going to a specialist and hearing the same sad news about her future, I was so sad. I remember every night for months I would lay on the floor with her. I would cry some nights and hold her ankle and pray for God to help her heal. I would put her ankle between my hands and pray; some nights my hands would get so hot that they would begin to almost burn and I would have to let go. It took several months and the vets called it a miracle, but that dog went on to retrieve over six thousand ducks, geese, and pheasants before she passed away many years later.

Boots was bred, and the first year I worked on the island, she gave birth to a litter of seven puppies. Only one was a female. I kept her, and we called her Maggie May. She was light brown almost blonde, and I felt that she would keep Boots company. I thought it would be great to rest one dog some days and use the other. But Maggie hated the whole hunting thing and never retrieved a duck in her life. When a gun would go off, she would run for the truck. She was more of a lover and not a hunter, and I accepted that.

Bill was a good man to work for, and he was generous. I would call him once a week or so and give him progress reports, which the supervisor disliked. At Christmas, I received a ten thousand dollar bonus that year, and overall my first year went well. It was great fun and hard work that first year, and I would not have traded it for anything. When we had shoots, many famous and wealthy guests would have lunch with the dog handlers. We would tell hunting stories back and forth. I met many interesting people.

I did have my problems on that island and tried to do too much. I was overwhelmed a lot of the time. And if I asked for help in coordinating the positioning of shooters or whatever, it fell on deaf ears, and on occasion I would explode in anger. Most of the anger was fear-based that I would look bad if the shoot did not go perfectly.

March came, and we did the last shoots for the year, and I began to think of renewing my contract. I would want more money for sure. I had proved myself and thought that I would be entitled to at least a raise of ten thousand. After all, I had gone above and beyond what was in my contract with all the extra weekends and late nights, some weeks over eighty hours. Yes, I deserved it.

I had a meeting with Jack, my supervisor, in an office one day and could not believe my ears.

"I think things went as well as expected the first year, and it was a learning curve for us all," he said. He went on to tell me that I would now run just the waterfowl program as Bill wanted to hire a Scottish gamekeeper. A raise of twenty-five hundred came my way, but the boat and the truck that had been provided were no longer mine to use. I wanted to leave, but I stayed and carried some huge resentments. The new gamekeeper and I would come close to blows on several occasions in the following months. They have a great saying, "Let go or be dragged," and I should have let go and saved myself a lot of anguish, pain, and humiliation and quit that job. But I didn't and I learned a lesson that would eventually change my life.

That summer I had more time to relax, but it did not seem to help my marriage, which had reached the point of no return. Mary was sleeping in the guest room, and we did very few things together anymore. There was a hurt in me that I could not explain. A lack of communication, trust issues, and the fact our sex life had been practically nonexistent for a year was tearing me apart. I was obsessed with the job at the island and worked far too many hours. We had drifted apart, and I thought if I hung in there maybe it would get better. There is a soul sickness that happens when you get to that place, almost like a cancer. No one can see it, and you pretend it doesn't exist, but it wears you down. One day, we argued. It was one of those arguments that I hated, and I asked Mary to stop and said we would continue it later, but she followed me around the house yelling. I cannot even remember what it was all about, but I reached the breaking point and the anger turned into rage. I grabbed a stainless chafing pan off the counter and slammed it down, crushing it like it was cardboard. I wanted to hit her with it, but I didn't and said, "That's it, I can't take it anymore, I want you to leave." Now, I had said this before, but this time I meant it. There would be no turning back. I was relieved and saddened at the same time.

The next few months we were at the lawyers, and Mary T and I continued to live in the same house. Those next few months were the hardest for both of us, and finally in November Mary T left one afternoon. She packed her things and took what she wanted, and as I sat in my living room with my dogs Boots and Maggie, she looked back and said, "You are going to end up just like your father, lonely, sad, and all you will have in your life is your dogs." Then she closed the front door and she was gone.

I never forgot that line, and there have been times since then when I've looked down while watching a movie with my dog in my lap and remembered what Mary T said that day. The funny thing is, sometimes I am sad and fearful that I may end up alone with my dog, and other times I laugh to myself and know in my heart there is nothing wrong with living like that. I am blessed to have something that loves me the way God intended us all to be loved: unconditionally.

For two weeks I was like a kid. I would come home at night and do whatever I wanted to. While I was married, I cooked dinner, did my own laundry, and did the food shopping most of the time anyway, so nothing changed there. While I was married, other married friends would tell me their wives did all of that, and at times I might have been resentful, but I liked doing at least the food shopping and cooking.

It took about two weeks before my new independence started to wear thin and loneliness came to stay. I had had a woman in my life through most of my adult life, even when I was drunk out of my mind. Now I was forty and alone, and many nights some movie would trigger an emotion. The tears would roll down my cheeks, and I couldn't stop. I missed Mary T. She had been there at night when I came home to hear about my day, and although there were lots of problems, that was something I missed. My dad had passed a couple years before, and without Mary I felt more alone than I ever had in my life. I barely saw my brother Eben. He had inherited a fair amount of money when Dad passed and was on a mission of self-destruction with alcohol and coke. My mother was in la-la land, and if I had something going on I would bring it up, but she would never give me feedback. Instead, she would talk about something she had bought or a cocktail party she had gone to. That shit got old quick!

I thank God for George, though. He was always there for me, along with some other friends in the program who gave me support.

An important thing I learned in getting sober was that anytime I was having a tough time and was into myself, it was a good time to get involved in the program and work with others. One night at a meeting, an announcement was made. It was a commitment to be a chairperson for Twelve Step meetings at the jail in Riverhead. After the meeting, I approached the man and asked if I could be involved. "It's a two-year commitment, every Tuesday," he said. I thought for a second, it seemed like a long time, and then I said, "Well, I will just do it one Tuesday at a time." I began the meetings that winter and it would prove to be an important part of my sobriety and life.

The new gamekeeper began demonstrating his skills on the island that fall, and as I summed up from talking with him through the summer, he was all talk. His Scottish accent and arrogant ways made me angry, so I tried to just do my own job with the waterfowl, but he would interfere wherever he could. The deer population on the island had been diminished by many days of hunting, so the corn was growing well and I looked forward to hunting ducks that winter. I came to work one September morning to find that almost all of it had been cut down. I was not even told about it and went into a rage when I found out. The new gamekeeper had decided it interfered with his pheasant drives. He smiled when he told me it was his show now. I wanted to drop him right there! Many days, it was like a bunch of male dogs marking their territory on that island.

My dog Boots loved to retrieve pheasants at the shoots, and I went from running the shoots to being a dog handler. I did it because Boots loved it so, but at times I felt humiliated, and to say the least it was very humbling considering where I had come from.

At one of the first shoots with the new gamekeeper, I was working my dog behind Bill on the drive of the northwest meadow. It was a typical fall day on Long Island, the wind blew from the northwest, and except for a few cirrus clouds the sky was deep blue. The new gamekeeper did not blank the pheasants toward the meadow with beaters like I did. I said to another dog handler, "Watch this, it is going to be a disaster." I knew that when it was cool and breezy, the birds did not like going out on the meadow. They would rather stay protected up in the woods, which is why you had to drive them into the area and then bring the shooters in behind the wall of birds. The new gamekeeper did not do that.

I think fifteen pheasant flushed and flew over the shooters, if that. At the end Bill looked at me and said, "What happened? Why were there no birds?"

"You have to ask your new gamekeeper that one," I told him as I walked away. Boots and I walked a few hundred yards and I looked back when we cleared the meadow. The gamekeeper was waving his arms about, and he and Bill were in a heated discussion. My ego loved it. After all, the right thing would have been to ask me how I did certain things there, but he knew it all and never asked, so I never told him. He thought he would retire on that island too, but he was fired after his first season.

It was an experience I will never forget working on Fantasy Island. Guests came to the island from all over the world, many of them very wealthy and some famous. My ego loved it all. I lost myself on that island and would come to learn something very valuable that would change my life forever. It came in the spring of '95 when it was time to renegotiate the terms of my third contract. Many of the benefits of having a company truck and boat were taken away. I had even gotten my captain's license so I was able to ferry guests back and forth from the island to the north or south forks, and now I was wondering why I had taken the time to do that. My supervisor met with me and said that because I would be working less time there with the waterfowl program, they wanted to pay me by the hour. I asked Jack, "What person in their right mind gives up a business to work here, is paid by contract for two years, and then gets paid by the hour?" He had no answer. It was unfair, and I was bitter for some time. I felt that I had given them many contacts, and I had coordinated contractors that I knew, as well as decoy makers, I built many duck blinds and pit blinds, provided a list of dog handlers and dog trainers for their shoots, and it went on and on. Who wouldn't feel used?

I left the island that day and never went back. It was early April, and I did not want to go back to the house painting. I felt lost and slipped into a depression. I had many expectations, I guess, because I was deeply disappointed, but more importantly, I started to realize my depression was linked closely to my lack of self-esteem. I had gotten so obsessed with the island, the people, excitement, new projects, money, power, and all the control that somehow I had lost who I really was.

My marriage failed and now my career had failed. I must be a failure, I thought, and all I could do was go from one day to another, go to meetings and talk about it. I was back in therapy again. It helped, but this was an inside job I had to come to terms with. Working on that island being a gamekeeper was how I made a living and should have had nothing to do with who I was as a man.

George was there when I needed him. Many hours did I talk about the loss of the job, what I would do, and how I would make it. He said one day, "You are great at catering those clambakes. Why don't you invest some money and hire more staff and see what happens?" I heard many years ago that God speaks through people, and to this day I truly believe that. I did what George suggested. I invested thirty or forty thousand dollars into advertising, purchased some new equipment, and hired the staff. I love the movie *Field of Dreams* where he hears, "Build it, and they will come." I built it, and they came.

That summer, my business doubled from the year before. The next summer, it doubled again. I was stunned and grateful all at the same time. A year or two before I was working at the island, I would visualize that my life would be wonderful if I catered events May through October and then hunted in the winter and had a bit of traveling in the spring. I surely would be "living the dream."

THE GIFT

They say sobriety is a gift to an alcoholic, and I know this to be fact. How could someone like myself, who spent every waking moment obsessing on drugs and alcohol, come to a place where the thought of using would not enter his mind? God, it amazes me that with all the work that went into it I had any time to enjoy life. Ah, that's right I didn't enjoy my life. I forgot that...

Eben had been smoking enough crack to bury a small town since my father had died in '92. I had village police, town police, and state troopers who would stop me or call me and tell me that I had to do something before it was too late. Eben had gotten five DWIs by then and assorted drug charges, and he'd been hospitalized several times for auto and motorcycle wrecks. I had gone to where he lived with guys who he knew had gotten sober to try to talk some sense into him. Never did it go anywhere. One such summer I talked with him at the house he rented. He was in shorts and his legs were so thin that his small calf muscles distorted the look of his legs. His skin was taught against his cheeks, his face sunken, and his pale skin had a tint of yellow. He was 5'8" and could not have weighed 140 pounds soaking wet. We spoke our piece and voiced concerns for him, and then he asked us to leave as he had done all the times I tried to help him.

It seemed like the only time he and I were close was a period of eight years after my parents had divorced. We drank and drugged together mostly, at times hooking up with a couple girls, and we thought it was fun.

Hell, some of it was. I got sober, and my brother lost me. I had to protect myself from all the drugs and drinking he was doing, and the only way I learned how to accomplish that was not to hang with him. It was hard. I think I tried to explain once what I had to do so I wouldn't pick up, but I don't think he ever really got it. After my dad died, even though Eben lived a mile away, we never saw each other. I had heard he had gotten his sixth DWI, and a week or so later he called me in tears and said, "Please help me and bail me out of this place. It is terrible here." He was in jail, and his bail was fifty thousand dollars. But even if it was fifty dollars, I would not have done it. He needed to find his own way. I cried after I hung up the phone, knowing that enabling him further would kill him. But in my heart the shame and guilt ran thick.

Around '97, we began talking. He asked me to help him. Eben wanted to go to a meeting, which we went to, and he wanted to work for me that summer. We were starting to communicate; it was all good. Then one day a month later, a detective came to the house looking for him. I asked what it was about, and he said a warrant had been issued. He assured me that all he wanted to do was to bring him to court and he would not be arrested. Eben explained that his lawyer had not gotten paid the latest installment and had not shown up in court. He said they were going to arrest him. I assured him it was going to be fine and that the cop had given me his word. I called the detective a day later and was given a date to bring him to court in Riverhead.

Except for the feds taking me to court for the migratory bird case in '93, I had not gotten so much as a parking ticket in twelve years. It amazed me when I thought about it. Shit, I had been in and out of the court system since I was twelve, and when I got sober I was so grateful not to have to look back. I had this problem, and still do, with authority figures, so going to court with my brother meant I had to put aside those resentments and do what I could to help him. He had no one left, and I thought being sober for many years and all the people I had helped would account for something.

I wore a three-piece suit and drove Eben to the court. I kept assuring him that the detective gave me his word he would not be thrown back in jail. As my brother and I stood side by side in the back of the courtroom, I could tell the judge was none too happy to see my brother. Then the judge began telling my brother that the only thing he thought would help him was to spend some years upstate in jail. I asked the judge if I could address the court, which he allowed. Now, going to court is always easier when you are not the one being nailed to the wall. I was not fond of the system then, nor am I fond of it today, but I knew my brother needed me. I felt that I might never get this time again, and I prayed for honesty and the words. "Your honor, I am Philip Gay, Eben's brother. I am a recovering alcoholic and have been sober for over fourteen years. I also run a Twelve Step meeting at the correctional facility here in Riverhead every Tuesday night.

"I will tell you that I would not lie for my brother, and everything I am saying is the truth. Over the years of being sober and chairing the meeting at the jail for several years, I have seen many people die or be incarcerated for long periods of their lives. Many of them never get to a point in their life to have an honest desire to stop drinking. My brother has been going to meetings recently. He wants to change. Your honor, it would be a terrible fate if the only time in his life he wants to change and get sober, he is put behind bars for years. Please, see a way to give him that one chance," I pleaded.

The judge was silent for a few seconds, then he said some things, and I was distracted as Eben began to give me his watch and wallet. Then I noticed one of the court officers walking toward the back of the courtroom as he put on his gloves. They don't put on the gloves unless they are taking you to prison. Then the judge said, "I will take this under advisement and reach my decision on Monday morning, court adjourned." I felt terrible as I walked from the courthouse to my truck. After all, I had promised my that he would be coming home with me, but instead he was off to jail again. That officer who put on his gloves walked up behind my brother, handcuffed him, and took him away. The detective who came to my house had lied. What else was new?

The weekend could not go by fast enough for me, and I am sure my brother felt the same way. Monday morning came, so I put on the suit and tie and went to the Riverhead court for the sentencing. I said some prayers for Eben. He was just an addict and alky like me, and I hoped he would get the gift as I did.

I sat in back of the courtroom and waited for the judge. That is one thing I could never get then or even today—the time wasted waiting for the judge. They are always late. Christ, if you were late, you would catch hell, but it is fine for them. It just pissed me off. Eben was brought through a side door in handcuffs, and he had a concerned look on his face. The judge entered the room and proceedings started. Eben stood up, and so did I, even though I am not sure I was supposed to. He looked at Eben straight in the face and said, "Mr. Gay, I have thought about this a lot. Your brother is your guardian angel, and if he can go through all that he has and gotten sober and stayed sober, then you can do it too."

I sighed a bit of relief and felt that a miracle was about to take place, and then it did. "Mr. Gay, I am giving you one last chance. I am putting you on the TASK program. You must attend meetings, and the most important thing is that you stay out of trouble. If you come back to this court with any violation in the next two years, I will give you at least three years upstate. You can count on that, my friend."

My bother couldn't say thank you enough times, as did I.

Eben was taken by court officer in cuffs back to jail to do the paperwork for release, and I was to pick him up the next day. I drove home from the court, and tears of joy rolled down my cheeks. How wonderful it was to mean something. All those years of doing the right thing…the gratitude I felt that day was enormous. To be there for my brother when he needed me, to finally begin a sober relationship with my brother who I loved…

it was all about to happen. I could feel it. And wherever my father was, he was smiling down on us.

The only thing that broke the silence in the truck as I drove up to Yaphank Jail to pick up Eben was the wipers slipping back and forth. I looked back at my life and Eben's life and how it had happened, and I thought that the only person who could have probably pulled this off was me. It was my honesty, it was my devotion to help another alcoholic who was still suffering, it was the responsible man I had become. I felt respect, I felt self-respect, and I smiled with tears in my eyes. I knew it was a miracle that he was being released. I knew Yaphank Jail well; I had spoken there at many meetings. As I pulled into the parking lot, I saw Eben running from the edge of the building toward my truck. It was like a movie. He was running in slow motion. As he opened the door, the tears streamed down his face. He grabbed me and held me tighter than he ever had before and said, "I love you. Thank you so much for helping me, thank you, thank you." The two of us hugged each other and sobbed like children for a while. It was a moment I will never forget. Then he said, "No one would help me but you, I promise I will do whatever it takes, I will never get high again, I will do anything."

Those are the magic words that anyone who helps someone trying to recover loves to hear. I know what it means to say them, because I said them more than once. When I got sober, if the people in the meeting said that I had to sit on my head in the corner of the room for an hour each night to stay sober, I would asked which corner. When you are at the jumping-off place, when it seems it can't get any worse, when your world shrinks and no one is there for you and you want to commit suicide on a daily basis but you don't have the balls to do it because you think you will screw that up too, then you are ready. Sometimes I am baffled by stories I hear, the ones of the high-bottom drunks or a person who comes to recovery before the arrests, jails, detoxes and physical demoralization takes place. I spilled more than a lot of them drank, yet they come to meetings and have the only requirement: a desire to stop drinking. My brother was far from a high-bottom drunk. Death was knocking at his door. On this rainy afternoon as I drove home, I looked at him and hoped Eben was ready, and I hoped it was his turn to receive that wonderful gift of willingness.

My brother had done a job on himself. He owned a couple pairs of jeans and a broken-down motorcycle. I knew also he carried some deep shame for spending all of the money my dad had left him. Also, he was unable to visit my dad much when Dad was on his deathbed. That had been a gift for me to be there emotionally at that time, and I knew that if I had been drunk or high, I could not have handled it either. I never blamed him, ever.

He went to meetings, got a job, and rented an apartment and worked for me sometimes catering parties. I know I was angry when I got sober, but in comparison to Eben's anger, I was a saint. Sort of. Some young kids who worked for me at that time could not believe I could curse through a complete sentence. Eben was no different...those fucking cops, that fucking boss, and on and on. It was the Motor Vehicle Board, or TASK, or hell, he might of hated me too, but he never told me to my face! TASK was a type of probation where he had to drive an hour up the island twice a month and be interviewed and piss in a cup. He hated it.

He went to meetings, and after work, he would hitchhike to therapy in the next town. One day a girl showed up at my house looking for Eben. She was an old friend from when they were teenagers. I had a bad feeling as my brother was not sober very long, but wild horses could not keep them apart. I let it go. He had to find his own way. The summer went by, and it was good to see him getting back on his feet. He respected me and I respected him and I was proud that he was doing well. As I am thinking back, I remember when we were drinking at the same party and I would hear him say, "My brother this" and "My brother that" as he talked to people. It made me uncomfortable, and I think I yelled at him once, saying he should live his life and stop living out of my shoes. Now, when I heard him say it to guests while he was working at a party, it was different. He was proud of me and still is to this day.

It was about a week before Labor Day when I smelled alcohol on my brother. He denied it. I was like a bloodhound. I could smell booze on someone from ten feet away, pot too, and if you had a gram of blow in your pocket, most times I could smell that too. I still can!

I knew that the task program was coming to an end, and I knew that if he got off having to piss in that cup he would be off to the races again. I knew his councilor where he went to group each week, and I dropped a dime on him. I explained the situation, and he then called Eben's TASK officer. She was helpful.

A week or so later, I got the phone call from my brother. He was on fire and said, "Did you call those TASK people and tell them I was getting fucked up, 'cause now I have to go there and piss in the cup every week for months."

"Of course I didn't call them. Why are you getting fucked up?"

He did not answer me.

"Maybe it was someone you were getting high with, you know you just can't trust those people," I told him.

"I was having a couple with Jimmy at the corner the other night, that son of a bitch," he told me.

"Yep, there you go," I told him.

So, for the next nine months, he was like the mailman—neither rain nor snow nor sleet would keep that boy from peeing in the cup three times a week. Sometimes his sponsor John would drive him, but many times he would have to hitchhike or take the bus each week, and then twice a month he was off to Haupauge to see the TASK woman, as he called her.

Eben's sponsor, or confidant if you will, was a man I had known when I was drinking. His wife had called me many years before and asked me to talk to him and take him to meetings. I did for a while. He hadn't had enough yet, and after a few weeks, he never called and slipped away like many do. A year or two went by and I got another call from his wife. She wanted me to help him again. Reluctantly, I took him for a while, and he wanted it this time and got some time together. What an amazing thing it was, how my brother hated most everyone in recovery meetings, yet this one man became his friend and helped him find his way. What would have happened if I had not gone there those times to help John? Would my brother have found someone else? Who knows? I do know that when I do the right thing, it comes back tenfold, and I am blessed that John was there to spend countless hours listening to his ranting and raving.

Fear is life's curse. Society and the world are impeded from reaching complete joy and freedom because of it, and alkies get obsessed with worry, lack of faith, and control. I have battled with this myself and still do sometimes, but it has gotten much less over the years. I called George when I had fifteen years and explained the fate of my future to him, saying this was going to happen, then that would happen, on and on. George would listen for a few minutes and say in a kind and loving way, "You know how many times you have been right in the fifteen years that I have known you?"

"How many?" I asked.

"Never, you have never been right, ever," George said.

Now, we have had this conversation a few times since, and it always is false evidence appearing real, over and over. I was worried about my brother. Shit, I wanted him to live, and calling TASK and throwing him under the bus might save his life.

I am not sure what it is with alkies, why they think that if they do not control, manipulate, obsess, and scheme, that things will not work out well in their lives, but they do. You would think that we would look back and see what a total cluster fuck of a job we did when we were drinking, but we don't. Maybe most human beings do the same thing, but I wasted many hours, days, and sadly maybe even years of my life projecting what would happen in my future. I try not to go there as much today; living in the moment is key for me. Also key is being grateful, and when I am appreciative for every small thing in my life and living where my feet are, fear cannot occupy the same space in my head. That is truth.

THE SINGLE SOBER LIFE

I had not been single and alone much since I was a teenager. I always seemed to have a girlfriend, but at forty-one I found myself without a relationship. They say if you want to get to know your character defects, get into a relationship. This is somewhat true, but to find out who you really are, be alone for a while. One night I was taking a guy to speak to my jail meeting, and we were talking. He was bitter after a tough marriage had dissolved and he had been sober a long time and had started drinking again and had been back in the program a few months, maybe a year.

"You know, alkies are not supposed to be in relationships, we are supposed to be alone," Bob said. I will never forget that comment. It came from a time in his life when he did feel that way. Hell, I have felt that way many times myself. Today, he is married several years to a nice woman who has been sober a while also. They are happy. He has a successful business, and life is good.

I always say that drinking was just a symptom of my disease. It saved my life on one hand and almost killed me on the other. I feel that growing up, I carried many fears. The lack of intimacy in my house had done some damage, along with never feeling accepted for who I was and having almost no self-esteem. When I was young, I had nightmares of dying and slipping into nothingness, feeling like I was falling off a deep cliff. Faster and faster I would fall into the darkness, and then I would wake up in a sweat. Dying was total abandonment for me, and at this time I think the fear was still somewhat present, but the nightmares were gone. I have felt unconditional love from my dogs, and it is the reason that my father loved them too. Dogs look into your eyes, and they are not only devoted to you, but if you treat them with love and care for them, they are always happy to see you, ride in the truck with you. They trust you with their lives and would do anything for you. I never had that feeling growing up, and unfortunately, I have not had many relationships where this was present. It was not my fault. I think I am guarded, and any time I was with a woman, even Mary T, I could not let the wall down completely and become totally vulnerable.

So there I was, sober fifteen years and looking for love…needing to be loved. I carry a fear even today that I might never be loved by a woman before I die. So a few months after Mary T left, I was looking for love. Maybe we should call her a victim, maybe I would be the victim—hell, you know the deal, someone was going to be the fucking victim. There I was at a show in the Nassau Coliseum, there were ten thousand people there at least, and I bump into an attractive young thirty-year-old and I was like a moth to a flame. I've always had a problem with hot women. A kind of listening impairment takes place, when lust was in my eyes and in my pants, and I could not hear what the Coca Cola Girl was saying. I called her that because she drove a huge truck delivering Coca-Cola. She was tough, tomboy like, and she drove a tractor trailer. She had long blonde hair, nice firm breasts, a beautiful smile, and ocean blue eyes.

So when we were getting to know each other, she started to tell me about her relationship with her father, how he mistreated her, rejected and abandoned her, how she was molested by a family member, how her ex-husband abused her physically, and how she had almost no money, a child, and on and on. Now, in my head, while this conversation was going on, I was saying, "Yes, uh-huh," like I am listening to every word. But in fact, I have a movie going on in my sick mind. The movie goes like this: "I can save this one…my friends would love her…she is funny…the guys will think I am cool 'cause she is hot…she and I can have kids together, it will look like

I have it all together...I can take care of her financially...I will knock her boots off when she has sex with me and she will never leave me...the end."

I saw her for a few months, and of course it did not work out, but we were very friendly about it and I was always good to her. Maybe at times I was too good and I gave up a lot of who I was, but we parted as friends.

It was spring and back to the world of East End Clambakes, coordinating events for the summer residents, hiring staff, preparing equipment, and three months of one hundred–hour weeks. There would be no time for dating.

That summer was far crazier than any summer as far as work went. After the smoke cleared, my accountant summarized things for me. My business had doubled again, for the third year in a row since I left the job on the island. The saying that when one door closes, a window opens is so true. I did not know how I would exist without the job on the island. Back when I worked there, I thought I would retire there on that dock, fishing with my dog sitting next to me. I loved the challenge of catering , talking through the event with the client, coordinating all the particulars, lining up the staff, ordering all the party rentals, tents, and equipment, booking bands and DJs, ordering the food, prepping it all out, loading all the grills, coolers, and bars in trucks, and then sending out the staff to cater the event. I work well under pressure, although I do have meltdowns from time to time. I always find the answer and solve whatever issue comes up. I loved cooking for two hundred and coordinating it all so they had dinner exactly when they wanted to have it. I have catered events in the best of weather and the worst.

Once I was catering an event for a close friend—he actually was Eben's councilor when he quit drinking. It was a wedding for his daughter. She was in her late twenties and was marrying a local boy. The wedding was at an estate in Hampton Bays over looking Peconic Bay. It was a beautiful place for a wedding, the house and huge lawn sat on a bluff some sixty feet above the water. The tent was erected as usual a day or so before the wedding, and I was busy with all the preparations the day before. We set up the tables and chairs for 170 guests under the tent. We had generators for power as the tent sat at least one hundred yards from the house. That night, it began to rain and blow out of the northeast with the remnants of a tropical storm that was coming up the coast from the Carolinas. Long Island juts out to the east quite a bit into the Atlantic, and I knew when there was a storm coming up from the Carolinas it was trouble, but I was hoping it would pass offshore a couple hundred miles. It didn't.

That Saturday morning in October, I wanted to be somewhere else. Torrents of rain came down sideways, with northeast winds of over 70 mph. I was not looking forward to working in that weather, but I knew we had to keep moving, there was food to prep and trucks to load. At around ten o'clock that morning, I got the call. The stakes were pulling out of the ground on the tent, and I needed to get the tent company staff there quickly. I called the tent company and got the foreman and told him to meet us there. I grabbed three men and some sledgehammers and other tools and headed out to Hampton Bays. The roads were flooded, and it took us a while to get there. As I walked toward, the tent I could see the tent flaps waving up and down, snapping in the wind. The stakes had pulled out. It had rained over two inches and the ground was soft. Over half of the stakes had pulled out of the ground.

I stood inside the tent and panic set in and I wanted to run. The tables were wet, the chairs had blown over, the wind was blowing right through the tent, and the huge pole tent was swaying side to side. Just then, the man from the tent company showed up, and he too was stunned at the sight of it. It never fails that when you don't want the client to see a disaster in the making, they appear like magic. Walter, the father of the bride, walked into the tent just at that second and said, "In my worst fucking nightmare, I would have never believed this." He turned and walked out of the tent. I followed him and tried to assure him, saying, "Walter, it is going to be all right, we will get the tent tied down, don't worry." He kept walking. Hell, it was like watching your house burn to the ground and having the fireman telling you, "Don't worry, it will be as good as new one day!"

I returned to the tent. The men were staking the tent again, but it seemed that after they would stake one side, by the time they got to the others they had to go back and do it over. I told the foremen of the tent company that he needed to call for help, which he did, and an hour later there were three men from the tent company and three men with me.

Another thing that never fails to happen is that someone will come to me when all this shit is happening and ask me questions. In this case, it was the florist. She kept saying, "Phil, this is a disaster. You need to move this to a catering hall somewhere." At first I dismissed the thought. What about all the tables, chairs, and generators? There would not be enough time to move equipment. A few minutes later, I was on my cell phone trying to find a hall. I called several, but they were all booked. I felt it was a sign. If there was one available, I would have tried to make it happen, as long as the client was good with the decision. I said a prayer to God to give me strength to make it through, and then I walked over to the florist and said, "Every place is booked. We are going to make it work, so do what you have to."

It took an hour and a half, but the tent men finally figured the only way to keep the tent flaps from pulling out of the wet ground was to tie a pipe between each pole on each of the side flaps. It started to work, and I took my staff and told the others to keep at it as we had to go back and finish loading equipment.

We got as many towels as we could pull together. We dried all the chairs and tables, started the propane heaters in the tent, and within a few hours we were almost ready. About this time, the tent staff said they were leaving, but I threatened them with what would happen if they did. They said they would stay, and they did until it was over. Around five o'clock, it was time to prepare appetizers and light the grills. The rain was still coming down as the valet parkers with their white umbrellas guided the guests into the house, and I sent some of the staff up to the house to begin setting up raw bars. The wind had calmed down to thirty or forty knots, so keeping the grills lit was still next to impossible. We had to make room in the cook tent and roll the huge barrel grills inside. The smoke was so thick when we put on the steaks and chicken that I could have used a respirator.

The house was pretty big, maybe five thousand square feet, but it was still cramped quarters for 170 people. I had to stay down by the tent because when I was up at the house the bride kept asking me how it was going. One of the times I answered, "It was a disaster, but now we are in good shape." She was not assured, but it was the truth. I had catered over a thousand events by that time and never seen anything as bad.

Then a miracle happened. The rain stopped and the wind subsided a bit, maybe down to twenty-five knots. I sent one of my staff up to guide the guests down to the tent. It was quite something to watch the expressions on their faces as they sighed in relief when they saw the beauty before them. The tent was seventy degrees, the band was playing soothing music, the candles flickered ever so slightly on the tables, flower arrangements looked eye-catching, and even though the wind blew outside, inside that tent the air was calm.

The bride and groom were announced. They had their first dance, and we served a delicious dinner. Lobster, clams, mussels, grilled rib-eye steak, grilled marinated chicken breast, and grilled vegetables were presented and dinner was served. I always feel like a weight is lifted after dinner is served, but this night I sat down and finally took a deep breath. My eyes filled with tears of gratitude. I had never given up, even when others told me to give up. My staff and I pulled a rabbit out of a hat that night.

I stood by the exit of the tent when many of the guests were leaving, and at least forty people came up to me and said it was the best wedding they had ever been to. I got a huge hug from Walter when he left and he said, "I don't know how you did it, but you did it." The bride gave me a kiss on the cheek and told me that it was her dream wedding and that she could never thank me enough.

But that is why I do what I do. It is a challenge, pulling it all together. Yes, there is no doubt that if someone did not know me, they would call for the men in the white coats sometimes when I have meltdown. But I stay focused and determined and know that all problems will work out if you keep at them, one at a time.

THE GIRL IN THE RED DRESS

The winters are long on Long Island's east end. The summer people have long left, only to be replaced by tens of thousands of Canada geese that feed on the few farm fields where they haven't built huge mansions yet.

The goose season had been reopened, and I was again guiding a few hunts a week with one guide working with me. Other than hunting, I enjoyed my home at night with a warm fire and a nice dinner of bay scallops that I caught myself, or maybe an oyster sauce over pasta from oysters I had caught a few days before. It was the beginning of December, and I called George just to check in. While I was talking with him, he was chuckling in his sick way and I said, "What are you laughing at?"

"Nothing really, just that Vera has a friend here, and she is showing Annette her tits in the pantry."

I had dated Vera a bit when I was first sober. We found we were better fishing together than sleeping together. We actually caught a 351-pound mako shark on my twenty-foot boat. Vera and I were friends for years. "What does she look like?" I asked quickly.

"She is about six foot tall with blonde hair and a nice set of tits," George chuckled.

"Put Vera on the phone," I blurted out. Vera picked up the phone and said hello, and I said, "So you have a hot lady out here and I don't hear from you, no calls, nothing? Who is the girl you have with you?"

"Her name is Jean, she is my sponsee from Florida, and she has a year and a few months," says Vera.

"I want to meet her," I said.

She laughed a deep laugh like she does and said, "How about going to the Sunday morning meeting and then we could go to lunch?"

The hunt was on, and I was excited to meet this hottie with the nice rack.

Sunday morning I walked up to Vera's door, knocked, walked in, and said, "Good morning, Vera, how are you?" I gave her a hug. She said something, but to be honest I do not know what—all I could see was a six-foot blonde with a tight pair of jeans coming down the hall.

"You must be Jean," I said, smiling. "I am Phil."

She was *smoking* hot, and a couple times I had a tough time putting a sentence together. We climbed into the truck, and we were off to the meeting. You know how sometimes you meet someone and you like them from the very start? It did not hurt that Jean was a ten-plus, but she was full of energy and had a wonderful sense of humor. The meeting was uneventful, except that I couldn't help notice all the snakes at the coffee pot clocking Jean as we walked in.

After we drove to the Corner Bar in Sag Harbor for lunch, I could not keep me eyes off Jean. She was cool with me, though, and I could tell she liked me. It was Jean's last night here, and then she was flying back to Fort Lauderdale where she lived. We talked for a while, and then it came to my mind that I had made plans to cook wild duck for a girl I was not really into. I looked at Jean and said, "I made plans to cook duck for a girl tonight, but I would rather cook duck for you."

Jean smiled sexily and said, "I would rather you cooked duck for me too."

I got up from the table and said, "I will be right back, have to make a phone call." I called the girl, cancelled the duck dinner, came back to the table, and said, "Dinner at my place tonight."

Vera spoke up, "What time should we be there?"

I had forgotten she was even at the table, let alone that I was asking her for dinner.

Well, I could not get rid of Vera, and that was cool. We had fun. I did not cook duck, but I cooked a great dinner. The best part was that before dinner I had some brie cheese and crackers on the table and Jean took a Dorito and applied the softened brie to it and ate it. I had never seen such a thing, what a wonderful concept: brie and Doritos. I knew right there that I had to bring her to meet my mother. Mom would probably pass out seeing that trick! I loved to torture my mother. Christ, she had it coming.

The three of us watched a movie after dinner, and then they both had to get going. I started to feel panic. I could not let Jean slip away. At least I had to get her phone number in Florida. I got her number and gave her a hug and they left.

I thought about Jean off and on the next day, and then I had to call her. She answered the phone. She was upset. I tried to comfort her and listen to her. She had to get off the phone so I told her I would call her the next day. The next day, she was in worse shape and crying. I guess she owed money to someone. She had no work and said, "I had so much fun back there with you guys, I just want to get out of here."

"Why don't you come back up here to Southampton?" I said.

"Where would I stay?" she whimpered.

I could not believe she said that. Could it be that easy? "You could stay here. I've got plenty of room at my house. Come on, I will buy you a ticket, what do you think"?

"I will call you back," Jean said and hung up like she had another call or someone at the door. My mind raced. Would she come up to visit? Did I come out to fast and tell her to move in and scare her off? Did I blow it?

Then the phone rang, and it was Jean. "I will be flying into McArthur tomorrow at two thirty in the afternoon."

I wanted to jump through the roof I was so lit up. "Great," I said. We talked for a while more, and I told her things we could do together. She laughed.

I could barely sleep that night I was so cranked up. I called George and told him that she was coming to spend Christmas with me. He laughed and said what he always said when he saw trouble on my horizon: "Go easy, my friend."

The next day, I picked her up at the airport. I was high on endorphins as my feet barely touched the ground when I carried her bags back to my truck. She smelled great and gave me a big hug and a kiss in the airport. Shit, I wanted to knock her boots off right there in the parking lot.

So much for getting to know someone—it wasn't an hour after we got home that we were having wild and crazy sex.

Jean was hot, thirty-two years old, sexy with long legs, an ass you could bounce a quarter off, and had energy and a sex drive that would not stop. I later found out she had been a dancer at Solid Gold in Fort Lauderdale. To keep her out of trouble, I got her a membership at the gym. She would have guys trying to pick her up every day we went, and of course my ego loved it.

I gave her one of my trucks to drive so when I was at work she could do what she wanted. She worked out just about every day with or without me, and she could stay on the stair master for over an hour straight. She was fun to be with, and we laughed a lot in the beginning. My brother liked her. She was a good egg. My brother came to the house to meet her for the first time, and she was dressed in tight shorts and a T-shirt that was cut off just below her tits and no bra on, her nipples popping through the shirt. His eyes almost fell out of his head, and he had a vacant look on his face as all the blood left his brain!

"Har are you?" he slurred. She had that effect on men; their tongues and brains did not function when you first met her.

Never did she care what other people thought, and she said whatever came to mind, sometimes making guys blush. I loved that about her.

George and Annette had invited us to a Christmas party at their house a few days before Christmas, so Jean and I went. That night she walked down the stairs from the bedroom with a bright red, low-cut, and very short cocktail dress. With her blonde hair, she looked like a Barbie doll. I introduced her to everyone at the party. She made quite an impression, and many women were keeping their eye on her, or maybe I should say they kept their eye on their husbands or boyfriends. She was hot and knew it, but not in the snobby way many New York women have. Jean was confident with her sexiness, and when guys would flirt with her, she played along and made conversation. She was no dummy.

I was happy for a while. Some of the best sex I ever had was taking place. Looking back, there was something always missing with me, and if I had a beautiful woman on my arm, it would complete me and I had it all together. Of course, I didn't. I was insecure, fearful, and lacked a lot of self-love then, but I didn't really know that then. She and I would go grocery shopping together. She loved food as much as I did, maybe more, and we would come home and cook a nice dinner. Jean was different than other women, who were obsessed about her bodies. She ate as much as I did, if not more. I put on over seven pounds in a month, but she never gained a pound, I couldn't understand it.

The night I saw the red dress, I just knew she had to wear it to my mother's Christmas party. It was always on her birthday, December 27. She had a party for herself every year. Maybe forty people would show up, and they were always boring. It was a lot of alkies with red noses and blue-haired wives who wore much too much perfume. You could tell them the same stories if you met them two days later, because they were too drunk to remember or listen, and they did not care what you said anyway. I could not wait to see the reaction Mom would have to Jean.

The night went just as I expected. My mother was aghast at the dress, and in a matter of minutes, Jean was holding court with several old guys and having a blast. Their wives, as usual, were off to the side making comments about her boobs, with her nipples popping through the dress, or the way she towered over the short old men with her high heels. Mom was embarrassed and I was in heaven…

DEEP DENIAL

Denial is a strange thing. It is there. Sometimes others see it, and if they love you, they point it out to you. Sometimes no one sees it. Sometimes you just go through life like it isn't there and all is good.

A few weeks after Christmas, Jean was cooking some chicken soup at night, which I thought was strange. I came down from taking a shower and sat talking with her in the kitchen. A couple of minutes went by and she was talking crazy. At first I thought I was losing it and I was crazy. I started to sweat for a minute, but then she told me she needed to lie down. She went into the living room and passed out on the sofa. She was stoned, on what I was not sure, but she was out there. I called Vera. "Hey, you need to come over here right now, we got a problem. Jean's high and passed out I think."

"What was she taking?"

"How the fuck should I know? Just get over here." Vera came to the house a half-hour later, and Jean was still out. We walked upstairs to the bedroom, and Vera started looking through her shit.

"What the hell are you looking for?" I asked.

"Pills, she has been taking pills," Vera said. "She likes Xanax."

I did not know much about Xanax because they came out with that shit after I got clean. I had just heard that it got you toasted like Quaaludes did. Vera found an empty bottle of Listerine in a draw under some of her clothes, and then another one in another bag under the bed, then a couple empty vials of pills. It was Xanax.

"What the hell is she doing with all the Listerine?" I said as I pulled empty bottles one after another from under the bed.

"She is drinking it, Phil. What the hell do you think she is doing? Wake up over there," Vera blurted. I was still puzzled. How or why would you drink mouthwash? I had heard about it, but never had I met someone who drank it. Same with vanilla extract…Christ, I thought there was not enough alcohol in that little bottle to get a fly high!

"What do we do now?" I asked. "We got to call George, maybe he can get her into rehab."

George owned the rehab in Westhampton, and in the years since I had gotten sober, he had given scholarships to so many sick and suffering people that if he had been paid back, he would be a million dollars richer. I can think of at least a dozen people he helped for me alone, and I am forever thankful.

George called us back and gave us the go ahead to bring her over to the rehab. Vera and I got her in the car. She was like a rag doll, her head bobbed from side to side between Vera and I on every corner.

Over the years I had taken a lot of people to treatment hospitals, and I had seen it all. There is a recovery hotline number you can call if you need help or just want to go to a meeting. One time a guy in the program called me, and we went to pick up a guy in Sag Harbor. He was toast when we got to his house.

You sometimes would get the call to help a person and not know the exact address, but after doing a few of them, you got good at spotting the alky house. It would be April and the Christmas tree lights were still on the tree outside, or it would be August and the lawn would be a foot high. We always found them. It was pathetic. They never washed and would be unshaven and their house would look like a bomb had gone off in it. You were scared to even touch anything. Empty bottles would be everywhere, along with half-eaten slices of pizza on the floor with green mold growing on them and dirty laundry. It would always bring me back to my drinking days; I was in the same shape as these guys. You were never supposed to go alone, that was the rule, because you could end up drunk or the guy could pull a gun. You never knew what you were walking into.

Another time on a Twelve Step call, Tom called and wanted me to go to a motel to talk to a guy who wanted to commit suicide. The guy was drunk. I was sober several years. Tom was new, and when we got to the door of the motel, he knocked on the door and said, "What if he has a gun?"

I quickly said, "Don't worry, Tom, he won't have one."

Just in case, while he knocked, I slid down to the cement wall a few feet from the door. We heard from inside the room, "Come in."

Tom opened the door and stepped back, looking at me with a vacant look. "I don't think we want to go in there," he said.

I looked around the corner of the door and inside the room. There stood a tall, naked man with tattoos all over his body. I guess living a crazy life, with guns pointed at me, being the only white guy in Harlem to pick up drugs, or robbing shit from houses or cars, this shit did not faze me. I walked in and Tom followed. His name was Kenny. He had white hair and was about six foot four inches. He couldn't have weighed 150 pounds soaking wet and had retired from the Long Island Railroad. We talked for a few minutes and asked him if he wanted to go to a meeting. He accepted as long as he could have a drink first. Kenny's hands shook as he poured a tall glass full of seven and seven. It brought me back, seeing him shake like that. I was a shaker too. My shaking was in the morning mostly, but I would spill the shit all over like there was an earthquake.

I looked back at Jean. She was still passed out and her head rested on my shoulder. I thought about how she was going to make out, how much shaking and quaking was she in for? I was not sure what the detox was like coming off of xanax, but I was sure it would not be pleasant for the poor girl. She was so sweet and why did she need to...I knew the answer she was an addict and a alcoholic and it was what she knew best I guessed.

We finally arrived at the rehab in Westhampton with Jean. She was starting to come around a bit, mumbling some sort of talk that only the spaced-out could understand. We parked and woke her up. She was toast. When we told her the people there could help her, Jean seemed relieved and smiled and then her eyes rolled back in her head again.

After a half hour, we left her in good hands, and Vera and I drove back home. The whole way home, I talked about how stupid I must have been to miss it. It was like when I lived with Mary T and she was using all those years.

"I should have known, Vera. Christ, I am sober over fifteen years. Did I have blinders on?" I said.

"Phil, I was with her the other day, I didn't know either, go easy on yourself," she tried to console me.

It was my own fault, for God's sake. I had the girl jump on a plane without knowing anything about her. It was my thing. Some people had told me I had a broken picker, and it might have been true. I have said it over and over: put me in the dark with ten thousand women, and I will pick the one with issues or hang-ups.

My therapist always told me to ask questions of women. Find would what she liked, what she did not, what kind of relationship she had with her father, maybe even her favorite color. But when I saw Jean and met Mary T, my mind went blank. I had probably slept with a hundred women and never knew what their favorite color was, for God's sake.

I visited Jean several times. I even went into a family program for the codependent issues I had.

Each time I went there to visit, we talked. She looked better and sounded better as each week went by.

After twenty-one days, she was out, and I brought her back home. She stayed for a week, but then said she needed to get back to her place in Lauderdale.

We talked often, and she came back for part of the summer. It was good to have her back, but I was working far too many hours and she felt ignored and resentful, even though she never talked about it.

I was never very good at communication with women. I would sense the tension and ask if she was all right. They would say they were, so I would ask again and then go about my business. A few days later, an argument would come up, and they would say that just because I asked if they were all right did not mean I cared. I was never very good at it. Shit, I had nothing to go by. Growing up, my parents had drinks on that sofa in the living room sitting as far from each other as they could and maybe saying a sentence to each other every five minutes.

That winter, I thought of Jean from time to time. I missed her and began thinking about the good times. It is hard for someone like me. I felt like a broken toy from the broken toy shop again. Time went by, and I started to envision us together again. Then my life would be full, it would have meaning, and most of all I would not be alone and the fear deep within me that I would be without love for the rest of my life would lessen. I had dreamed about most women I had been with, and I could not understand why they did not want to get back together with me and start fresh.

But you just can't start fresh. There is history. Words were said. Feelings were crushed. There was pain. Most women were not willing to put themselves through more pain to take a chance that it might work out or not. The most important thing I didn't understand was that the relationship was based on a brief period of crazy sex and infatuation and never did we really get to know each other. We were not in love. Love? What the hell did I know about that? I never saw it between my parents, never felt it really. I thought I did, but obsession, wanting, longing, and infatuation were all I knew.

I was heading to Florida for a week, and I wanted to surprise Jean. I knew it could go either way, but I took the gamble. I stopped by to see her at her house and knocked at the door. Some guy came to her door and my heart sank. He was in his twenties, good-looking, and had a cocky attitude. I disliked him from the moment I saw him. I asked him if Jean was home. He asked my name and went inside. She came out wearing a pair of daisy dukes. A faded T-shirt hung on her wet breasts, and her hair was wet from taking a shower. The memories rushed back of all the laughs and the wild sex we had.

I wanted to get back with her in the worst way. I never once thought of any of the heartache, the arguments, or the time she relapsed and I took her to rehab. No memories of those hard times came to me—they never do. I told her I missed her, but she said nothing. A half smile came across her face, and she looked away. I immediately got that knot in my stomach. It was that familiar knot that came before the pain would hit me. She told me that the boy at the door had moved in a couple weeks before and it was serious.

"Do you love him?" I asked.

"We are different than you and I were, he understands me," she said with a tear in her eye.

I needed to run; I could not break down in front of her. It hurt that she felt I did not understand her. It hurt being rejected again. Tears rolled down my cheeks.

"I have to take off," I said. I gave her a hug, and that was the last time I ever saw Jean. I sobbed like a child driving down A1A toward my hotel.

It came to pass several months later that she was not sober. It was better not to be involved again. I knew it in my heart, but I still missed her just the same.

I always wondered what would have happened if she had not slid back into the pills that night. Maybe it was God's will not to put me through what I had been through with Mary T…who knows?

I came across a story in a book years ago. A copy of it is on my refrigerator. It is my life.

AUTOBIOGRAPHY IN FIVE SHORT STORIES, BY PORTIA NELSON

I walk down the street.

There is a hole in the sidewalk.

I fall in

I am lost…I am helpless

    It isn't my fault.

It takes me forever to get out.

I walk down the same street.

There is a deep hole in the sidewalk.

I pretend I don't see it.

I fall in again.

I can't believe I am in the same place

    But it isn't my fault.

It still takes me a long time to get out.

I walk down the same street

There is a deep hole in the sidewalk.

I see it there.

I still fall in…it is a habit.

My eyes are wide open.
I know where I am.
It is my fault.
I get out immediately.

I walk down the same street.
There is a deep hole in the sidewalk.
I walk around it.

I walk down another street.

LOSS OF A FRIEND

Life was good, and my catering business was doing well. I had not been in a relationship for a while, and I was somewhat content. It was June. Summer approached, and the weather warmed to the eighties during the day. Peconic Bay was warm in the seventies. Many days, I worked late and went for a swim in the bay just south of Robin's Island. I had Boots, my dog of seven years, and her daughter Maggie to keep me company, and I would laugh to myself when I was home alone with a dog on each side of me, hoping for a handout as I ate my dinner. I would hear what Mary T had said to me years before.

I started to notice that Boots was not eating her dinner some nights, and after a couple days I had took her to the vet. I liked my vet; he had always been good to my dogs, and Boots liked him. They did some tests on her and called me to come and talk with the doctor. He had a serious look on his face when he entered the room. My heart sank, my face flushed, and my eyes flooded with tears.

"What is it?" My voice shook.

"Boots has a growth on her liver, it looks like cancer. I am sorry, Phil."

I broke down. I loved her with all my might. I sobbed for a while, and then he said, "You could take her to a specialist in Plainview. They might be able to do something more than I can."

I sat there sobbing in the examination room for a few minutes. I was stunned and looked into my friend's yellow eyes. She did not like me to be sad and looked at me as if to say she was sorry she was sick. The made me sob harder.

The vet continued, "Boots has severe arthritis in her spine, and I am amazed she has been able to swim or run at all."

I got the number for the hospital in Plainview and called when I got home and made an appointment for two days later.

I thought about our time together, Boots and I. I thought about all the years she had probably been in severe pain.

The dog brought me joy and loved me. She protected me, my trucks, and my home. She spent the last years of her life in pain every time she had to retrieve a duck or goose in the ice-cold water, and never did she give up or show she was in pain for fear that I would not take her with me hunting. I thought of the times she crawled over sunken logs in the swamps of upstate New York chasing down wounded wood ducks, or the hundreds of geese with just a broken wing she had to do battle with to bring them back to my hand. Retrievers always had my respect, and this dog was one of the best I had ever had.

That night, I was scared to lose the last thing connected with my dad. He had given me the dog when she was just a puppy on Christmas Eve. It had been the best Christmas present I had ever gotten. I thought about the arthritis and how long had she been in pain. Dogs are like that—they just want to provide happiness for you, be your friend, and love you through thick and thin, and never do they complain like humans do.

The next day, I was with her all day. I called Mary T and told her how sick she was, and Mary came over to the house. Boots had not seen her in a couple years, but she wagged her tail and greeted Mary. We talked and cried for almost the whole visit. I feared it would be our last day together and decided at sunset to take both dogs for a swim. It was something they loved. Chesapeakes love the water, and although Maggie was chickenshit of swimming in the ocean, she loved the bay. It seemed a good place to go. Driving there, my mind wandered and I remembered the boat trips to work on the island with Boots' feet on the gunwale of the boat, her brown ears flapping in the breeze.

I parked the truck on the beach and helped Boots out of the bed of the pickup. Her weight was no longer over a hundred pounds, and I could feel her ribs as I lowered her slowly to the sand. Maggie jumped out and was in the water in seconds. God, it was a beautiful night, the sky was just beginning to turn pink, and the sun setting over the bay like a huge orange ball. It was early June. I dove into the bay, tasting the salt on my lips. The water was warm, and as I floated on my back for a minute, my mind focused on the moment and all fears faded away.

I began to swim toward the sunset, maybe twenty yards off the beach. The dogs followed me along the beach. They walked slowly and kept up. I knew the feeling of being in a surreal moment, but I have never felt it like that night. I had a strange feeling this would be the last time Boots would go to the beach, the last time I would have her with me to protect me, to love me and be at the beach. I knew she had to go to Plainview in the morning.

I did not want it to end, and tears rolled down my cheeks. I looked back at the truck, now over a half-mile back. I wanted to just keep swimming forever, so I would not have to face tomorrow. Another fifty yards, I would think. The dogs swam out to me, thinking they better save me before I drown. I had one dog on one side and one on the other. I swam closer to shore in waist-deep water. Boots swam up to me like she always did when we swam together. She hopped up and placed her huge paws on my shoulders. I hugged her and kissed her on the head. "I love you," I told her. Her big pink tongue licked my face, and we all got out of the water. We began walking back down the beach to the truck. There was a couple walking on the beach, and as I approached the truck they came to me, smiling. "That was the most beautiful thing I have ever seen," said the woman.

The man said, "It was amazing how they just walked slowly with you the whole way while you swam."

"They are great dogs," I said as I smiled and picked up Boots and lifted her into the back of the truck. Maggie leaped in and wanted to play with her mom, but Boots was tired. It was all she could do just to stand there panting. Her liver had enlarged to the point where her lungs could not expand and breathing was getting more difficult.

I believe that animals know when they are dying. They stay with their masters, and even if they are in pain, they never let their masters know. They are scared to leave their heroes behind on this earth. They feel their job is to protect us and care for us and give us love and joy. They sacrifice their whole life for us; they are God's angels.

I have had many dogs in my life. I hope they are all there on the other side waiting for me when I go. I know we have been each other's heroes. They are amazed at what I do and what I do for them. Whatever you want to call it, I was Boot's hero. I knew that, but most of all she was my hero and I would remember her and stories would be told about her my whole life. It is what we do. Our dogs, especially hunting dogs, are like people we have known and we tell stories about them forever. The only difference is that not once, never in their lives, did they ever hurt us, say hurtful things, or wish bad thoughts about us. Their only fault is they maybe loved us too much and sacrificed their lives. This is why they are my heroes.

I came home and made some dinner, although I did not want to eat much. I cooked some meat for Boots, but she did not eat it.

It was late morning the next day, and I had an hour-long drive to Plainview Animal Hospital, so I walked to the truck with Boots and lifted her into the front seat of the cab. Dogs love trucks, they do indeed, and Boots loved to look out the side window. At times, her ears would flap in the breeze and make me laugh.

This day was different, though, and Boots did something she never did before. She lay on the seat and just looked at me as I drove with her eyes filled with love.

She knew what I was doing, she knew where she was going, and she knew what was going to happen. Her eyes full of love because she knew that what I was doing was the hardest thing I had ever had to do. She seemed to say, "I respect you and love you, you have been a good friend and I will miss you forever."

I arrived at the hospital and waited only a few minutes before I met with the doctor. He looked her over and wanted to do another sonogram, so I left her in the examination room and went out to wait. It was only a few minutes before the doctor brought me back in and gave me his opinion. Boots had a tumor that was making it difficult for her to breathe. It would cost three thousand dollars to try to remove the growth. Their were no guarantees she would make it through the surgery, nor that it would help her that much in the long run, but there was a possibility that she could live another year or so.

I asked if I could take ten minutes and go outside with my dog to think about it. I walked my friend to a grassy area with some shade and sat down with her. I got on my cell phone and called my brother. My heart was breaking as I talked to him and tried to come to a decision. I did not want Boots to suffer, but I could not put her to sleep either. I cried like a five-year-old boy and looked at her yellow eyes. She looked up at me as if to say, "It is okay if this is the end of our time. You have given me more love and adventure than any master could have ever given me." I kneeled a few feet away. Boots got to her feet and sat next to me and licked the tears as they rolled down my cheeks. She didn't want me to be sad; she never liked it when I cried. I told her I loved her and gave the big brown dog her last hug and brought her inside the hospital. I signed some papers, and she was to be operated on that afternoon. Before they took her inside, I knelt next to her and hugged her. I kissed her head and whispered in her ear that I loved her and told her she was my hero. I called as many people as I could on the way home, wondering if I had made the right decision.

At ten o'clock that night, I was leaving my brother's house when I got the call. It was the hospital. They had opened her up, and the inside of the poor dog was riddled with cancer. They could do nothing so they just sewed her back up. She died a few minutes before they called. The doctor told me how sorry he was and that she did not suffer.

It took me a long time to accept she was gone. Maggie missed her and kept looking for her mother around the house for days; it tore my heart out. Weeks later, I got her ashes and spread a few of them where my dad's had been spread years before, on the marsh where she loved to go clamming. The rest were placed in the fields and ponds where she used to hunt. It seemed like a fitting place for them.

RACEHORSES

The summer came and went. It was a blur, working a hundred hours a week most weeks. I was used to it, but it felt like I was doing time. It's exciting, demanding, and physically draining to cater several events and parties each weekend. It was good, though, and kept me from getting stuck in the sadness and loss of my friend Boots. Clambakes were more and more popular. There was plenty of Wall Street money—some guys were receiving million-dollar bonuses and renting houses for the summer and throwing money everywhere. I got my share.

Dating during most summers for me was impossible. I worked too many hours and had things come up at the last minute, or I just did not have the interest to get involved with a woman. After the summer season was over, it was different. When I would meet someone, I would get infatuated and it seemed to always get complicated.

I spoke to a man who was happily married one night at a meeting. The topic of my dating life came up, and his response to my problem of finding the right woman was the choices I was making. It seemed obvious.

"Your problem is you keep picking the racehorses, you need to stop doing that," he told me.

I had been out with many very attractive women, and I admitted I could not help it. I was attracted to them. The blonder, the hotter the bodies and sexier the smiles...yes, they were my downfall, these racehorses. I met another one that fall at a recovery meeting. Kate was a friend of a girl I knew, and from the moment our eyes met, I wanted to get to know her. She was from the city, an aspiring actress and model. She was hot and intelligent. It was not long before we went out, and I fell for her in a huge way. She was wife material, or so I thought, and after a few weeks I was truly infatuated with her. I thought she was perfect, but mostly she was evasive and played the game, which triggered feelings. I now know that what came up was neediness, the fear that if I lost her, I would never be loved. But I did not see the neediness then. And like they say, when you exchange fluids everything changes. We went weeks before we had sex. There was a lot of rolling around like teenagers in front of the fireplace on the living room rug at my house, but no sex. It got more and more important to have sex with Kate. I was good at sex; for me it "sealed the deal." Give them a few good orgasms and they would never leave me, or so I thought.

I had become more vulnerable with Kate than any woman except my ex-wife. But Kate had the same thing keeping her from finding someone as I did: a huge fear of commitment. It all stemmed from her fear of abandonment related to issues from childhood. She, like almost all women I had dated, had a father who was not there emotionally for her. I think that, intellectually, she wanted to be with someone like me: an honest, compassionate, funny, kind, caring, and successful guy who was sober and had respect and integrity (don't let me forget attractive). But in her unconscious mind, something never let her trust that or feel like she deserved it, nor did she believe someone like that would be interested in her. So we did the dance. I would come close and say something to reassure myself that she was not going to reject me as we lay there wrapped up in each other's arms. I would say something like, "You know, maybe in the winter you and I could go on vacation together to one of the islands in the Caribbean."

It would have been cool if she had brought it up, but she was gun-shy and I had known her for only a month. She would feel suffocated and tell me she needed some space and not to call her for a couple days. I would get anxious and needy and push her, wanting reassurance with an urgent need to "seal the deal." This shit unfolded slowly over weeks and months of pain and obsession.

We did have sex one night. It was one of those times when it just did not go as planned. I wanted a replay for sure. Sometimes sex isn't perfect the first or second time…I knew that. She was busy and working, but I felt I had done something wrong. I always felt like this when I fell for the race horses. At times I could not even be myself. I was a fucking chump of a man who seemed to almost whine on the phone, "When can I see you?" Fuck, I hated that needy shit when it came to the surface.

Not long after. I wanted to see her. I arrived at her house in a panic, which is far from my personality. I like to be in control, but this night I was helter-skelter and fear was making me crazy. I was losing who I was, so the person she liked was no longer there. It was the needy dude with tears in his eyes. We talked, and she told me I was making her uncomfortable and that she did not think it was a good idea that we see each other anymore. I said almost nothing and walked to my truck. It was raining, and between the water on the windshield and tears from the sobbing, I could barely see the road driving home.

Then it started and did not stop for over a month. I felt absolute abandonment and rejection, coupled with no self-worth or self-esteem. I would have beaten someone senseless if they said to me what I said to myself every minute. You would have thought we had been dating for years not months. But it did not matter, as I had dropped my guard and let the walls down, thinking this was what Kate wanted to see. I could barely eat. In a month, I lost over fifteen pounds. I could not sleep more than an hour some nights and many nights not at all.

I remember one night I was watching a movie, and it reminded me of my time with Kate. Hell, when you are hurting even the fucking commercials make you remember the hurt. At one point, I found myself on the rug in the fetal position sobbing so hard I thought I would break a rib. God, it hurt like nothing I had ever felt. I had a constant knot in the upper part of my stomach, like someone had punched the air out of me. I would call people sometimes and it helped, but they would get tired of listening to me. My brother later told me he would talk to me for a minute, then put the phone down and walk away for fifteen minutes and I would still be talking when he came back to pick it up.

I began reading books. *The Road Less Traveled* helped, and there were many others. I had not been much of a reader, but now I was like a sponge soaking up water. I wanted relief, and it was all that seemed to keep my mind occupied and helped pass the time. I found that when I was sobbing, I sounded like a five-year-old boy, not a man at all.

One night I picked up the phone. It was Mary T. I was crying. I told her I couldn't talk to her and hung up. She called right back. "Are you all right? Is it your health? What is happening?"

I did not want to talk to her. It had been months since I'd heard from her, and to this day I do not know why she called. I finally broke down and told her I was hurting, that I had broken up with Kate and that I had been crying for days and could not sleep or eat.

"This is great, you are so lucky, you are doing the work!" she told me.

"What the fuck are you talking about? Shit, I feel like I have been punched in the stomach a hundred times and can't do anything, and you think it is a good thing?"

She told me that breaking up with Kate had brought up my abandonment issues from years ago. It made more sense than anything else I had heard.

It is sad when you are going through pain and all you can do is keep talking about the night you were at dinner, the candlelight. You remember every word that was said, the times you were intimate...all you can do is focus on those times. Most people were tired of listening, but Mary T stayed on the phone with me for over two hours.

I got off the phone and was somewhat relieved. Mary T said my heart would heal and that the best thing was that if the feelings came back another time, in another relationship, it would not hurt as much and take less time to get over. I could only say, "I hope so." Over and over, I could say those three words to her: "I hope so."

Sometimes I would wake up and think of Kate, then I would sob until I did not have the energy to sob anymore. Other times, I would be crying in my dreams and wake up crying. I was in bad shape.

After another two weeks of dealing with the feelings, I could not take it anymore. I did not want to drink or drug—that never came up. But thinking of putting a gun in my ear did, and one day I made a phone call to the Caron Foundation. I was sober almost twenty years and was a basket case. I had attended the family program when I was a year sober, and I knew they had an alumni program. Hopefully, it would get me back on my feet and help me deal with this rejection and abandonment shit.

They were very busy and it usually took a couple months to get in, but they had just had a cancellation and I could come in three days on a Sunday.

TALKING TO THE PILLOW

It was early November when I drove down to Wernersville, Pennsylvania, to the Caron Foundation. At times I wanted to turn back and head home, but I didn't. I remembered what happened the last time I was there, how they broke me down into a puddle of piss by bringing up hurtful childhood memories that I had somehow kept hidden and then tried to put me back together again. I was scared to face it all again.

The first time I was there, I was newly sober. Although I did get something out of going there, I was in the dark about any feelings whatsoever. I knew this time it would be different. I had not even thought about how much courage it took and the amount of desire I had to change. I just wanted the pain to stop. I was sick inside my stomach; it had been sour for weeks and food did not even appeal to me, not even sweets.

Orange and red leaves lined the driveway and blew up the sides of my truck as I drove up the long driveway into the parking area. Anxiety started to take over, but it was too late. I knew I could not turn back, so I turned off the engine. I just sat there, wondering if this was a mistake. I was almost like a little kid with a toothache who arrives at the dentist's office and lies to his mother: "The pain has gone, I am really alright now." I took a deep breath and got out of the truck and grabbed my small suitcase.

Unlike rehab, where you can talk about booze or drugs and rant and rave, this shit was the real deal. I would be put on the hot seat. They would rip me apart and then try to put me back together again. There would be group therapy, and some shithead, a much sicker member by the way, would try to tell me what my problems were. At some point, I might come close to grabbing him or her by the throat. I would open up, break down, and everyone would see what a wimp I was as tears ran down my cheeks. Why the fuck did I want to put myself through this shit again? I breathed in more country air. I hadn't realized until then how my breathing had become so shallow. I had barely been able to fill my lungs with air for weeks.

I checked in and went to my room. I was early and took the best bed and got settled. My roommate had not shown up yet. That was another thing I hated—a fucking roommate. I was used to my own room. I hoped he wasn't an asshole and that he didn't snored or do some other shit that would upset me. He probably was driving and thinking that same thing!

The real shit would not hit the fan until Monday. That first night, we would be broken into groups. My group turned out to be three men and seven women. We were all given name tags and introduced ourselves, and our councilors introduced themselves. My mind wandered, checking out the better-looking women in the group. I could not help myself. After a short meeting, we went to dinner and then to bed.

We would get up at six each morning for six days and not be done with group therapy, psychodrama, role-playing, or whatever other torture they could dream up until nine or ten each night. I think in two days I might have talked in group for five minutes total. I listened to the other people in my group, who I determined had far more problems than I did, and I became more unique, at least to my own thinking. On Tuesday, the councilor said, "Phil, what do you think?"

I thought for time and then looked at her and said, "Well, to be honest I do not think I belong here. I really am not that bad."

The members of my group hooted and hollered, and one woman said, "Are you fuckin' kidding me? You are twisted up, brother." At first I wanted to grab her, but then I sat back in my seat and decided that maybe

I was in denial. The group members pointed out things I had shared and why I needed to be there.

This was what I loved about those places: you got to hear it from the crowd. Yeah, they might have issues and were pretty fucked up, but if they could see that I needed help, and the councilor did also, then I would hang in for at least another day.

Role-playing is where someone in the group plays your father, mother, husband, or whoever, and you interact with them. Sometimes there were several members involved, and almost always it seemed that I was picked as someone's alcoholic father or husband, which in the beginning seemed interesting. I felt needed and important, but after a few days, I got burned out. It amazed me how when a person was working through something, they actually would begin to think they were angry with you. One time, this thin-framed woman in her forties snapped and came close to swinging at me as she acted out her piece. I finally got to a point when I told the group I no longer wanted to play the role of an angry family member.

Many of my issues dealt with abandonment and rejection. They were core issues. I could not recall many of the ways I had been hurt, but they were present and kept me from being happy.

I was one of the last ones to work out my scene. It just happened that way, and one day the councilor asked if I would like to do work. I did.

I minimized my issues compared to the sexual or physical abuse that many others in the group were dealing with. One important issue that was brought up while I was there was the face that silence abuse was as powerful as the others and more difficult to recognize. If you were beaten or molested, you could remember it. I did know there had been some physical abuse until I was twelve years old, when I began to put my hands up, but I thought I deserved it and it was what all children went through.

When I worked through my scene, it was with my mother. I picked an older woman who seemed angry for the role. The councilor helped us get started. At first I just sat there. The woman who played my mother stood over me in a chair to simulate the power she had over me growing up. As I began to talk to her, the councilor whispered something in her ear and she looked away. I kept trying to get her attention, but she ignored me. I began to get angry, and she started to look away more. When the woman said anything, it was in a condescending tone with disapproval and disgust. This is what I had felt as a child. Also, just as I thought I would get my chance to say my piece to her, she would hold up the pillow. The pillow represented the disease of alcoholism, the councilor would say. "You are talking to the pillow, she can't hear you."

I would persist, crying and yelling. I remember losing it at one point, and I tried to get up from my chair to reach for that pillow so I could be heard. But the councilors held me down. I went from yelling and screaming into a rage and then back to crying and sobbing as I fell to the floor. I could not get through to my mother. She ignored me as if I did not matter. She was the important one. I came to realize later that I never felt accepted, loved, important, intelligent, or even good-looking as far as my mom was concerned. There was a huge hole in my soul, and when I met these racehorses, I needed them to love me like my mother should have. This would put a huge amount of pressure on even a civilian out of the program, but many of the women I was dating were recently sober and full of issues themselves.

It angered me, what my mom had done. I let it fly that week. I punched shit, beat pillows, and screamed until I fell to the floor in a heap, sobbing like a child. One week at a place like that gave me a great amount of understanding. I would continue seeing Glen, my therapist of many years, when I returned home, but this shit doesn't go away. I was given great advice by Glen to always call out the fear. Naming it takes away its power. It does work, but it takes lots of practice.

One of the classes at Caron had to do with horses, equestrian healing I think they called it. My group went outside and met on the side of the property with a horse. As the councilors explained what would happen before we went out to meet with the horse, almost all of us had tears rolling down our faces. Shit, they had opened up our hearts. We were all more vulnerable then we had ever been, so if you told us anything we would have started to weep. What happened was really interesting. We were instructed to stand next to the horse and place our ear at his side and listen to his breathing. Our hands were placed on his side to feel his heart rate. We were told to close our eyes and let ourselves go. The large old horse was gray and white and showed no reaction to all of this. He just stood there looking straight ahead, probably thinking, "Here we go again with these nutty fuckers." Each of us took a turn. I took my turn, and I felt close to the huge animal and for some reason started to cry. He seemed to understand the pain.

There was one girl who had a particularly painful past of sexual abuse and physical abuse and always looked so sad. I felt so bad for her. She was a badly broken toy. When it was her turn to stand beside the horse, she began to sob, as most of us did. What was different was the horse started nuzzling her side and arm as if to say, "I know it hurts, I love you, it is okay, I know your hurt."

I thought it was amazing how animals know when you are hurting.

I made friends there. We exchanged phone numbers. We were going to stay in touch, but we never did, and as time has passed I do not remember their names. I only know that the time we shared there helped me get through one of the hardest, if not the hardest, emotional depressions of my life.

I wish I could have said it was all fixed, but it wasn't. I left Caron that sunny November morning and headed home, hoping that what I learned would help me avoid doing the same things over and over and expecting a different result. There would be more racehorses, but I would have more insight and hopefully I would not get torn down again. I drove back home from Pennsylvania, quiet in the truck, and I did not even turn on the radio until I reached Long Island. I thought about my life and my childhood, wishing parts of it had been different. But again I came to realize that I could not change what had happened over thirty years ago, nor could I change my mother's alcoholism or the demeaning way she spoke to me. Her arrogant, know-it-all mentality drove me crazy. I hated many parts of her, but many of those issues I could never change. It was now evident to me that not only would she never change, but that she was hurting in a different way and it was the only way she knew.

Driving down my long driveway, beneath the seventy-foot white pines, toward my home always makes me feel safe, and this fall afternoon even more so. Sometimes I would forget the mail and walk to the box in the dark. Walking back, the house seemed tucked away, the lights glowing from the windows and the green landscaping lights making the pines glow. I would sometimes say to myself, "I wonder when the people who live here are going to take it back?" as if I did not deserve the beautiful home I had built. Over the years, these thoughts came to me less and less, but occasionally it amazed me that they came at all.

The next few weeks were difficult, but they were better than the weeks before I went to the alumni program at Caron. I began to see Glen again. There were days all I could do was talk about what had happened with Kate and me. Many times I would ask, "Does that not sound like she at least wanted to be with me?" Rejection was confusing and painful. I would want to know what I did wrong, if I could have done something differently, or if I should have spoken about the fear I was feeling.

They say hind sight is 20/20, but not always.

I had a dream one night of seeing Kate and talking in the warm sun at her house. She looked beautiful, her golden blonde hair shining in the sunlight, her skin browned from the Florida sun, and her deep blue eyes looking into mine. I had run the scene in mind time and time again. Months had gone by. I was different now, not as needy I hoped, and I could just be myself.

I went through Christmas, and after New Year's I planned a vacation. I wanted to go somewhere warm. I knew Kate was in Florida staying with her mom. I had the address, and I needed to see her, to show her I was different. I wanted her to see that I was now in control of my fear, that the neediness was gone. I took a deep breath and sighed. I wondered if she would be alone, or would there be someone she was in love with at the door? I walked up the steps and knocked on her door.

My throat was dry. I swallowed deeply as the door opened and an older woman with blonde hair answered. I introduced myself to her mother. She was an attractive woman in her sixties. I waited while she called for Kate. First impressions tell a lot. Kate smiled as she walked toward me, but in a controlled, serious way that let me know she was guarded. My heart sank.

It was strange. We sat on the patio across from each other, almost as I had seen in my dream weeks before. She was dressed in daisy duke shorts, my favorite and a ripped T-shirt that hung well below one of her shoulders. My heart skipped as I told her what had happened in my life since I had seen her. I wanted her to know that I understood why she did not want to be with me that winter, that my fear of rejection had made me become fearful. I told her that the more I worried, the more I needed reassurance from her that we would be together in the future. Maybe I did not say forever, but I might as well have

"I know it made you uncomfortable, I know you were scared," I told her.

Kate said, "It put huge pressure on me. I wanted to be your lover, not your mother."

I explained where I had gone and about the work I had done, the awareness I had now and how I was different. I was honest as I could be, but she could still see that I was a broken toy from the broken toy store and the parts that were broken had been glued and put back together with new paint. In my heart, I wanted to be as good as new, maybe better. I hoped that the glue and paint would not show, that she would see that I was more secure and less needy.

I could feel the uneasiness taking over. I finally got the nerve up and said, "You know, I am here for two weeks and would love to go to dinner or go to the beach with you. Could we do that and maybe start over? I just need another chance, it will be different, you'll see."

Kate's eyes looked down toward the grass for a second. I knew her answer already. Then she said, "You know I can't now. I am seeing someone here. I'm sorry."

Then it came, the knot in my stomach, just below my chest. I knew it well, but I had not felt it for several months. It had gone and now it was back like it never left. It started the second she looked down at the grass. I did my best not to break down crying in front of her. It was all I could do to keep it together as I backed out of her driveway—I had told her I understood. Had I understood? Hell, I did not understand. "Why again?" I thought as I waved to her and pulled away. "Why does this keep happening?"

I sobbed out loud as I drove down the street and tears streamed down my face, their salty taste on my lips.

In the program, they say not to get into a relationship for the first year. It makes sense. We were both sober and adults. She had six years, and I had close to twenty. In my case, they should have told me to avoid relationships for the first two decades. I was not equipped to know what to do, how to act, how to be, how to feel. I was still a child. I was wasted all the times I dated and had girlfriends as a teenager. I think when the first girl I cared about dumped me I was sixteen, and I never talked about how it felt to anyone. I never let many girls and later women get close because I was scared they would hurt me again. It was nothing I thought to myself. It was just some sort of uneasiness that would come over me and I would find fault.

Maybe she was too into me. Maybe she said she loved spending time with me. Oh shit, this one has to go. Plus, her legs were too long, her lips too fat…whatever it was, I would find it.

I dug deeper into the past with Kate; I wanted to understand it all. Many times, there is no answer. It is the way life is. I wondered how civilians made it through life. Maybe they found women who had it together and made little civilians together. Maybe they all just went through life.

As I turned into the place where I was staying, I shook my head from the noise in my mind.

That night, many feelings came back. I was sick. I could barely eat dinner and only slept a couple hours. The next day, when the feelings and negative self-talk came up, I did not let them take hold of me and struggled to keep busy. It passed in a day or so. I wish I could say they never took hold of me again, but that would be a lie. They did, however, begin to lose their strength.

I stayed with my brother's girlfriend, Lisa, in Fort Lauderdale for a week or so. Lisa had an apartment on the beach. She and my brother had been seeing each other for a year or so, and they had their problems from time to time. She wanted Eben to be someone other than he was sometimes, and one of the issues that bothered her was his spelling, of all things. She showed me a letter he had written. "See? He misspelled account. Can you believe that?"

I could hardly believe she was making an issue about it.

"Why don't you buy him a dictionary?" I said. Eben was a year or so sober, and I worried about him and the relationship. But who was I to talk? I had my own shit going on.

OUT OF THE FRYING PAN

The spring arrived, and as always, there were many things to do. I had to get ready for the clambake season and prepare equipment. The calls began to come in, booking weekends for the upcoming summer.

I always liked coming home after my vacation and seeing my friends and my dog and going back to meetings where I knew everyone. I had been feeling better, had read many books, and had insight and awareness of what had happened emotionally a few months before.

One night I bumped into a couple girls I knew. Both of them were in their early thirties and early in sobriety and very hot—I liked them both as friends. One of them, Julie, was always crying it seemed. She was full of anger. She had been in a relationship with a guy who had dumped her and she was torn up. She couldn't sleep and was obsessed with the guy and why he had left her. I talked with them both after a meeting one night.

"Julie, I know how you are feeling. I just went through this with Kate. You probably keep going through scenes in your mind over and over again about him and what he said to you. 'What could have gone wrong?' you keep asking yourself. I bet you are not eating or sleeping either, and it is difficult to work. It is all you find yourself talking about."

She looked at me like I had been reading her mail. "How do you know?"

"I know because I just went through it. I know it hurts. It makes drug withdrawal a cakewalk."

She began to cry and said, "I don't want to feel this."

"I know, but look on the good side. It is a learning curve. It will make you more aware of yourself and what you want and need in your life. I have some books I read last winter that helped me. I will give you one tomorrow. If you want, call me and I may be able to help you."

Julie was another racehorse. She was over six feet tall with golden blonde hair, a sexy body with great tits, beautiful blue eyes, and a wonderful smile. She was like a wild horse in every sense of the word. At the time, in all honesty, I wanted to help her and no doubt I wanted to one day have wild and crazy sex with her. But for now, I knew her pain and wanted to help her through it. I knew she would need someone to talk to.

Julie called me that night around ten o'clock. It was close to one in the morning when she said she thought she could sleep and said good-bye. We talked almost every night before going to bed; we did it for weeks.

In late May, things were heating up. Spring had sprung in the Hamptons, and the late-night talks with Julie were heating up as well. She told me she did not want to be in a relationship, but my ability to hear that was gone. She needed work so I hired her to work catering. We had worked some parties together, and we would flirt like teenagers some nights. It was a full moon one night and we were catering a beach clambake. After serving dinner, Julie was sitting on the tailgate of the truck facing the ocean. Her blonde hair shined in the moonlight, and when I walked up to her, I just kissed her right there, in front of God and everyone. I could not help myself. I felt like we were invisible, although she didn't, and finally we calmed down a bit.

I asked her to come over to my place after work, but she said that she couldn't. A few days went by before I was busy with work and wanted to call her, but I didn't. Then I got a phone call from her asking if she could spend the night as she had rented her apartment for the weekend. The first night I laid on the floor of my guest room for an hour talking with her and then left and went to my room to go to sleep, but I can say that it was hard to sleep. The next day, Julie thanked me and said she was staying at her girlfriend's that night. I had to cater another beach party. It was almost eleven o'clock when I finished and took a shower, and as I walked downstairs I heard voices on my deck. Julie and her friend were sitting on my deck, and she wanted to know if she could spend the night. We talked, then went downtown to get ice cream. We sat at the beach in my convertible truck, watching the stars, laughing, telling stories, and laughing some more. Life was so easy at those times. I never wanted them to end.

When we got back, Julie said good-bye to her friend, who she drove away. Julie and I were finally alone. What followed were some of the most erotic events I have taken part in. Our deep, passionate kisses seemed almost electric. Time seemed to stand still, and it was close to sunrise before we got to sleep.

Infatuation is a powerful emotion, and I don't think my feet touched the ground for days. There were times over the next few weeks when she would come over, I would light some candles, put on a Barry White CD, and we would spend hours having sex, talking, laughing, and having more sex.

June arrived and the weather got hot; it was my favorite time of year. I loved to head to the beach on Sunday. It was always slow as far as catering parties, and my brother and I met at the beach near Shinnecock Inlet in Southampton. This day, Eben and I sat in our beach chairs by the water talking about life and enjoying the heat, and even though the water was cold in June, we dove in from time to time to cool off. His girlfriend Lisa was up for the summer. They had been seeing each other again, and things were getting better. Actually, I was about to learn how much better.

He said, "I have something to tell you, Captain."

Since I had gotten my captain's license, that was what he and many of my friends called me.

"What's that?"

"I am getting married," my brother said with a smile.

I choked on my soda, and I was silent for a time trying to muster up excitement. It kind of shocked me, and then he said, "There is something else, you are going to be an uncle."

Now I was really at loss for words. I wanted to be supportive, God knew he needed that from me.

"Have you thought about this?" was all I could come up with.

"I thought you would be happy," he said. "I have made the decision and it is what I am going to do." He was almost forty years old, after all, but emotionally I did not think he was ready for marriage, especially kids. I congratulated him, and we started to talk about the wedding plans. He was happy, and although I felt it might be dicey to say the least, I smiled, thinking that being an uncle would be cool. My sisters never had any children, and neither did I. My younger brother would be the first to carry on the family name.

Eben walked down the beach, and I sat there thinking of the journey he and I had taken. The years of not seeing him, the calls from jail, the times when I used to have to send him away at Christmas because he was too high or drunk…it all brought tears of joy. Their sweetness touched my lips. I was so grateful and blessed to know that God helped me, my father, and then my brother receive the gift of recovery. I tried not to go the place of this being far from a good idea; that was not my place. He would have his own journey and learn, as I had. He asked me to be his best man. I was proud and knew Dad was also proud, wherever he was.

I told Julie about the wedding. She loved my brother and she accepted my invitation to come to the wedding. It was to be on Shelter Island, and a bunch of us were going to go over and stay in a hotel there and make a weekend of it. She wanted her own room, so I booked two rooms next to each other. That was always her game. We would be having off-the-wall sex in every position known to man, yet she wanted her own room. It puzzled me, but I did not make a deal of it.

Weeks went by. Julie and I saw each other at meetings and played the game of sitting apart, like no one knew. Shit, they all knew we were knocking boots. Sometimes I would call her twice during the day, leave a message, and then call her again at night. She would say, "You called me three times today, do you know that?"

I would tell her I had not been counting. At the time, it was more from a place of happiness that I called than from a place of neediness. That would come later, unfortunately.

In mid-July, Julie said she wanted to stop dating me for a while, although she still wanted to come to the wedding in early August. I did my best not to project, but it was no use. I kept projecting how we would be lovers again, hot and heavy.

The weekend finally came. My Uncle Ted, by then the judge, did the ceremony, which was at Bull's Head on Shelter Island. It was a beautiful blue-sky day when my brother and his new bride were married and Julie was there at my side. She looked amazing in her beautiful dress. Her skin glistened brown, and those long legs and full lips looked so inviting to me. She was the most beautiful woman there. It was the first time she and I had been together as a couple in weeks. She wanted everyone to realize we were not a couple, but that was hard to convince them as we were sitting at the same table and walking around together. Many people came up at different times through the afternoon and said, "Don't tell anyone, but you two are the most beautiful couple here today." I would give Julie a smile, but she would wrinkle her nose a bit as if to say, "I don't want to hear it."

We laughed talked about the memories we had and shook our heads in amazement that my brother was now a married man. It was all good. I asked her to dance, and finally she said yes. I held her in my arms tightly and closed my eyes. I loved the way she smelled. She was beautiful, and all I do was wonder if we would have sex when we got back to where we were staying.

It was fun teasing each other at the wedding, some sort of broken toy foreplay, I suspect. She was telling me we weren't a couple and meanwhile flirting like a horny schoolgirl who didn't want her parents to know and who was going to knock my fucking boots off when this was all over!

We had fun at the wedding. The time went by so fast, and Julie and I headed for the inn where we were staying. She had her room, and I had mine. All day at the wedding, it was all I could do not to kiss her full, beautiful lips. She smelled so good as I held her close dancing, but I resisted temptation. Arriving back at the inn, we went to her room. She and I laid on her bed laughing like teenagers. We were both high with excitement. I am not sure when it happened, but I kissed her deeply, and she pushed me away. It was like she would hold one hand against my muscular chest and the other hand would coax me toward her, it drove me crazy.

"We can't do this," she said.

"Can't do what?" I said.

"Have sex, we can't do it," she said. It went back and forth this way for at least an hour. We finally made a pact: if we had sex, I could not call her and she could not call me. It was perfectly dysfunctional. I agreed to the terms quickly. God, it was great to be with her again. We went at it all night, and after almost a month of not having sex with each other, we were fortunate not to bang each other's brains out that night!

I awoke the next morning in my room. Julie had left early in the morning to go to work. I stopped downstairs and had breakfast on the lawn. It was a warm August day, the sky was blue, there was slight breeze, and I just sat there smiling. I took a deep breath of the summer air. The sweet smell of summer was everywhere. I drove my convertible Chevy Blazer to the ferry singing to Barry White's "Never, Never Gonna Give You Up." Crossing the bay on the South Ferry, I got out and walked to the rail, watching the gulls whirl about in the wind over the choppy bay as my mind wandered. Would she be with me now? Did this seal the deal? Maybe one day, my brother would be my best man at our wedding.

God, I had never felt that way before or since, or had I? I questioned other times when it had happened, the infatuation that I mixed up for love. I had lied to myself those other women had been in love with me too. Then I dismissed the thought, this was different.. I had what I always wanted. Whether it was love or if I was just infatuated in a huge way, I did not care. I wanted the feeling to last forever.

It was Monday, and by Wednesday I wanted to see her, wanted to call her. I was having trouble sleeping. I was obsessing about being with her, but I kept myself from calling her. I knew the deal we made—as childish as the deal was, I would blow my chance with Julie if I caved. That evening, I went downtown. I walked into the park in the village. A band was playing, but I was anxious and couldn't sit still. I saw Julie and wanted to talk to her but didn't. I left and went down the street and sat on park bench. I said to God, "If I am supposed to talk to her, have her come to me."

About five minutes went by. My mind wandered as the summer breeze blew through the trees lining the street and I looked up. There was she was, walking toward me and smiling. My heart skipped and my face flushed.

"Fancy meeting you here," she said, smiling as she sat on the end of the bench. I felt like I was a teenager as I sat staring at the cars driving slowly by with my father's twinkle in my eye. After a pause she said, "You know, you have a big fan club."

"What do you mean?"

"I mean that every person that I talk to about you loves you and says that I must be crazy not to be with you," she said.

I wanted to jump up and cheer, but I didn't react and just said calmly, "What do you want to do about it?"

"Part of me wants to be with you, I really do, but I am scared, I am not sure if I can trust it, I keep looking down the road."

We got up from the bench, and I walked her to her car. We got there and embraced and deeply kissed on the hood of her car, looking up at the stars for an hour talking and telling each other what we wanted.

"I am going to try to do this and try not to screw it up," she said. We talked about things we would do together. She told me what I had been waiting to hear, that she wanted to be with me. I had waited weeks for her to say those words. I asked her to come home with me that night, but she said we would see each other tomorrow. I kissed her one last time and walked to my truck. My eyes were filled with tears and I thought how lucky I was to be in love with such a beautiful woman. I was happy. I felt complete again.

The next few weeks were mostly magical. One night, there was a big storm. Julie called. Her electricity had gone off, and she wanted to come over and stay the night. We sat at the dinning room table after dinner. She did some paper work and paid some bills, and I worked on some paperwork of my own. I had never done this with any woman. It was comfortable, and it seemed perfect. It fit, and my mind thought how right it would be with her in my life, one day living with me, being my wife. It was what I was missing. I felt more whole. Later, we went to bed, made wild and crazy love, and fell asleep. I noticed that for the first time in my life I was able to sleep with a woman holding me. I never once felt smothered. It felt perfect.

A few days later, we went to a show at a horse farm. A man was a horse whisperer, just like the movie with Robert Redford, and he was planning to break a wild horse. The trainer announced what a wild horse was like, how you must ignore them at first, then very slowly let them get close to you, and when they run away, just let them run and trust that eventually they would always return to you. I could not help thinking that these words explained exactly what I was feeling the last few weeks. I kept looking over at Julie. I smiled and said, "Sound familiar?" She had a habit of slapping me on the shoulder. The girl was strong and almost knocked me off the bleachers a couple times. Julie knew she was just like that wild horse and I was the whisperer, trying to ignore her and slowly letting her get closer and closer.

264

There are things that happen in life just exactly as they are supposed to happen. You could not have written anything better than the dialogue of the horse trainer describing what had to be done to calm that horse. At one point, a formation of geese flew right over the show. It was a sign. I pointed them out, and again Julie punched my arm.

As we drove home on that beautiful August night, I teased her about what we saw at the farm. She tried not to act as if it had anything to do with us, but inside she knew it was right on.

At home, I cooked some lobster fra diavolo while she sat in the kitchen and watched me. There was silence for a couple minutes, and then she said, "You know, my friend had me write a list today about what I wanted in a man."

I tried to not show a lot of interest. "Really, and what was the list?" I said.

Inside, I wanted to hear magic. I wanted so much for her to want to be with me, I ached for it.

"I want a kind, loving man, compassionate, great in bed, happy, successful and good-looking and fun to be with, a great sense of humor, someone I can always trust."

I smiled as I stirred the sauce, never looking up, and then I said, "Do you think I have any of those things on the list?"

She hesitated for a second and then said, "You are the list, everything I want is you."

I turned around. She stood up and we kissed. Tears rolled down our cheeks. We fell to the rug and hugged and passionately kissed. Finally, I had everything I wanted in life. I was loved for who I was. Again, I was complete.

Through my drinking days, when I was dating a woman I ran from commitment. I would feel trapped, and when they wanted to hold hands walking across the street or have their arm around me lying in bed after sex, it felt like I was choking. With Julie, it was so different. I was not sure what was happening, why it was different with her, why I could hold her or walk with her, lay with her in bed after sex and not want to call her a cab. It felt right. It was right and I knew it, and as long as she affirmed that we would be together, I was without fear. I let so many walls down. I was more vulnerable than I had ever been in my life—more vulnerable than with my wife, and I had lived with Mary T for over six years.

I talked with my brother about Julie. My friends liked her, and most of all, I was falling in love with her.

As fall approached, things with Julie and I were going well. We had a couple times where she pulled back. She would start thinking about us down the road and the fear would come. There were times she had financial fear, and I would talk her through it and be as supportive as she would allow. There were times we would have sex, and after we would lay in bed talking and she would say, "I don't deserve you, you are too good for me."

She too struggled with abandonment and rejection, and thus came her fear of commitment. Her stuff was from her father, mine was from my mother—we made a great pair of broken toys.

As a young girl, her father would tell her that he would be home at seven o'clock, but he would stop by the bar after work and get drunk, and she would wait by the kitchen window. Headlights would approach the driveway, and she would perk up for a second, thinking he had come home. But instead the car would drive by. She would wait for hours until it got late in the night and her mother would make her go to bed. She logically loved the man I was, but in her subconscious, she felt she did not deserve me, that I was too good for her. She had dated many guys who were unavailable and not there for her. I was present, consistent, and kind to her, and it scared the shit out of the girl. She did not trust it.

I was working through my own shit also. Julie was perfect for me: beautiful, smart, sexy, strong-willed and the real deal. I wanted to be with her forever. I talked to Glen about her when I went to see him. I told him that when she pulled away, it brought up fear and anxiety. I worried that if it did not work out, I would be alone the rest of my life. He tried to make me understand that it was all right for her to look down the road and dream, but when I did it, it scared her. I was not good at this. I needed it to be uncomplicated, but when is a relationship between two toys from the broken toy store ever uncomplicated?

One day it would be all good, we'd be laughing together, going to dinner, and having sex. What could be better? Then she would go through something with her family or her job, and she would appear distant on the phone or in person, and I would feel out of control. I'd be sure I was losing her. I would ask her what was wrong, but most times she told me nothing. The more she pulled away, the more I would want to be reassured that she wanted me, and my neediness would make me sick to my stomach. Sometimes I'd hear myself practically pleading with her.

Sometimes when she would pull away, I would tell myself not to call her. My friends would tell me to let her come to me, to stop pursuing her. The problem with that was that I would obsess about her, thinking of the nights during the summer we were close, when it was good and we were making love. Days would go by. I'd get an hour of sleep here, three hours there. I lost my appetite and began to lose weight. I had been down this road before. My friends were right: every time I stopped insisting on seeing her for dinner, a movie, or whatever, she would call or see me and want to be with me.

One period, we were apart for a week or two. We talked on occasion or I would see her somewhere. I was getting worn down. I would go back over our time together, trying to figure out what I had done wrong, I would talk to my brother and my friends for hours about it. She had not abandoned me, she had not rejected me, yet that was what I felt each day. The nights were the worst. I would toss and turn, trying to sleep. This infatuation had as much power over my thoughts as any drug ever did.

I had been talking to a friend for a few days straight about what I was going through. He listened to me, and thinking back now, I don't know how he had the patience to listen to it over and over again. "What should I do?" I asked him. It always ended around midnight.

"Try and get some sleep," he would say.

Then the next day, Julie called. "Hey, what's up, Phil?"

My heart rate climbed as I said, "I am just hanging out, why?"

"I was going to stop by." And she would. We would talk for a few minutes, then have make-up sex for hours…it was wild. Then she would leave and I was back to my old self. I was happy, hungry again, and when my friend called that night and asked, "How are you making out?" I said, "Great, things are good. She stopped by and we worked it all out."

The guy could not believe it could be that easy. "Are you sure?"

"Yes, I am good." I told him the story of how we talked and worked it out. In actuality, what had been worked out was nothing. We barely spoke for fifteen minutes, but I could not really explain what we worked out. All I knew is that I felt better for now, and that was all I cared about.

It started to happen again. When we would make love, she would have tears in her eyes and I would ask her, "What's the matter?"

She always said she didn't deserve me; it was like a broken record.

I have heard this many times at meetings: "You had a hard childhood. Well, it's over, get over it, move on."

I know on a conscious level that, yes, I have moved on. I worked on the Twelve Steps, forgave my parents, made amends to those whom I harmed, at least the ones that I could locate, and I tried to conduct my daily life in a mature and sober way. Yet when I met "the one," you know, the one I thought could complete and enrich my life, the one who fit into the picture I have in my mind, it would start to happen. I'd let down the walls and become vulnerable. The fear came after that. I'd be afraid that if I messed this one up, I would be alone forever, which was complete abandonment and it terrified me.

Julie said she needed to visit friends to sort through some feelings and would be away for a week. I was anxious, but of course I did not want her to see that. I told her I would see her when she got back. I wanted to call her that week in the worst way, but I stopped myself.

She arrived back in town, and I called her. I asked if she wanted to get together that night, again hoping we would have sex. The sex always made me feel better and removed the fear that I was losing her. Julie said she wanted to be alone.

The next day, I could not take it. I had barely slept the night before, and being the twisted guy that I was, all I could think of was her being in my arms.

We would make love, and it would seal the deal for sure.

Late that Sunday afternoon, I finally got her on the phone. I wanted to see her, but she kept telling me she needed some more time to sort things out and that I needed to give her some space. I hated those words. Never in my life had I dated a woman who said she needed some space and it had worked out later. It was always a fucking train wreck.

"Why don't you just tell me you don't want to go out with me anymore?" I said on the verge of tears.

"'Cause I don't want to tell you that, it is not what I want right now," she said.

I am not sure how many times I said it over and over again, but I know I could not hear what she was saying, and eventually after a few minutes of tears and yelling, she said, "Okay, I don't want to see you anymore!"

When she said those words, I remember not being able to breathe. Choking and sobbing, I hung up the phone and fell to the floor. I had done it again.

As time went by, I always wondered what would have happened if I was able to keep that fear of rejection and abandonment at bay. If

I had given the girl space, given her time to walk through her pain. Would she have found me on the other side and accepted all the good in me, accepted and allowed herself to love me? I will never know the answer.

The next few weeks were almost as painful as they were when Kate and I split the year before. There were sleepless nights. I did not eat well and lost weight. I had an advantage, though. Glen was there to help me with the hurt. I was better equipped to talk through what was going on, although most of what we talked about in the beginning was me examining what went wrong.

Of course, who has the answers? No one but our higher power. Maybe it is there and only there that I will know for sure.

A couple months later, it was spring and I had worked through some of the pain. I still dreamed about us at times, still wanting it. I went on vacation, and my mind wandered back to happier times with Julie. By the summer, I felt more at ease and saw her a few times. She did not have the power she once had.

I saw her one day and she told me she needed work, so she tended bar at a couple parties for me. One summer morning, I was sitting on my porch talking to her. I think she had come by my house to get paid, and she was telling me about a guy she was dating. She was saying how the guy had bailed on her and left town.

"Why can't I find a guy who is cool and wants to be with me?" She looked down at the lawn.

I waited a few seconds. I knew the answer. I looked up at her. and said, "I know someone who has always wanted to be with you and he is right here if you let him."

"Oh, Phil," is all she said and she walked to her car. I felt like she was talking to a lost puppy that could not get the picture. She drove down my driveway, never to return again.

I am not sure even to this day if I was in love with her or if it was my fantasy of what would make my life whole. Was I wrapped up in just another codependent relationship, or was it God putting someone in my life so I could work through more of my stuff? Hell, I think there is truth in all of it.

A WAKE-UP CALL

My life the next year was mostly wrapped up in work. I made great money that summer and catered lots of parties and weddings for the summer people. I thought of the previous summer often, and I missed Julie, her laughter and her smile. I wished it had worked out. Since Julie, I had met a couple women and dated for a while, but it seemed that issues would always come up between us and a something would tell me to back away.

That fall and winter of '99, my health was not right. I was tired a lot, and some days I could barely keep my eyes open while driving. I had a lot of tests, and a few weeks later, I was told I had hepatitis C. I had either gotten it from mainlining smack when I was sixteen or from sharing a straw with someone when snorting coke. Regardless, I was devastated and angry. Now I had two diseases to deal with. Alcoholism seemed like plenty, and now this threw me for a loop.

I was given a phone number to a specialist at Stony Brook Hospital. I felt like I had been going through life working like a dog most of the time and saving money when I could—not that it was a lot, mind you, maybe I had twenty or thirty thousand put aside besides my retirement—but I thought, "What good is saving all this money if I may get sick and not be able to enjoy it?" A week later, I heard about a place that organized vacations for sober people at Club Med resorts. I looked into it and booked it. Then I booked a month in Key West. I rented a house there, took almost all of my money, and took off two weeks later. In the back of my mind, I was scared of dying, scared of not enjoying my life, and I was going to have a blast...sober. I made an appointment with the liver specialist at Stony Brook when I would return two months later.

The sober vacation was going to be held at a Club Med in San Salvador on an island called Columbus Isle located in the eastern Bahamas. The staff welcomed my group of about a dozen people as we arrived from the airport. They walked us around the club and toward our rooms, passing the pool. There were guys and girls in bathing suits dancing around in the pool, doing something they called the sun dance. They were swaying their arms from side to side. They looked silly, and I said to myself there was no way I was doing that shit! I was too cool for that.

There were five hundred recovering men and women from all over the world there. It was amazing. I was nervous, not knowing anyone and not sure if I would meet some fine young girl. This could be a bore, I thought.

That night, I walked into a meeting and a man said, "Welcome to paradise, and if you don't have fun here, it is your own damn fault." I will never forget that. It was like he was talking just to me and reading my mind. Would I be the one who would not have fun? The thought bothered me.

I met some people at dinner. They seemed nice enough. We had dinner and talked about program stuff and sobriety, and I felt a bit more at ease.

The next morning it was raining. The turquoise ocean was a blue gray color. It was damp and people were reading and playing cards. Many were not happy with the rain, but they tried to accept it. After lunch, I was walking back to my room to read and take a nap. I walked by a cute blond talking to a guy who I thought was her boyfriend. Her Brooklyn accent made me laugh. I smiled and said hi as I passed them. The blonde said, "Hey, young fella, where are you going?"

"I am going back to my room to take a nap."

"Are you going to the spin dance class at two o'clock?" she said as she did a little spin. She was now following me down the hall. Spin dance class was like doing the sun dance by the pool. I was too cool for that shit. Yeah,

I loved to dance, but usually late at night to some loud music with a hottie. And hell, I did not know how to spin. I would rather die than be embarrassed.

"I don't know how to spin dance," I said.

But Laurie was convincing. She was a bit shorter than me, maybe five foot five, and she had a great body and blue eyes. As she followed me a bit further down the hall, I could tell the guy was not with her at all.

"Look, kid, just remember that you may never see any of these people ever again, so who cares what happens?" She had a point, but I continued walking to my room and said I would try and make it.

I began to doze off reading my book, but at five minutes before two o'clock, a voice in my head told me I was going to miss my chance. I threw on a T-shirt, shorts, and a pair of sneakers and was on my way to spin dance just in case. Maybe...

I was late, and Laurie already had a partner. My heart sank a bit, thinking I had missed out, and I turned to leave before she saw me. Christ, it was like going to the charm school dance when I was twelve. I was too late. A blue-haired, four-and-a-half-foot-tall woman with glasses like my grandmother used to wear caught me.

"My name is Mitsy. You can dance with me," she said. She grabbed my hand before I could hit the door. I smiled and acknowledged her, but I really felt that my worst fear was coming true. I would be dancing with this shrunken woman and be the laughing stock of everyone!

"I don't know how to spin dance, Mitsy."

"Don't worry, honey. I grew up in the forties, so just follow my lead and do what I do and you will be fine."

She had a sureness about her, and I did what she said. My eyes searched the crowd, and finally Laurie saw me and smiled. I smiled back. It was like being a kid in dance school. Laurie was right, though. I knew no one there and would never see them again, so what the hell, who cared? The instructor showed everyone the steps. I was lost, but Mitsy held my hand and told me to watch her. When the music started, I felt clumsy and wanted to run, but I didn't. My blue-haired lady knew her shit, and after a few minutes, I was spinning like a pro. She was actually the best dancer there and made me look like I knew what I was doing, which was far from the truth. Laurie smiled, and I could tell she was impressed, even if I was not. The instructor announced it was time to switch partners, and Laurie had my hand before I knew it. We were laughing, dancing, spinning, and having a blast. I actually thanked her later for talking me into it. We walked and talked after and made a date to have dinner later that night.

As I look back now, she was the perfect woman for me to meet that trip. She had a fun side to her, and she was a tom-boy. We had dinner together, and she told me about the guy she had been talking to in the hall. He had been trying to hook up with her, but she did not like him. We hung out that night, and by midnight we were telling each other our life stories. It was something broken toys did. I told her many things about my time drinking and drugging, almost to see if she still wanted to be with me. A woman not in the program would probably head for the hills, but nothing fazed Laurie.

I remember lying on couches by the pool. The stars seemed so close you could reach out and touch them. We rolled around kissing for a while, and then she said, "I really want to have sex with you, but how am I to know we will never see each other again?"

I knew she had a good point, but I liked her and wanted to see her more than just this one night, even as horny as I was.

"I could tell you we would be together tonight and later when we get back home, but that would be a lie as I don't know that for sure. What I do know is that I am here right now. I want to have the time of my life here on this vacation, and you are part of enjoying it. Let's just be here in the moment, enjoy each other, and not look into the future and spoil the time we have here, right now."

The words popped right out of my mouth. It was all true, and she took a second before she said, "You're right. Let's go wild and have fun."

And that is what we did. We went deep-sea fishing, sailed Hobie Cats, swam, and had some great sex for that week. It was all good.

YOU CAN DO IT

One day, she came back to the village and was wild, telling me about fishing and catching the biggest tuna of over a hundred pounds. I loved her animation describing the struggle with the rod and the huge fish coming over the side of the boat. I told her that a few of us had booked the boat for the next day, and she wanted to go. We went deep-sea fishing with four other people in the program. It was a beautiful afternoon in the Bahamas, about eighty-five degrees. The sky was dark blue with some wispy clouds here and there. A light wind of less than fifteen knots made it an easy run out to the fishing grounds. The thirty-two-foot boat slowed as it approached a reef maybe twelve miles from shore. It was from here that the depth of water fell, and the area was rich in baitfish and birds. The captain was excited about the look of the water; he told me to keep an eye out for frigate birds as they usually would spiral in tight circles above tuna and other game fish. It wasn't long before we had knock-downs on our rods, including several double- or triple-headers.

Laurie let off a scream every time we hooked up or brought one to the boat. I had never been fishing with a girl who got as excited about fishing. I laughed every time she screamed out. Wahoo, nice yellowfin tuna, some over sixty pounds, a couple of twenty-pound mahi, and a blackfin tuna came over the stern the next few hours. I helped the captain gaff the fish and get the lines in when we caught fish. Many on the boat were amazed at the experience I had from years fishing back home. It was a great day of fishing, and all of us on the boat had our chance to reel in a fish or two.

A guy from the city was reeling in a fish and wanted to give up; it was giving too much fight. I tried to coach him. His technique was all wrong. "Use your legs, pump the rod, and use your legs," I told him.

Sweat ran down the man's face, and his arms shook as he struggled. "I don't think I can do it, the fish is stronger than I am."

"Don't think that way, you can do it, I know you can."

Finally, the tuna was close to the boat. We gaffed it and brought it aboard. It was foul hooked, which was the reason for the struggle.

"See you did it, you won," I told him. He thanked me over and over again for the next hour, saying, "You know, I wouldn't have been able to catch him if it was not for you. I believed you."

I loved watching people catch fish. Shit, I knew he would tell the story a hundred times in his life. It was getting late.

"Another ten minutes of fishing and we need to head in," said the captain. Two seconds later, we had a knock-down. I saw the huge splash out of the corner of my eye when the fish hit the lure; it was a big fish. The reel screamed, Laurie screamed, and the next guy was ready in the fighting chair. It was a stand-off for about twenty minutes, even with the captain backing down the boat. The captain now respected me as a fisherman, as I had gaffed fish through the afternoon, located birds that led us to the fish, and was a good mate.

"I think it is a marlin," he said.

"It might be, I saw it hit, and it was not a tuna," I told him. Our angler started to lose strength. Shit, we were all tired with the fish we had caught that afternoon.

"Phil, I think you should take the rod, I am losing it," he said. Then he rested the rod on the stern of the boat, and the line almost touched the hull.

"Don't let the line touch the boat, we will lose him."

"Please take it, I can't..."

I knew he had had it. I took the rod, got in the chair. and started to pump, using my legs. I began to gain line back on the reel.

"Woo hoo!" cried Laurie. "Phil, get him, you can do it!" She yelled right in my ear!

Others on the boat cheered me on as I struggled with the fish. In my life there have been only a few times when people thought I was a hero, and this was one of them. It pushed me beyond, to a place where physical strength did not matter. I had been given something more. They believed I could do it, and I could hear them behind me, yelling, "You can do it!" Laurie rubbed my shoulders as I took another few feet of line back on the reel. Then it happened: the line went slick and the huge fish was gone.

"Ohhhhh," they said. Then there was silence for a minute. I reeled back the line, and we examined the wire leader. The leader looked like a slinky, tightly wrapped circles.

"Marlin," I said. The captain concurred. Sometimes when a marlin hits, they strike the bait with their bill, so the line wraps around the bill, and although the fish is not hooked that well, it will stay on the line for a long period until the fish starts to swim toward the boat. Usually, that's when the wire slides off his bill.

"Bill wrapped," the captain said as he looked at the leader. "You did a good job, my friend." He grabbed my strong shoulder. I was let down for a minute—everyone on the boat said it was too bad we lost him. Laurie and I climbed the steps to the tuna tower and joined the captain for the ride home. We were high and full of life. Laurie high-fived me and the captain, screaming "Woo hoo!" one last time.

The wind had died and the seas were calm. We skimmed across the water to the dock. Occasionally, a flying fish would jump from almost under the bow and fly out over the water, going fifty feet before splashing back into the sea. Laurie and I talked about the day, the excitement, and the best fishing day that a girl from Brooklyn had ever had. I climbed down the ladder and went into the cabin for a drink. The man who gave the rod to me when the marlin hit was sitting in the cabin and said, "You know, if there was anyone on this boat who could have caught that fish it was you."

I smiled, and that was all he said.

My soul smiled that evening as we approached the inlet. To have people who believed in me and respected me...well, I was not used to it. I did not think about why I never got respect or felt it growing up. Nope, I just cherished the feeling and thanked God for that day. It was a gift for all of us! When we arrived back at the dock, many locals had heard of our great day on the radio. We unloaded three wahoo, a half-dozen nice yellowfin tuna, four or five mahi, and a blackfin tuna. A night later, the chefs at the Club Med prepared platters of sushi and grilled mahi and wahoo for everyone.

I needed to relax, unwind, not think about my hep C, not do anything but live in the moment, and most of all, I had the time of my life. If there was someone who did not have fun that week, it wasn't Laurie and me, that is for sure. I liked her a lot, and before she left, I asked her to join me in Key West.

A couple weeks later, she flew down to the place I rented in Key West and she stayed a few days. I took her tarpon fishing the second day. I had never been, and after two hours of watching boats catch fish all around us, I gave Laurie the rod and walked to the side of the boat to take a leak. As soon as I started to relieve myself, I heard a scream from the girl from Brooklyn. And there, twenty yards off the stern, was a hundred-pound tarpon, tail-walking on the shimmering blue water as the line screamed of the small light-tackle reel. It turned out to be the only tarpon we caught that day, and Laurie was sure to tell everyone we met how she was the best fisherman. I concurred with a smile.

I dated her a bit when I got home. Things are always different when you meet someone on vacation, although we stayed friends, and even after many years passed, she still occasionally sent me an email. She married a few years back, I think. She was a good one.

GRAB YOUR OWN BAG

I arrived back from vacation in April, and a few weeks later, I went to a specialist in Stony Brook who was one of the best in the field of liver disease. I was scared that I would hear I should be put on Interferon, a chemo drug that knocked the shit out of you. It's what they used then to treat hep C. I knew some people who had been on it for as long as a year, and it brought on high temperatures and made you sick, like having the flu. I met the doctor, Elles I think was his name. He was younger than me, maybe in his late thirties, but he was a nice man with an easy way about him. He made me comfortable, and as he looked over my blood work, he told me that I had a genotype of hep C that did not react well to treatment. There was less than a 20 percent rate of success with Interferon, and I would have to be on it for over a year. Cirrhosis or liver cancer could happen eventually, but 15 percent of patients lived out their whole lives without it ever affecting them. Smoking, drinking, raw seafood, and caffeine all had to be avoided. I knew I was good to go. I had not had a drink in seventeen years, I'd stopped smoking ten years before, and I had not drank a cup of coffee in over ten years. But sushi was one of my favorite foods, and I did not want to give that one up.

A month later, Dr. Elles wanted me to have a liver biopsy, so and I went to the hospital where he did the procedure. A needle over ten inches long was stuck between my ribs and into my liver, where he took a core sample of my liver. To this day, I have not had the nerve to go back and have another because it hurt so much. They gave me a local, but the pain was something I would not want to recall. A week later, I went back to his office, where he told me that my liver was very healthy, with no scarring, and a healthy pink color. I was relieved, and I made up my mind that day that I would be one of the 15 percent. I left that office and prayed for God to help me stay healthy.

One thing they found was a high iron count in my red blood cells, and they wanted me to have some more blood work done. A week later, the doctor called and told me that I had hemochromatosis. It was a blood disorder, and I needed to have phlebotomies to drop the iron to a safe level, otherwise I had a good chance of dying from liver cancer. By letting the blood, the liver would take iron from the liver and bone marrow to make new blood cells, thus dropping the iron level. Having liver cancer scared me; it had taken my dad and my Boots.

I went into a rage for a few days. I was bitter and angry that not only was I an alcoholic with hep C, but now I also had a liver disorder. I knew that drinking and drugging had given me the hep C. Maybe it was a straw or a dollar bill I shared with someone. The liver disorder was inherited from my mother or father, and because my dad had died from liver cancer, I thought it must have been from him. People of European descent seem to be the only people who get it here in America. I went to the hospital every two weeks for over two years before the iron level dropped to a safe level. There was a woman there each time I was there; I recognized her from meetings. She was sober a long time, maybe over thirty years. I think her name was Virginia. Her level of iron was so high that she had been going for over five years. Her arms were frail and thin, and many of her veins had collapsed. I felt grateful to not have to go through what she did. She died not too long after from liver cancer.

A new place opened where I could go and get a phlebotomy in Southampton, so I began to go there. I was angry some days. "Why me?" I would think. The other patients were all hooked up to IVs, and I could not wait to get out of there. I was so into my shit that I did not even realize until after a year that almost all the other patients were there for chemo. All I had to do was drain a pint of my blood while these people were all struggling with cancer. It has been over six years since I began going—now it's only twice a year—but I am happy and grateful to have what I have and not cancer.

I heard this saying once: "If we all sat in a circle and put our problems in paper bags and threw them all into the center of the circle on the floor, whose bag would you want to pick up?" I know what is in my bag. I may not like it all, but it is my stuff. I try hard to work on what is in my bag and I do not want anyone else's.

It was a huge awakening for me to learn that, no matter how unfair life is and no matter how bad I think I have it, I have it better than most. When I am grateful for everything that makes me who I am—including the faults, defects, character flaws, and issues with my health—it does not have power over me. There are times life gets tough and sometimes I wonder why this is happening to me because I live a good life, do for others, give generously of my time…I don't deserve it.

Just because I live life in a good way, a spiritual way, I am not free from unpleasant situations, difficult days filled with frustration, and days when it seems like my life is just a struggle. Life is not a plot, and I am just doing my best with what I have been given. Years have gone by, and I am so grateful when I am at that office to give up a pint of blood and not hooked up to chemo. Trust me when I say I am blessed.

THE WILD WEST

Since I had gotten sober, I left my house on Long Island almost every winter for vacation. In 2002, I decided to go to Costa Rica. I spoke no Spanish, but I talked to some people who had been there and they said it was not that important as many of the people were beginning to speak English. I loved it there. It was like being in the Wild West back in the 1800s. It was full of adventure, and the beauty of the jungle was something I had never seen. It was amazing to go white-water rafting on the Pacuare River and see butterflies of every color and size, birds, monkeys, toucans, and macaws.

I rented a house for six weeks on the Nicoya Peninsula on the west coast, near Samara. I flew into Liberia and rented a four-wheel drive and started the three-hour drive to my new house. I always travel with my own CDs, and James Brown was cranking as I was flew down the highway with a smile on my face. I was alone. Some friends were to join me in a week or so to do some fishing. I'm not sure what the speed limit was, nor did I care, but I glanced at the speedometer and I realized 120 kilometers an hour seemed about right. It wasn't. I came over a hill, and there in the bushes I saw a small car. It was a cop with a speed gun in his hand. Another cop walked out into the road and motioned for me to pull to the side of the road. I was laughing as the five-foot-tall Tico cop with mirrored sunglasses walked to my window. I knew as much Spanish to ask where is the bathroom, so I knew this would be good. He knew how to say license and registration, and when he saw my license he said, "Ah, New York."

I just sat in the car and smiled. Shit, I had not been driving for more than a half-hour. My short friend showed me in a book that my excessive speed could cost me $100 in court, or I could pay him $20 and receive a warning. I pulled a twenty out, and he motioned with his hand for me to drive slowly as I pulled away. In five miles, I was going 120 kilometers an hour again, still not knowing how fast it really was, but figuring I would not see a cop for the rest of the two hour drive. I didn't.

I followed the directions and eventually found the sign for the driveway to the house. The road sign, weathered gray from the hot sun, hung from a tree. The dirt road wound back and forth for close to a mile. Lower and lower I went, until I was at the deep blue sea and my house was there, about forty feet from the Pacific Ocean. I had rented the house from a friend at home. It had two stories and a thatched roof with some solar panels and no windows. Beautiful palm trees shaded the house on the ocean side. The front porch had an awesome sixteen-foot table that was four feet wide and two inches thick. It was made of local guanacaste wood. The shaded porch was decorated with beautiful hand-carved chairs where I would have my breakfast for the next two months looking out over the sea. Teak, mahogany, and guanacaste are just some of the wood found there. In the States, these pieces of furniture would cost thousands of dollars. There, they cost just a couple hundred.

My days consisted of deep-sea fishing three or four days a week. I would charter local boats in Garza, a town ten minutes drive away. In the huge cove there were small, twenty-five-foot center-console boats, and after a fifteen-mile run, we would be fishing. During February and March, it is a rare occasion when the wind blows more than fifteen knots, and if it is blowing a bit at sunrise, by ten o'clock the wind dies and the sea goes glassy. The water temperature I could not believe. It was eighty-five degrees or hotter. Fishing was awesome. Pacific sailfish would sometimes reach 130 pounds, and on thirty-pound tackle they put up a show, tail-walking and jumping out of the deep blue seas. On occasion, the captain would locate a school of porpoise, which sometimes hid huge schools of tuna underneath. One such day we came upon a huge school of porpoise. They were mostly white belly, but many spinner dolphins jumped out of the water and spun several times like they were showing off their talents. The school, which was a mile wide and a half-mile long, was followed by thousands of sheer waters, frigates, and other sea birds, all diving into the water to feed on bait the dolphin and tuna were forcing to the top. We trolled our baits through the commotion; it smelled at times like the chicken coop I had to clean as a young boy in Water Mill. The wind was light so the seas were calm, but in the pod of dolphins, the water was wild with excitement. The smell of fish was present, and occasionally a huge yellowfin or bigeye tuna would seem to fly a few feet out of the water as they crashed the bait. I was fishing with a young guy and his girlfriend I had met on the beach the day before in front of my house. They were from the state of Washington, and neither had any experience deep-sea fishing. It seemed many times that taking a green horn was good luck and we would have great fishing; sometimes the green horn would catch the biggest fish.

We trolled for over an hour through the dolphin with no luck. A couple other boats heard about the action on the VHF radio, and two or three were trying to hook up, but no fish had been boated. I told the captain to let out more line from our reels so the baits would be further back from the boat. I used to do it on calm days back home, and it would work. As we made a turn, our baits sank deeper, and bang, two reels screamed as tuna grabbed the baits. The fish I fought turned out to be a fifty-pound yellowfin. I fought it for fifteen minutes, pumping the rod in a belly gimble back and forth until it came up toward the stern. A belly gimble is a belt with a cup that locks the rod in and keeps the butt end of the rod from digging into your gut. I saw the fish as it came near. It was a beautiful fish, and as it circled beneath the boat it glowed, the sunlight shining gold off its flanks.

The mate gaffed the fish, and congratulations were heard. But after a half-hour more, the fishing novice was still struggling with his fish. He had only been able to return half the line to the reel.

Deep-sea fishing has always been a battle between fish and man, a battle of endurance. You need to be in good shape and have technique. After a month of fishing, my arms would get stronger than they ever would get lifting weights at the gym. Once I had fought a 150-pound tuna in the hot sun for five and a half hours; the fish was foul-hooked in the side of the head. The mate and my friends on the boat occasionally poured water over me and gave me a drink of water so I would not melt down. In the end, as happens more often than not, the line snapped as the mate tried to gaff the fish close to the boat. The fish swam off and I dove over the side into the water. I was spent with exhaustion and I slept for an hour below when we ran to the beach.

I can't even remember the thirty-year-old's name, but I gave him encouragement and kept telling him he could do it. "You almost have him, don't give up," I said.

No one wants to give up the rod. Others had asked me that day I struggled for hours, fearing that I would make a mistake because of exhausting, either tightening the drag or touching the line on the hull of the boat and comprising its integrity. So I knew what he wanted to do; we all want to catch the big one. It would be a memory you could share with others until you grew old. I have shared this dozens of times, and I am sure the kid from Washington has told the story many times also. Fishing stories are what fisherman love to tell: the fight is longer and the fish in the story grows larger each time you tell the story, as does the amount of time you endure and struggle with the fish.

The kid did well, and he hung in there. Shit, it was over one hundred degrees in the sun. Sweat rolled down his face, and the muscles in his arms and shoulders bulged from the strain. There is always distracting commentary from people on board...the kind of fish, the size, is he getting tired...

then all the line you have spent twenty minutes gaining back on the reel screams away in seconds and you start over reeling all over again.

This kid was at the end, and his girlfriend coaxed him on, saying, "You can't give up, keep going, you can do it." He motioned a couple times for me to take the rod as I stood next to him, occasionally holding him from going over the side as the huge tuna would burn more line from the reel on another run. He was a strong, two-hundred-pound, six-foot-tall guy, in good shape with strong arms, but I knew that strength does not make a fisherman. I had seen many give up a fight after just a few minutes, while I had fished the Canyons off Long Island years before and reeled in dozens of tuna in a day. But this was no fifty- or eighty-pounder; this was a slammer.

Finally, after an hour, the fish made another run and the kid fell to his knees on the deck. The rod rested on the gunnel, and he said, "Take it, I am going to loose him." I motioned to the mate to give me another belly gimble and tightened it up.

I took the rod, slid the butt into the gimble, and leaned back. I felt the strength of the huge tuna, and the thirty-pound rod bent with the tip almost touching the water as I arched my back again, trying to retrieve some of the line lost from the last run. For thirty minutes, it was a standoff. I would get line back, and then the fish would take it back as I groaned and my arms ached with the strain. Then it started to happen. Some call it the circle of death or the tuna circle. They begin to circle deep below the boat, around and around. I began to pump the rod slowly and gained a foot of line or more on each circle.

Then we finally saw the fish; it was over a hundred feet below the boat. The water off Costa Rica can be the some of the clearest water in the world, and seeing a hundred feet down is typical. More commentary continued on the size of the fish. At least now we could see that it was a tuna. It was the largest yellowfin I had ever fought. I struggled, my arms shaking each time I pumped the rod. Wearing just a bathing suit with my brown body shining with sweat, I would try to wedge my knees against the side of the boat to get leverage. The adrenaline really seems to take over when I am in that place. I felt no pain really, just strain. Voices were distant, almost coming from another time or place. The hundred-pound leader began to clear the water.

"Leader! Leader!" cried the captain.

The mate reached for it, but I could tell the fish was not done.

"No, not yet!" I yelled, and the fish made another run. Moaning, I began to struggle. I loved the battle. I was strong, stronger than him, and I knew it now. I was confident he was mine; I felt it. The kid slapped my back and said, "Don't lose him, Phil, you got 'em!"

Again they yelled for the leader, and this time I felt the time was mine. As the huge monster circled for the last time, I led the leader into the hand of the mate.

"Easy, easy," I yelled to him.

William was the mate's name; he had lived his thirty years a few hundred yards from the beach in Garza, and fishing was his life. Many years before, he had been working a long-line boat and the engine went down. With no radio, they were found a hundred miles from Panama three weeks later. He said he had lost almost thirty pounds, which he was never able to put back on. He was thin-framed, maybe five-foot-five, but strong. I had seen him wrestle with many two- to three-hundred-pound marlin I had brought to the boat.

William slowly brought the fish closer to the boat, and the captain struck the gaff almost perfectly, hitting the fish just behind the head. The brilliant yellowfin was ours, with tears and laughter and high-fives for all. The fish settled down, and we pulled him aboard. The picture hangs on my wall of the kid from Washington, the mate William, and I straining to hold the huge tuna in our arms. We never weighed the fish, but Captain Ed and I figured the fish to be 230 pounds. He was a beauty, and the sushi was enjoyed by most of the town for the next few days. Life is good when you win, it really is. The kid shook my hand after we got him on board.

"I knew you could do it," he said. I smiled in thanks. Although many things happened with the big fish, many are lost at the boat.

I have never told the story of catching that fish other than exactly how it happened, just as I have written, but I always wonder if, when the kid from Washington tells the tale, he mentions that he and I shared the honor of fighting that tuna to the end or if he was the one to catch it alone. Fishing stories change over time…they always will.

WHO AM I?

Alejandro was a Tico (Costa Rican). He was a thin man, maybe twenty-five years old, who became a friend. He would come to the house and talk almost every morning—or I should say try to talk with me. I did not know the Spanish language, so it was difficult for a while.

I had a Franklin translator that helped. In the morning, he would come over after   breakfast, and I would teach him English and he would teach me Spanish. I became friendly with many local Costa Ricans and played basketball several times a week late in the day to get a workout. The temperature would drop by five o'clock to around ninety degrees, which after the rest of the day seemed cool. Local kids used to come and watch or play sometimes, although their game was soccer.

I shopped a few days a week. The local fruits and vegetables were awesome, and I had all the fresh fish one could want. The best *piña*, or pineapple, comes from Costa Rica; I ate several a week those two months.

My day would start with me brushing my teeth, putting on a bathing suit and a pair of boat shoes, and I was ready for the day. I would have some fruit, maybe some fresh eggs and toast, and on days I did not go fishing, I would read a book and look out over the blue ocean.

I was not sure what was happening then, but it was different there. I felt free. Free from having to impress maybe. No one cared that I owned a house worth a couple million dollars. No one cared about the business, the equipment, and the fact that I had catered events for some of the most famous people in the world or the fact that I had been written up a dozen times. None of it mattered.

They saw me as who I was and they enjoyed my company, just for me. I had to humble myself many times. I had to listen, and I tried to understand rather than be understood. I enjoyed simple things and lived in the moment, once in a while thinking of home, but not often. There was no TV or radio. I would read books some nights. When I had friends visiting from home, we would go out to dinner.

A local girl used to come in six days a week to do laundry and clean the kitchen, for the cost of a dollar an hour. I gave her $40 when I left, and it made her cry.

The house was so close to the ocean that it took me a few nights before I could sleep as the waves crashing on the beach would keep me awake. After a few nights, I slept well and had many dreams. I dream a lot more when I am away, I am not sure why. One such night I had a dream. It was in color as many of my dreams are and I saw myself standing under a red tent. I was at a funeral ceremony on the Shinnecock Indian Reservation. Brad Smith had died in the dream; he was the cousin of Peter Smith, a Native American and a great friend of mine for years. We had gone to school together. The service was near a church, and I was never sure where the red tent came in, but that was how I remembered it in the dream.

When I was back home two weeks later, I saw Brad coaching a Little League game. I stopped the truck, backed up, and said, "Hey, Brad, how are you?" He said good, and then I asked, "Have you been all right. I had a dream about you."

Puzzled, Brad said, "Yes, I have been good. What was the dream?"

I did not want to tell him, but he insisted, so I said, "Well, you were dead, but I see that you are good. It was just a crazy dream, I guess, sorry to tell you, take care." I waved and drove away.

Dreams are funny. They sometimes don't seem to connect with anything, and they are very bizarre. Sometimes the meaning is deep. Sometimes the dreams take place in the future, sometimes in the past. A year later, I got a call. My friend Pete Smith, Brad's cousin, had died from a heart attack. The funeral would be at the Indian reservation two days later. As I stood there listening to the service I looked up, and there I was, standing under a red tent. It was just as I had dreamt the year before. A chill came over me, and then a man moved closer to me. It was Brad. I nodded to him, and moments later, I whispered, "Brad, this is the dream." He nodded back. "I know," is all he said.

Many years have gone by now, and on occasion I see Brad and yell out the window as I drive by, "Hey, Brad, I had a dream about you."

He usually says, "Don't want to hear it, sorry." He smiles, waving at me not to stop. I probably scared the guy.

Those six weeks, I had three groups of friends come down and stay at the house in Costa Rica. We did tons of fishing under that hot sun and caught lots of fish. I never met any women really. I had twin local girls who used to stop by the beach a lot in front of my house. Alejandro said they liked me. They were sixteen years old. Both were beautiful and loved to smile. I was friendly to them, but they were far too young for me. I would try to speak Spanish to them both, and they would laugh as I tried to speak the words.

Something happened to me down in Costa Rica. I was more at peace with myself than I had ever been. It was almost like I began to lose myself and become someone else. Or was this who I was all along? It confused me. The new me was calmer, quieter, more content to watch and listen. Most of all, I had such respect for people, how they lived, and the way they smiled even though they had nothing. Yes, they had homes, but no cars, no TV for most of them, no phones, and rarely did I ever hear them talk about what they had done or what they were planning to do next year or next week. They were all present in the moment, and almost everyone I met was grateful and happy.

I had eased God out (EGO) living in New York. Like everyone there, I was wrapped up in work and money, and a lot of the time fear played a role in my daily life. I worried about how things were going at work, my life, my relationships, my family, etc. I now looked back at what a waste of time it all was. I spent a lot of time listening to my rich clients and guests talk about their winters in Aspen, their new ten-million-dollar house, the new kitchen, the new whatever. I knew I was not that bad—or was I just like them sometimes? I questioned what was really important now that I did not have to worry about any of it. I talked more about work and money when I was at home, but I could see that what I was becoming was not what I had just been experiencing. I liked the new me. He was kind, he was fair, loving, and understanding, and most of all, he was liked and loved for just him. None of the stuff like how much jing I had made, how many things I owned, and how hot my last girl was mattered to these people.

The day I left, Alejandro came to say good-bye. He had been my friend, and he had tears in his eyes as he said, "I will miss you my friend."

"I will miss you too," I said to him. Except the days I went offshore fishing, he and I spent every morning together learning to communicate. I left with him the translator and told him to practice his English, and he told me to practice my Spanish. I left him as he waved good-bye.

HAPPY TO SEE ME?

Relations with my mother were distant and disappointing at that time of my life. I was feeling free, comfortable, relaxed, content, confident, and grateful. I was enjoying more self-love and self-respect that at any other time in my life when I returned home from two months in Costa Rica. I had not seen my mother in over three months. I called her, asking her if she would like to go to dinner at a local restaurant in Southampton. She accepted, and I met her there. She was always early, and I walked in. She gave me a less-than-warm hug, which was her usual way, and we sat down to order. I had not seen her in months. My skin was dark from the tropical sun, my hair was bleached blond, and I was feeling better than I had in years. I had been deep-sea fishing and horseback riding, had seen purple butterflies the size of softballs, fought three- to four-hundred-pound blue and black marlin, seen white-faced and howler monkeys and crocodiles, flown in ultralight aircraft along the cliffs of Costa Rica's Pacific Coast, met wonderful people, and learned to speak Spanish. At least I could put a sentence together now.

I had even gone swimming one night in the sea just after a thunderstorm in front of my house. I swam out a hundred yards, lay on my back, and watched the lightning bolts as they flashed offshore. I wanted to share so much of what I had been through, what I had seen, and what I had been through. I had a lot of courage to venture off on my own to try new things, to meet new people, and to live as I lived then.

"How have you been?" my mother asked.

I smiled. "Good, Mom, I went through—"

Before I could finish my thought, she interrupted me—she was famous for that shit—and began to tell me how her fucking furnace went out and how much it cost to fix it. Then there was a story about her friend whose son was sick, then another story about a great cocktail party the week before. I let her go on and on. I just listened. I wanted to see if she would talk about herself without being even slightly interested at all in me or my vacation. I knew she'd had a couple of drinks before she met me and that she had not seen me for months, but for not giving me any attention and taking no interest in my life, that night stunned me. I said maybe twenty words in the hour or so we had dinner. After dinner, I walked her to her car. She walked up to a car and tried to put her key in the door of a car that did not belong to her. I just shook my head, then I walked her to the right car.

I said goodnight. I wanted to call a cop so she would get a DWI, but I didn't.

My feeling of self-worth, happiness, and gratitude disappeared, and anger, sadness, and disappointment returned. I became angry, and after a couple days I went to my mother's house and I laid it on the line.

It was a spring day, the grass was beginning to green up and there were buds on the trees as we sat on her porch overlooking Peconic Bay.

"Mom, I have to say something, and I want you to listen and not interrupt, can you do that?"

Eunice acknowledged that she could. Her name always seemed to have some sort of power and control for me, but now it was just a name. I would be heard, and I did not care if what I had to say hurt her or not.

"Mom, I want you to know that I am upset and hurt about what happened at dinner the other night. I had not seen you for months. I said literally twenty words for the hour and thirty minutes we had dinner. You never asked me once about my trip to Costa Rica, never once did you care enough about your son to listen to my experiences, what I went through, what I saw, and many things you have never seen or done. No interest came from you. I have to tell you that you are the most self-centered, narcissistic woman I have ever met. My whole life means nothing to you. Yes, you love to talk about me to your friends, like some sort of boost for your own ego, but the truth is you don't know who the hell I am and never have, mostly because you are so damn obsessed with yourself and your world that you can't even listen and learn about me.

"It is not just me. You have pushed all your children away, and the thing you fear the most will come true one day. That is the fear of dying alone, with no one there for you, no family, no friends, because everyone is too disgusted and bored with you. Someone who never listens to anyone else and talks only about themselves is a real bore, and that is what you have turned into. I do not have a relationship with anyone that forces me to work as hard as this, and I do not want to do it with you anymore. I do not want you to call me for dinner or anything else."

Mom paused and looked out over the bay, with the breeze blowing through the thin limbs of the willow tree in the front yard. She looked up at me and said, "You really are just too sensitive. It is not like that at all."

It was her way of turning it all around and pointing out that you were thin-skinned. She would do mean shit and be degrading, but if you reacted, you were the nutty fucker, not her. I was sick of it and I stopped her. "Yes, it is just like that, and it is hurtful. It has been going on for years. You are an alcoholic. Christ, you couldn't even find your own car when you left the restaurant the other night. It is one of the reasons you have no interest in any of your children's lives. I do not want to be with you if you are drinking, so make a decision, and if you would like to go to dinner, then remember that I want no part of it if you are drinking."

I walked away down the steps toward my truck and looked back at her on the porch. She looked out toward the bay in silence.

Taking my power back was hard, but it felt good. Letting her know I wanted no relationship with her was hard. She never called and wanted to have dinner. Months went by, and I did not talk to her. I felt guilty at times, but at almost fifty years of age, how long would I allow this in my life? I was done.

"If you had a tough childhood, it is over, get over it and move on."

This was easier said than done. My interactions with my mother kept me stuck. Maybe it was her unavailability or her lack of interest. At times, I thought maybe she was right and I was too sensitive, but I almost always felt worse after seeing her. I had spoken to George and Glen about what would happen. They both asked me if there was anyone else in my life who made me so uncomfortable. Of course I said no. Then they asked, "Why then do you do it with your mother?"

The answer was always the same: "Because she is my mother."

I struggled with codependency, and I still struggled with relationships, many times picking unavailable women. At times I just felt like being alone. It was easier and less painful and far less work.

THE SWEEPSTAKES WINNER

A year or so passed after I stopped calling my mother every couple of weeks. She never called me, and I found that the guilt passed eventually, and I lived my life in a more comfortable way.

Then one spring I had been away. I had a habit of calling Mom to let her know I was back in town. So I called her, but I did not expect anything from her. I just wanted to catch up for a bit and that was it. I said, "Hi, how are you?"

"Okay, but I can't talk long. I am expecting a phone call. I just won a million dollars. They are coming today to bring me a check."

"Really?" I said. "Sounds great. How did you do it, win the money?"

She said she had entered a sweepstakes and that they had called and said someone would be there to drop off the check. She then cut me off and said she had to get off the phone in case they called. I shook my head laughing to myself and thought, "Shit, maybe they will drop by my house too."

Over the next two hours, I went about my business, making phone calls and looking over my two months of mail. But the call with Mom bothered me. I needed to go to her house. Her second husband had died, and in his will it was stated that she could live in their house until she passed. It was a cute house with a beautiful view of the bay not a hundred yards away, at least until a wealthy new neighbor across the street decided to plant a bunch of shrubs and a hedge, which almost blocked her view of the bay completely. The front of the house had a wraparound porch with a wood ceiling made of clear cedar, and the redwood deck was lined with a white railing. As I drove up her driveway, Mom was sitting on the porch in her chair wrapped in a shawl.

"Hi, Mom," I said as I walked up the path from my truck. She smiled. Her face looked much thinner than I remembered, with aging brown spots on her face, and her lips were cracked from dehydration. It was sad seeing her like that.

"Have they brought you your check yet?" I asked with a smile, knowing in my heart it was some sort of scam.

She had a sad look on her face and looked down at the lawn. "No, but they are coming today. They promised. This time it is different."

Nothing is sadder than someone who is close to the end of their journey in life, hoping that money will somehow make it right. Hell, I wanted to win the damn sweepstakes for forty years! I brought her inside, and we sat down at her dinning room table, which was littered with mail. I had not been there at her house for over a year at least. I wondered what had happened. It did not take long to realize that her mental sharpness had almost vanished. I looked around and checked the fridge. I poured out expired milk and cream cartons. Some of the food had turned a pale green color, and my heart sank. I had heard from other people about how their parents had lost it and had to be taken care of, but my dad took care of himself almost to the end of his life.

I was not ready for this, but I think no one is ever ready for it. To see my mom panicking over this damn sweepstakes money that was never coming, coupled with her loss of understanding stunned me briefly. I paused and thought, "What should I do next?" I always have been good under pressure. I was able to snap into gear when others would just sit back and be silent. I began to look through the mail as I asked her about the sweepstakes, wanting to know when it started and how much she had spent.

There were dozens of envelopes on the table, all wanting money to win big. I got angrier and angrier. Mom was like a little girl. She knew she had been doing something wrong, and she realized she did not have a clue what she had done. I asked to see her checkbook.

"Do you understand that I just want to help you, Mom?" I said. "I am angry about people taking advantage of you. I am not angry at you, and I want to help you." I looked deep into her eyes. She nodded and understood.

Mom had about thirty thousand dollars in a checking account, and I later found she had about seventy-five thousand in her UBS account. Looking over her checkbook, I realized that over the last six months she had given over ten thousand to scam artists. The scammers would either call her or write her, telling her she had placed in the winning jackpot for a million dollars. They just needed her to wire the tax money so they could get her a check. There were checks for twenty-five hundred dollars and some for less. She had been going to Western Union and, the day before, had wired money to San Jose, Costa Rica. There was a phone number. I called and spoke to a man. He guaranteed me it was legit. After a couple minutes, I was thinking it might be on the up and up! I wanted to get his address, which he gave to me, and then I told him I had people in San Jose who would be there shortly to visit him. The line went dead.

Mom was never great with money. She had pissed away over a million dollars making one poor business decision after another, mostly with land she owned. Hell, I had offered many times to help her, but I was always denied. I had nothing when I got sober at twenty-seven, and now I was doing really well in business, yet she never asked me for advice. Shit, I could not even balance a checkbook when I was drinking, and now I had five checking accounts and owned two corporations. I had asked lots of questions of people I respected. The money did not fall from the trees.

My head went back and forth. I would be angry about the past and then I would look into her helpless brown eyes, the eyes of a little girl, and know I would have to help her. I spent a couple hours at her dining room table. I explained that she could not give anyone any more money.

"I am sorry. I did not know. It seemed that they were telling me the truth," Mom said. She looked like a young girl. Shit, it was so sad.

I left that day and explained I would help her and that she would not have to worry, and again she promised she would not wire any more money overseas. I hugged her and told her she would be all right and that I would call her tomorrow. She touched my head like she did sometimes and said, "Thank you, you are a good boy." Her cracked lips pursed slightly.

I drove down the long beach and had feelings of every dimension. I was angry at the scam artists and wanted to shoot them on sight. Then guilt got hold of me and told me I should have known Mom was going downhill. But how could I have known? Then I would feel scared and overwhelmed.

When you are in that place, you never think that this has happened to almost all grown children with aging parents. For a minute, I felt fear, and some of it was self-centered. I called my sisters and brother that night. Everyone said the same thing: "She is not living with me." No one had seen it coming, and no one had talked to her for weeks or months. God, it was sad.

I took some time that day and thought about what I should do.

I called Mom the next day. She seemed good, and we talked about the weather and when spring was coming.

The next afternoon, I called and she picked up the phone and sounded out of breath.

"Hi, Philip. I have to call you later. I have to go into town."

"Whoa, hold on! What is the hurry?" I asked.

"Well, I have to go to Western Union. I have to get there before they close."

I convinced her I was around the corner, although I was at home twenty minutes away. I said I would be there in five minutes and to wait for me. I must have been going 75 mph down the back roads and got there in eight minutes. Mom was sitting in her dinning room wearing a tan rain jacket and her gloves.

"Why do you have to get to Western Union today, Mom?"

"I have till this afternoon to get the rest of the money to Tel Aviv so they will send my million dollars."

My heart sank. This was like a bad dream. I couldn't believe we were back at this nutty fucking place. I was angry that I had spent two hours with her two days before and she hadn't listened to a word I had said. This time, she had been chosen to win $500,000, but the winner had been disqualified. If she sent another two thousand, she would then win the grand prize of a million dollars.

"Mom, you need to sit down. Please, Mom. I am sad to have to tell you that this is another con game, and you are close to losing another two grand. If it sounds too good to be true, it probably is. Please remember that, Mom."

Her face dropped and she wanted to leave, but I would not let her. I asked her to give me her checkbook. She did, and I explained that if she kept doing this, she would be alone with no money and would not be able to take care of herself. She got scared. Again, she had the look of a lost child who had done wrong. I gave her a hug and said I would call her when I got home, which I did. Then I called my brother and sisters for the update.

The next morning I got up and called UBS, where she had her investments. I knew it would not be long before she would head down there and start draining that account to wire more money overseas. I told them my Mom and I would be there in an hour and to have papers ready and that she would be turning over all of her assets to me. They questioned that Mom would do it. I assured them that she had decided it was best in her interest and to just get the damn papers ready.

Then I called Mom.

"Good morning, how are you?" I asked.

"Good, I am heading down to UBS to get some money," she said.

I could not believe it. She was possessed with getting more money to piss up a rope. I knew it. I tried reading her the riot act first, then I tried something else and said, "I would like to help you with your bills. Wouldn't it be nice if you never had to pay another bill? Would you like me to pay all your bills from now on so you never have to open another one and I will give you money anytime that you need it?"

"I would love that, I would," she said in a cheery voice.

It would be her money, but I would manage it for her. Maybe she thought I was giving her my money, but who cared what she thought as long as I could get her to do this?

"I would like you to come to my house and pick me up and we will drive down to UBS so I can do that for you, okay? And please bring the safety deposit box keys and your driver's license."

She began to tell me that she had no idea where the keys were. I told her to look in the clock on the mantle. They were always kept there. She had told me this years before. She came to my house thirty minutes later. She walked into my living room. I asked her to sit down, and I said, "Mom, I am worried about you and these scams you have gotten involved with. I would like to make it so you never have to look at another bill. I will pay them all for you, but you have to do one thing to help me do that. I will need to go to UBS sign some papers. I am going to help you. You trust me, don't you?"

With a kind smile, Mom said, "Of course I trust you."

"You have lost over ten thousand dollars in the last six months to these sweepstake scam artists. They are liars and were never going to ever give you any money. In a few months, if you keep doing this, there will be nothing left, and I do not know where you will end up. You don't want that to happen, do you?"

I explained we were going to move all her assets into my name so she would be protected. Knowing it was the best thing I could do for her and the right thing to do, I never questioned it.

"Thank you for helping me. I never wanted to be a problem, you know," said the little girl she had become.

UBS had the papers and asked her if she was sure it was what she wanted to do. She assured them it was, so the papers were signed and we went to another bank. At the bank, some woman gave us a hard time and said we would have to come back another time. I was not having it and I asked to speak to the manager. I can't remember what the issue was. I did not like that bank, and she was a perfect asshole to boot.

I knew Mom used to speak of stock in AT&T, Exxon, Verizon, and a few other companies, and I felt there had to be stock certificates somewhere. I thought that even though she had wasted a lot of money, she must have saved more than the $75,000.

Mom and I entered the small room to look through her safety deposit boxes. It was a funny scene. I opened the long gray box. It had many papers and envelopes inside, and one by one I looked at each one. One envelope said, "AT&T, 122 shares." Mom grabbed it and threw it in the garbage can.

"That's junk," she said in disgust.

"I don't think so, Mom, let me read it." I took the stock certificate out of the trash and put it in a folder. I opened another envelope that said, "286 shares Exxon." She grabbed it and again threw it in the trash.

"Let's get out of here, I told you it is a waste of time, you don't know what the hell you're doing anyway," she said.

There was part of me that wanted to say, "You know, you are right, let's throw all this shit in the trash and leave." The old me would have done that, but I knew reality was not being broadcast to the old lady anymore. She was getting a lot of static. I said with a raised voice, "Now you will sit there and be quiet. I will look through this whole box and will be only a few more minutes. You are not allowed to touch any of these, all right?"

Like a scolded girl, she looked down and never said another word until we left the room.

It was some mess. After dropping off the certificates at UBS a day later, we calculated Mom's net worth at $225,000, plus another $30,000 in the checking account, which we also closed. I opened another account and gave

Mom some cash. I asked the broker to sell stocks that were not performing well and buy bonds that would mature every few months.

In the next few weeks, we were able to hire a girl to be Mom's caregiver. Caregiver was an understatement—Karen was a godsend and stayed with Mom 24/7. She had the patience of a saint. She was also kind, about thirty, and hot!

Something was happening when I went to see Mom, but I could not put my finger on it at first. Karen was always there, and I liked flirting with her a bit. At first, Mom did not like her, and I found it amusing. Mom insisted that Karen knew it was her house and Karen could leave any time. Mom's nasty words and tone rolled off Karen like water off a duck's back.

We all decided my mother needed to go to the doctor for a check-up.

We took her and spoke to the doctor a week or so later. He suggested that she should not drink anymore. So it went from vodka and wine to apple juice. I thought that would throw her for a loop, but it did not seem to bother her much and she hardly ever mentioned that she missed it.

I do remember a Thanksgiving three years later when my brother, Karen, Mom, and I went to a restaurant on Shelter Island. When no one was paying attention, Mom ordered a vodka Gibson quietly under her breath to the waiter. It caught me off guard, and I had to tell the waiter to use apple juice instead. She took one sip and had a disappointed look on her face.

"This does not taste like a Gibson."

I laughed. "Just drink it, Mom. It is better than a Gibson."

It took dozens of hours every month to keep up with what she needed. Resentments flourished as my sister and I argued from time to time about the amount of time we were spending. I soon asked my brother to help sign checks, meet with contractors to install a new water heater or furnace, and repair and paint the porch. It was endless. Eb respected me, and he knew all the work involved and was a big help.

The years went by, and occasionally a health issue would come up. I was away one time when she got sick and was admitted to the hospital. She went in for an overnight stay after she had fallen. My sister and brother back home told me to get home as Mom was on her last legs and may go in a day or two. I was in Hawaii on my winter vacation and scrambled to the airport the next day and flew home. I went to the hospital when I got back and walked into her room. She was resting. I sat by her bed until she woke. It saddened my heart how tired she looked. Her hair was no longer was curled and perfect. Instead, her gray, straight hair laid on the pillow next to her head. I touched her face, her skin was dry and rough. Then she woke up and tried to focus on who was there next to her.

"Philip," she whispered.

"How are you feeling, Mom?" I asked.

"Not great. It's good to see you."

I held her hand. It was bony and weak, and the purple veins looked close to the surface. I made some conversation for a minute or two and then she was asleep again.

As I walked down the hall, my mind was consumed with fear. How much more time would pass before I would be laying in some hospital bed with family stopping by to make some meaningless conversation about the food, the weather, or the nurses? I would probably say, "The fucking food sucks, I hate this place, and what the hell do I care about the weather? I may just die here, and who the hell would give a shit?"

I decided it would be better for everyone involved if I died in my sleep like my grandmother had years ago. Then I started to think, "Who am I kidding? What family will come and see me? I will probably outlive my sisters. My brother and my nieces will come to visit, or will they? Will I be alone in that hospital bed?"

As I walked down the hall, I looked in the rooms and saw many old people with no one visiting them. They were sad. Would that be me? I shook my head and tried to stop thinking.

I drove ten minutes to my home and spoke to my brother about how Mom was doing. I tried to catch up, but I was exhausted from traveling.

As I was trying to fall asleep, I wondered if she would pass that night and what would happen next. Then sadness hit me. Years before, I had carried a lot of bitterness from the past and the fact that when I talked with her, she was never able to ask me anything about my life. She only spoke of cocktail and dinner parties and boring people I never met. But now the drinking friends were nowhere to be found. She was alone and almost no one had been visiting her. I was so angry but I wasn't sure at who or why. Again I wondered what had happened when she was a young girl. Was she not loved or appreciated? Did she go through life feeling she was unimportant and inadequate? That neglect was evident in her, and I figured that was why she had a deep fear of dying alone.

I learned over the years in the program how to get what I needed from people who loved and cared for me. I told her that afternoon on her porch that she would die alone with no one loving her if she did not change. I wanted to take it all back. Why had I said it? I was angry and felt justified saying what I did, but now I wished I could redo that day and take back the ugly words I threw in her face.

I fell asleep wishing things were different.

The next day I had breakfast and made the trip to the hospital. I have always hated the hospital. My grandfather was sick when I was a child, and I hated to visit. I was in my late teens and the smell of death was there. It scared me then and it still does. I had detoxed many times at that same hospital, and being there bothered me. I spent many three- or four-day stints there, hooked up to an IV and shaking and quaking. My shit was always self-inflicted, though, and I felt guilty about being there and taking up space. I had no self-control. I was weak, I thought. I was broken and could never be whole again. There was the feeling that I would just die there.

Death is so final and brings fear to me even to this day. Death is the epitome of total abandonment. I have talked with my therapist for years about it, the fear that when I die, I will vanish, like falling and falling and never getting to the bottom.

I walked down the hall to the elevator, passing visitors and patients, their faces drawn from stress and sadness. "No one likes ever being here," I thought. My mind was spinning with thoughts as I reached my mother's room.

Mom was propped up in her bed when I came through the door eating some toast. Her face lit up when she saw me. "Well, hello there! How are you? Glad to see you!" she said with a smile.

I was stunned for a second. I expected her to be feeble and weak, but she wasn't. This was not the first time my brother and sisters had thought she was not going to make it. I told everyone she was like the Energizer Bunny—give her a refill of juice and she'd be good for another ten thousand miles!

We talked for an hour, not about much. I might have told her about my trip or someone I had met. I was never sure she was retaining anything, but it did not seem to matter now and so we chattered away. She knew who I was, but I noticed she was losing memory of events, people, and the time of year.

Days later, she came home to Northaven, Sag Harbor. She was happier there for sure, and Karen took wonderful care of her. We were all so lucky to have her take care of the tasks that I am sure none of us were willing to do.

Maybe part of it was that she was my mom. It had been different taking care of Dad as he was a man, and when I bathed him it was not uncomfortable. Plus I knew in my heart that he was good and decent, and most of all he loved me, especially in the end. Also, my father was sharp as a tack right up to the end. Not so with my mom. I struggled sometimes with guilt because I could not do for her what I done for my father.

Some days, I had conversations with her about when she had lived in England, which I knew she never did. It was like a young child telling stories. I asked her questions about it. Half the time, it was pretty amusing. At times I was fascinated with the details and her description of this make-believe life, so much so that I wondered if maybe she did live there in another life. The dementia was getting worse. She was constantly telling stories, as long as someone would listen, and now she had Karen, who was all ears. At least Mom thought she was, and that was all she needed, so it did not matter.

The arrangement her second husband had made allowing her to live in that house was a blessing. The house was not what it had been after she renovated it. Now there was a musty smell about it, old stains on the carpet, and the paint was fading on the trim and walls. But the view from the porch was her favorite, as it looked over Long Beach and Peconic Bay, with the beach a hundred yards away. I had spent many fun and not-so-fun dinners there. I remember my engagement dinner there with Mary T, and for years every early September, George, Annette, and the family would get together for Mom's bouillabaisse, which she worked on all day. She knew how to stir the pot!

Yes, stir the pot in more ways than one. Years ago Mom loved getting reactions from us, and she knew how to push our buttons. George would be amused, being an outsider, but he was also relieved that he did not have to play the game. It was about control with her. She made us kids give up our power, even into our forties. She was as cunning and manipulative as any good alky mother could be.

If people talked with me instead of her at her dinner parties, she would bring up a night the police took me away or when she and Dad had to clean me up after I had puked all over myself. She did this from the time when I was first sober. It embarrassed and humiliated me, and I would get quiet and not react, as if to say, "You are right. I am still no good, a drunk, a failure, what was I thinking?"

People who are cursed with being an alky despise it when another alky gets sober. It means they have to look at their own drinking. It was confusing, because I heard from people who talked with my mother about how proud she was of me and how I was running the program and was some sort of president there. I wasn't, obviously, but it made the story more interesting. I was never really convinced that she was proud of what I was doing with my life—being sober, being successful, or just becoming a good man—as much as my success let her feel that her life had more meaning and that she was some a success also because of what I had done. I was bitter for years and resented that.

MORE RESPONSIBILITY

As if life was not handing me enough to take care of, I decided to buy a piece of property and a shop on the highway in Southampton. I had plans to open a seafood takeout shop and restaurant. I hoped I could "build it and they would come." I spent over $150,000 renovating the place, which used to be an ice cream store. I bought the place in March and had three months to get it done before I would open on Memorial Day. I bought all new equipment, including lobster steamers, fryers, a grill, a convection oven, sinks, and stainless work tables, and I renovated the customer area and made an office. I had been catering for years, but I had no idea what would go into a restaurant. How hard could it be? Hell, I had catered events for five hundred people many times. This would be a piece of cake.

Not only did I have my twenty catering staff employed in the summer months, I also had eight restaurant staff to manage, and in my spare time I managed my mom's affairs and made sure all her needs, repairs, and bills were taken care of. In addition, I was still chairing the Twelve Step meeting at the jail every Tuesday.

Well, I built it and they came—in a huge way. There were times when I knew how busy the staff was that night by the way the kitchen floor looked. Anyone in the restaurant business knows that when you are in the weeds and crazy busy, the kitchen is a mess at the end of the night. If the floor was dirty, with a couple dozen French fries crushed into the floor mats and pieces of shrimp and fish everywhere, I knew we did 150 dinners.

We had a learning curve we worked through, like any new place, but in the end it was a great first season. I remember in April, before I opened, seeing a friend and owner of a well-known seafood restaurant in Southampton one night. He had heard I was opening up that spring and he said, "Don't sell 'em cheap," meaning lobsters. Well, lobster prices had been consistent for two summers. Who would have guessed that the summer I opened, lobster prices would be 30 percent higher? I sold them cheap—too cheap maybe—but we did over one hundred lobster dinners alone each Saturday night, plus another two hundred other dinners on a good night. It was a success and customers loved it.

The catering business picked up that year, and the year after it was up another 50 percent. We were doing six or seven good-sized parties every Saturday night from mid-June through the end of September, plus a half-dozen more during the week. Most were private parties, with some corporate events, weddings, and rehearsal dinners. I started catering many events for the same clients each summer. Years before, I would spend over $50,000 on advertising in magazines and newspapers. After I owned the restaurant, I stopped advertising altogether. I did not need it anymore. I had over thirty people working for me and was going through seven hundred lobsters some weekends or more between the catering and the restaurant. One Fourth of July weekend, I remember grossing over six digits. I bought lots of catering equipment, plus I owned seven trucks and half a dozen trailers. I had a barbecue trailer custom-made for me down in Georgia; it cost $11,000. It was huge, and I could cook twenty chickens or forty shell steaks at once.

Many of my clients who owned houses in the Hamptons were (and are) my main source of income, but there were also a lot of people who would rent a house for the summer. The idea of having a clambake on the beach or at their house appealed to them, so they would call me. Someone told me once that more than thirty thousand cars a day drove past my place, and there was no better advertising. The first year I had the store, I had to borrow money. The second year, I borrowed a bit less, and after that, it took care of itself. We had customers who would drive out from the city and stop in to buy my homemade clam chowder, some platters for the weekend, and our lobster salad.

The first few years at my new location, my company was busier and busier. Many famous actors, movie directors, comedians, singers, musicians, owners of recording companies, and real estate moguls either threw parties I catered or were guests at them.

When I was a young boy, I dreamed of having my own store, although back then it might have been a candy store. When we were growing up, my brother always joked with me about how I used to have lots of candy and would sell him pieces for a nickel here and a nickel there. I was ten maybe.

The hardest part for me was adjusting from being on vacation in the tropics in the early spring to opening the restaurant in May. There are always problems running a restaurant, and I had my fair share. Something would always need repairing, whether it was a walk-in freezer, a walk-in refrigerator, refrigerated bay maries, display cases, soda refrigerators, the fryer, or a steamer.

There was a lot of stress to the restaurant/catering business. A cook would leave the freezer door ajar, and the temperature would be just around freezing when we opened the next morning. I would have to call a repairman on a Sunday. An easy fix would cost $350 if you were lucky. More involved fixes would run $500 or more. It never ended, until I closed the door in the fall.

I would work a hundred hours a week for four months, then close the restaurant for the winter in September. Then I'd travel a bit through the fall, go duck hunting in Saskatchewan in late September, then take a hunting trip in upstate New York for a week, then a few days in Delaware when the season opened there, and then I'd be back around Thanksgiving for our duck season. Then I would take clients hunting on farms and water blinds until February, and then I'd be off to the tropics again. I made a comfortable life for myself, and I was grateful to be able to do what I loved. Some days I still can't believe I get paid for what I do; I am blessed.

A NEW CHOCOLATE FRIEND

Two years after my dog Maggie died, I felt it was time for a puppy. I never could understand how, when someone I knew lost a dog, they could just go right out and pick up another. Since I have been sober, I have loved my dogs like they were my children, and living alone since Mary T, their sprit and happiness has filled my home. When a dog passes, the house becomes quiet and empty. Their spirit is gone.

My house had been empty long enough, and it was time to get a new Chesapeake. I had thought about it for a year, and I was scared at first. I am always scared to go through the loss when they go; the abandonment hurts when they leave this earth.

I located a litter from upstate. A friend had gotten a beautiful dog at the same kennel. I did not know what my new dog would look like. I wanted a chocolate like Boots, but I knew I would accept any color. Chessies are not usually dark colored; most of them are light brown. Dead grass is a popular color, but not many are chocolate. I was to pick up the puppy in Quogue, a twenty-minute drive from my home. I followed the directions and pulled into the yard to pick up my new dog. I was excited and a bit fearful at the same time. It was the right time, I tried to assure myself as I stepped out of my truck. The breeder Suzanne walked up the lawn.

"You must be Phil," she said. "Your new pup has been waiting for you."

Puppies are wonderful. She was six weeks old and had that funny swagger as her body tried to catch up to her feet. She rolled over, got up, and came to me. She was as chocolate brown as Boots. My eyes welled up with tears as I knelt down on the grass to play with her for a bit. "She likes you, she does not do that with many people," Suzanne said. I was not sure if Suzanne told that line to every person who picked up their new puppy, but she was right: the pup accepted me right there and then, and that was all that mattered. Her eyes were still blue, her ears seemed too long for her head, and her fur was soft as velvet. I brought her up to my face and smelled her. She had that puppy smell, and her short brown nose gave me a sniff at the same time.

"She is a cutie, Suzanne."

I never had a puppy who acted the way she did. It was strange. Usually they go through a period where they miss their mother and littermates, and they cry and whimper. They are scared of what will happen. My little friend laid down next to me on the seat of the truck with her head on my leg and slept all the way home. When we drive down the road today, she is either laying with her head on my leg the same way she always has or she sits as close as a teenaged sweetheart on the seat next to me. It is too funny. People laugh when they drive by. That summer was the best fun. I would walk with her on a leash at the beach, and young children loved to play with her. I spent a couple weeks searching for a name and finally came up with Ginger. I'm not sure if it was because I liked sushi and ginger or that she looked like a ginger snap, but the name stuck.

I waited until the fall, when she was six months old, before beginning any serious training. It was easier for me then as I would have more time to spend with her. She learned that the only place to go to the bathroom was in the woods past the lawn, and she hardly has ever gone on the lawn since she was a puppy.

I taught her slowly at the bay how to swim. I would lay in a foot of water, holding her so she would trust me, and when she got older she swam with me in the ocean. Some days we swam side by side, just past the breakers, for a quarter mile or more. She was different than some of my other dogs in that where I was, she was. If I was in my office, she was there. If I was watching a movie in the living room, she was at my feet. She was my shadow.

Ginger became a hunter when she was six months old. I was easy on her and did not demand a lot out of her, and she loved it.

Dogs are just like people, each one with its own personality. Ginger's is one of love; she is happy and loves everyone. I have never seen her get in a fight with another dog. She protects the house, but if she is out with me walking at night and she hears something move in the bushes, she will bolt for the porch with her tail between her legs.

In the summer, I take her clamming at least once a week. Mostly she swims around and around, sometimes for two hours straight without touching the bottom.

I have had so many dogs. I love when they are a year or two old. Ginger will be five soon, and I look at her and wonder how I will make it when she leaves me, how it will hurt me. I shake it off and try to stay where my feet are. I am one of those people who becomes very emotionally attached to my dogs. They give me what we are all searching for: unconditional love and companionship. I have lived alone the last sixteen years, with an occasional live-in girlfriend from time to time, but now it is mostly Ginger and I, which is fine with me. I am seldom a lonely man.

DOWN UNDER

So I had my new friend and business was doing better than I could have dreamed. There was a lot of stress in the summer, but come September, I closed the restaurant for another year. It was peaceful. I would go through the adjustment period and struggle with self-esteem, but I was familiar with that part. Catering close to one hundred events and parties, with dozens of calls each day and finding solutions to myriad issues, plus dealing with the finances to keep my mom's life going, wore me thin. I would regroup, take some time off, relax, and work out more at the gym, which I missed through the summer, and slowly I would feel better about things.

That fall seemed to scream by, and it was February again and time to go to a warm place.

I decided to head to Kauai for two weeks and then head down under to Australia for a month.

Kauai was beautiful, and I enjoyed getting up around eight and heading down to the ocean to pray for a bit before breakfast. I try not to make plans on vacation and just let things happen, do what I feel like doing. Maybe just heading to the beach with a great book is enough, or taking a drive to the fruit stand or snorkeling at some place I have never been. Some trips I would bring a woman, but this time I was alone.

This one day I went for a swim—usually I would swim close to a half-mile each day. This time I just wanted to do some snorkeling and swam a hundred yards off the beach when I felt a presence. I looked to my left but there was nothing there. Then I looked to my right and saw a huge leatherback turtle swimming along with me. We swam for another thirty yards, then I swam over to him and held his shell as he swam along with me in tow. It was an awesome feeling. The turtle did not seem scared at all.

I later found out there was a law that you could not touch or get close to the turtles, but I had no idea then and came out of the water smiling.

Wherever I travel, I get to meet people at meetings. I have been to meetings in eight countries. Sometimes they have been in Spanish, but still I feel connected.

After my time was over in Kauai, I hopped on a plane for Australia. I was excited, as I had always wanted to go there. I was in Sydney and Brisbane, and then I had a week in the Gold Coast. It was like being in Fort Lauderdale at spring break. There were lots of young kids getting twisted at night, but I did my own thing...I went horseback riding in the Numinbah Valley an hour or so drive from the coast. There were eight of us from all over the world, some younger and some older, men and women. It was beautiful and untouched. Barely did we pass a house or building on the trail. We had a cute young guide; she was a little hottie of maybe twenty. She asked me some questions about the States while we rode. Mostly all of us were silent, the beauty of nature had a hold of us and we took it in. There were rolling hills and trees unlike any I had ever seen. I was more relaxed than I had been on the entire trip. We stopped at a pasture and walked toward the river. An older man who was part of the staff had a small fire going and toasted some sort or bread and we also had tea. I walked up the rocks a bit and just sat there for a while and daydreamed. I thought about how lucky I was to be there, how interesting it was to meet people from all over the world, and how easily we all interacted in a comfortable way that March day.

After tea by that river, I had a spiritual experience. Later I thought they had put something in the tea, but that wasn't it. I felt right-sized, maybe for the first time in a long time, no better no worse than anyone else. As our group walked back to mount the horses, I began to cry and stopped by a tree in the pasture. Was this heaven? When I died, would I feel as free and unassuming of myself and others, never judging, just accepting? I was at peace. It lasted for several minutes, and I have never felt that way before or since. If that is what the afterlife is like, I should never be afraid of death.

I had learned how to be alone on my winter vacations. I organized trips and excursions, massages at least twice a week, and ate at some of the finest restaurants I could find. I have been to some of the finest spas and gyms in the world. I knew how to be good to myself. I deserved it, and very seldom did I ever feel guilty about the money it cost to live the way I did. Some trips I would meet a woman and enjoy it with them.

I felt the sacrifices I made in the summer were the price I paid for my winter trips. I always said that if I had enough money, I would leave in early February and not come home until late May, when it was warm back home and everything was in bloom. It never seemed to work out that way, though. I almost always arrived back home in early April for a last snowfall. "Poor man's fertilizer," the farmers used to call it.

I rented cars on occasion, but I was anxious about renting one in Australia as they drive on the left side of the road. I had come close to getting hit by traffic walking out in the street, not thinking and looking the wrong way. But I only needed a car for a week or so, and I would be careful.

I worked my way up the coast toward Cairns and then Airlie Beach, where I would stay for a few days, then I had booked two weeks at a resort on Hamilton Island for the end of my stay. It was a high-end, all-inclusive resort, and from what I had seen in brochures, it was quite similar to being in the Caribbean. The sea was turquoise, with desolate white sand beaches and palm trees hanging over the shorelines. There was sailing, snorkeling, and diving. Yep, it was right up my alley. The Aussies are fun people. I met quite a few of them in meetings during my trip. Sounding a bit like leprechauns when they shared, some of them had hard stories of being drunk and living in the Outback. They were wild stories.

The last day I was there, I had a good day. I went to the gym and worked out for an hour, played some squash, then had lunch and headed to the beach. I was brown as a berry by this point. I put on some 30 SPF block, laid down with a book, and woke up an hour later, around four o'clock in the afternoon. I felt good. I wanted to go to a meeting that night, so I headed back to my hotel to shower. I showered, changed, checked e-mails, and left for the meeting, in case I had a hard time finding it.

It had only been four days since I had rented the car, which was still strange to me. The steering wheel was on the opposite side of the car and the signal light on the right side of the steering column instead of the left. It took some getting used to. There was the issue of driving on the other side of the road and all the turnabouts, as the Aussies called them. Traffic funneled into them at thirty-plus kilometers per hour, which scared me at times. I told myself I would be fine, and I had only one close call in a turnabout. That night, I was relieved it was the last night I would be driving there, as I would be turning in the car in the morning.

I found the meeting easily. I was early, so I went back to the main road to gas up the car and waste some time. The meeting was at seven, and it was almost six thirty and just getting dark. The last thing I remember was putting gas in the car.

I came to in a room. My leg hurt, and my head hurt. "Where the hell am I?" I said to myself. I looked down and realized by the white gown that I was in a hospital.

My heart raced. Just then a nurse walked in and said, "I see you are looking a bit better."

"Where am I? What happened? How long have I been here?"

"Easy Phil, you are in Airlie Hospital. You had an accident, and you are lucky to be alive. You had no identification, no driver's license, so we did not know anything. You had the accident at six-thirty and now it is eleven-thirty."

"Was I unconscious?" My mind started to race. I was panicking again and full of fear. Who was I? Were people worried about me? Did I have children and a wife at home? Where was home?

"No, you have been conscience the whole time, but you were a bit confused for a while," the nurse tried to assure me. "You should rest. The doctor thinks you have a concussion. If you think of anything, write it down in this notepad. Just relax. It could have been a lot worse. You hit a bus, you know, head on. You are lucky to be with us. The police said you were lucky you had your seatbelt on and the airbag went off. It saved your life."

The nurse walked out of the room and down the hall. Was this a dream? I wanted it to be a dream. "Wake up, for God's sake?" I thought. I realized I asked all the questions, but I didn't ask what had happened to my head, my leg, and my side. I was hurting all over. I lifted the sheet and saw that my knee was bandaged. It was twice its normal size. There were a lot of scrapes and dings on my shin and up my leg. Fear struck me and tears welled up in my eyes. My breathing grew faster and faster. However, I knew that freaking out and reacting got me nowhere in situations like this. I tried to calm myself down. I knew I needed to get back home. The rest would work itself out in time, but I needed to get home.

Reality began to come to me. I was from Water Mill, yeah New York. Eben was my brother. I remembered his phone number, then George's phone number. I wrote it all down. Then it went blank. I had nothing. I was in Australia, but why? Where was I staying?

I heard once that if you fall asleep with a concussion, you could forget everything forever. You have to stay awake. "You've got to remember," I kept telling myself. I became more terrified. I was alone. Being in a strange country, what if they did not stitch up my knee correctly? Would I be able to walk all right? My mind just kept racing.

I had to remember where was I staying. It was something about a terrace. But terrace what? The nurse walked in; it was close to two in the morning, and I had not slept.

"You should rest," she said.

"I keep thinking of the word terrace," I said. "Maybe it is where I am staying, could it be?"

"Oh, yes, the Whitsundays Terraces in Airlie Beach," she said.

"That's it, that is where I am staying." I wrote it down on my pad.

"Now really try to sleep, okay?" She left the room again.

How could I sleep? Christ, my vet's hospital looked newer and cleaner than this place. I kept at it, and by seven in the morning I had almost two pages of information, including names, addresses and phone numbers. I had to get out of the hospital and get home to America where the doctors could do a better job of taking care of my needs. I would have to call the airline. Surely they would understand the urgency and let me change tickets. Dozens of thoughts kept spinning through my mind; it was hard to quiet them. I finally did get some sleep, and when I woke up I was able to eat something. Then I had to have an MRI. The nurse wheeled me into the room, and the MRI looked like something left over from the '70s. The green faded paint was peeling, and I knew I had to get home!

After the MRI, I had to meet with the doctor. I knew if I told him the truth about the pain and dizziness, he would want me to stay. I tried to pull it together when the nurse rolled my wheelchair into the hall to meet him.

"How do you feel?" the doctor asked.

"My leg is kind of sore when I bend it, but I would like to go home."

"How is the dizziness? Any headaches?" he questioned.

I lied and said, "no, I am good, just tired, and I need to get home. Did you stitch my knee up?"

"Yes, I did. You took quite a few sutures. We had to sew it in two layers because of the deep wound. You lost quite a bit of blood."

"How many stitches?"

"Close to thirty stitches, I should think."

"I have hep C, you know," I told him.

"I know. You told me last night in the operating room before we started on you."

I was stunned for a second, thinking that I was worried about their well-being even when I did not know who I was. I knew they needed to know about my liver disease.

"You were lucky," he said. "An inch lower and you probably would have cut your cartilage or ligaments in your knee. The laceration was in your muscle on the side of the kneecap, and in your case it is fairly thick. You have some bruises on your side, and I think you have some cracked ribs also. It would be a good idea if you spent another night here as you have had trauma to your brain and a concussion. I would like to keep an eye on you."

"I will be fine as long as I am home," I said. "I do feel better now, and thank you for all that you have done for me." I signed some papers, and the nurse rolled me back to my room to get dressed. For a bit, they could not find my shoes, the red crocs I had been wearing the night before. Finally, someone decided to look in the operating room and returned with them, one with dried blood still on it.

They gave me a pair of crutches, and I hobbled to a taxi waiting in front of the hospital. I grimaced as the pain in my knee shot through my leg when I had to bend it slightly to get into the cab. So many thoughts were running through my head. Hobbling around on crutches brought back memories of my father. How long before I would be able to walk? Would I be able to walk without a limp? Would I run and be able to work out? I tried to hold back the tears and stuff those feelings as best I could. I wanted to call Dad and tell him all about it, then I realized he had died years before.

I never even thought of my mother until I was in the air, not that there was anything she could have done. She was in the fog worse than me.

It was a hot Sunday in March in Airlie Beach. People were walking to the beach as the taxi pulled up the hill to where I lived. I had spent only a few days there and recognized the park and a restaurant where I'd had dinner the night before.

"Right here is good," I said, and the taxi stopped. I hobbled from the cab and had to climb one step at a time up to my room on the second floor. I let out a groan on each step as my knee was screaming in pain. Sweat ran down my forehead as I opened the door to my room. I was completely out of breath after walking up only a dozen steps. The day before, I had worked out for an hour and played squash for an hour, and now I could not even walk up a flight of stairs. The fear began to come. I had to stop myself because my cracked ribs sent shooting pains through my side. I called George first. He answered the phone, his voice bringing back the sobbing. I told him that I had hit a bus and needed to get home and how scared I was.

"Oh, Phil, are you alright?"

"No, I mean I am banged up. I've got stitches in my knee, and my leg and knee are pretty swollen. I have some cracked ribs and maybe a concussion. Otherwise I am good." I tried to laugh but grimaced when my side felt like someone was stabbing me.

"Phil, I feel bad for you, alone there so far away, is there anything I can do?"

"I am just scared, George." I began to fall apart again, with tears rolling down my cheeks, and my side twinged each time I coughed.

"Phil, you are going to be all right," he said. "You are lucky to be alive. Go easy on yourself. What are you going to do?"

"I am going to call the airlines and work on changing my ticket and go home tomorrow. I need to be home, George."

My home was my safety net. I loved it there, with my bed, my beautiful place, and my sweet Ginger. I would be all right if I made it back, but it would be tough to get there, I knew that. George was great and comforted me like he had for over twenty-five years. I began to calm down. He told me he wanted me to call if I needed anything. I called my brother; he was upset and wanted to know what he could do. I told him I needed him and my friend Eddie to get me at the airport when I flew in. I just needed to let him know when.

I hobbled back down one stair at a time and got to the hotel office. This was not the place for me. There were lots of steps and hills. It was painful, but I made it and asked to use the phone. The girl at the desk said, "You must be the one who hit the bus last night. The police have been calling, and they want to see you to fill out a report."

I thought, "Great, now I am going to be sued or some shit, maybe a violation."

The urgency to get out from Down Under was big now. The people at the hotel were wonderful. They helped me with calling the airlines and sent someone up to help me carry my things to a room on the ground floor. It took an hour, and I made arrangements to leave the following afternoon. The airline said it would cost an additional $500. I was pissed they had no compassion, but I made the deal with a credit card. I would take a shuttle to the airport and then fly to Sydney, then back to New York. It would take close to twenty hours. I did not want to think about it, I hated flying more than twelve hours at a time.

Situated in my new room, I put a plastic bag around my knee to keep the bandage dry and took a shower. What I took for granted—something as simple as showering—was a big procedure. What used to take fifteen minutes now took an hour. I scrubbed the dried blood from my leg and foot. There were lots of cuts on my leg from broken glass. The soapy water stung as I washed the cuts clean. Just as I got out of the shower, the phone rang. It was the front desk telling me the police would be at my room in a half-hour to fill out the report.

A few minutes later, I heard a knock at the door. I opened the door to a policewoman wearing a checkered hat; she looked familiar, like some sort of dream.

"My name is Officer Mcfadden," she said. "I was hoping that we could finish the report. Do you have the time?"

"Yes, sure come in. You look familiar in a strange way."

"Don't you remember talking to me last night about the accident before the ambulance took you to the hospital?" she asked.

"I am sorry, I just remember coming to in the hospital about 11:30. I don't remember anything about the accident. They say I hit a bus."

"That you did, head on too. You were very lucky. The bus was going forty when you drove in front of it. The bus crushed the front of your car and almost drove over it. You and the car were dragged over a hundred meters before it came to a stop. They had to cut you from the car. You don't remember? You were talking to us."

I had a lump in my throat. I was lucky to be dragged down the road and be only as banged up as I was. If I wasn't stunned about the whole ordeal before, I was now.

"You probably gave me a breathalyzer, didn't you?"

"Yes, we did. You were sober."

I knew the answer, but I got satisfaction from not having to worry about dealing with all that drunken shit from the past. She was nice and even kind of hot in her uniform, but I was hurting too much to entertain thoughts of lust for more than a passing second. She asked if I was going to be around for a few days if she had any more questions. I said I would be at the hotel, although I knew I would be on a plane with any luck before the sun set the following night. I wanted to get out of there. The cop said that no one was hurt on the bus. I was thankful about that, but I wanted to take no chances. I needed to fly, literally.

I thought about the accident after the police had left. It amazed me how I had no recollection of anything for those five hours. I prayed and asked God to never let me remember that night, ever. I have read how extreme pain, abuse, or trauma causes your mind to shut down and protect you. Thank God for that.

The trip back home took forever and a day, literally. I had filled a script at the drug store for Panadol, as acetaminophen was called there, the day before I left. They seemed to numb the pain. I thought it was some special drug they only had in Australia. I was worried about them and felt that I had to careful with the pills—until I got home and found out they were only Tylenol.

I was exhausted when I got back to New York. Eben and Eddie were waiting for me, and my eyes welled up with tears when I hugged them. A day later, I made an appointment with my bone and joint doctor. He took a look at the knee and took some x-rays, looked over the sutures, and checked my knee for mobility.

"They did a good job sewing up your knee," he told me. "Your muscle here that attaches to the knee is pretty large because you work out. I think you will heal fine, but you will need to see someone for therapy."

He gave me a script for physical therapy, and I saw Alan, a man who had worked with me when I had hurt my shoulder years before.

The day I went to Alan, I was feeling anxious about my recovery. Would I be able to do all the things I loved to do? After talking to me for a while and examining my knee for flexibility, I asked him what he thought.

"You will be back stronger than you were before you did this and doing whatever you want," he said.

Tears rolled down my cheeks, tasting sweet as they touched my lips. He did not understand. He held my arm and said, "What did I say? Are you all right?"

Choking with emotion, I said, "I have been so worried that I would walk with a limp and not be able to work out at the gym, go to spin class, and do all the things I love to do."

"With anyone else there might be a problem, but you are an athlete. The size of the muscles in your leg from working out saved you, and because you are in great shape the recovery will be fast."

Alan was great with me. He is a wonderful physical therapist, and within two weeks I was back at the gym, working out. A week after that, I started spin class again.

It took a couple months, but I was soon doing everything as if the accident never happened. My short-term memory was affected by the concussion, and as they had told me in the hospital, it would take a year or more for that to come back to normal. By the time that a year went by, my memory was better.

I have been through many terrifying things, but I had never been sober when something like this happened. Coming to in a hospital in a foreign country put a huge amount of fear in me. I had learned in the program to live in the minute, and that is what got me through. Another deep-seated fear I really had not gotten in touch with was the fear of being helpless, like my father was. God, I never wanted to have to rely on people—they failed you. Maybe it came from watching how my father struggled to walk sometimes. I always felt I had to be physically fit and strong.

MOM'S NEW HOME

When I began taking care of my mother's finances and her caregiver moved in, I knew there would come a time when the money would run out. I figured it would be about five years, and I was close. In the summer of 2008, I called my brother and sisters and we made plans to find a nursing home because her assets were gone. I explained to my mother that she was going to a place that could take care of her, like a hotel. I felt guilty lying and hoped that no one would tell me that story when I grew old.

I had found a nursing home months before and talked to the administrator and walked around. It was like many old people's homes, I guess. It smelled, and the patients were a bit nutty. Some yelled things while others sat in chairs with drool running down their chins. It was a sad ending to life. My father was blessed to have died in his home with us there to help him. My older sister lived far away; she did not want her mother with her. None of the rest of her children were willing to have her move in with them, including me, so the home was where she went. It was a difficult thing for me. I felt guilt and maybe some shame, and my own fear of abandonment would surface from time to time as I thought about my last years on this earth.

God, it was hard when I dropped her off. I could hear the abandonment in her voice when she asked when I would be coming back. By this point, she was almost eighty-four and had lived a long life, and while she was not as sharp as some, she was better off than most of the old people there. She had lost a lot of her memory and knew little of the real world. She made it up as she went, each day another story.

Mom had a room with a view of a garden, although most of the time she seemed to keep the drapes shut. The first few months, during every visit she would say, "When are you taking me home?" One day when I saw her, she told me she had called the house on Hampton Road in Southampton where she had lived as a child and later in life. She had remembered the phone number from thirty years before. I recognized it and was amazed. On my visits, I brought her imported chocolate and sometimes a book or magazine.

A transformation had taken place years before. She had changed from a woman who tried to control me, who was angry with what life had dealt her, to being a helpless little girl dressed as an old woman. I had let go of many resentments years before, and more of it began to subside when I was able to take care of her needs and watch out for her. Yeah, there were plenty of times I was overwhelmed and resentful, but out of that came forgiveness and love for Mom. She told me often that she loved me. She thanked me over and over again, and I would smile knowing in my heart that it was helping me far more than it was helping her. I heard those words, and I know she meant them. I think it was sad because the words came too late. I wanted to hear them years before, but at least I heard them.

Maybe I had hoped that one day she would get sober like my dad and we would have time to heal some of the hurt, but it didn't go that way. I tried to accept it for the way it was now, but it was confusing and lacked resolution. It was the same pattern I had been used to for years: vague, confusing, and inconsistent.

I was being a good son. I was looking out for her. I had told her years before that I would take care of her needs, and I was following through.

Some days as I drove to the nursing home, I wished it was different, wished that she was different. But it wasn't.

I used to ask myself what it would be like to tell my mother about a girl who had abandoned me. What would a caring mother say? The last person I'd ever turn for comfort was to my mother. I knew too well that she would dismiss my feelings like always and kick dirt on me as I laid helpless in the hole.

So now sitting in her room, I struggled to make conversation with her. It was hard, and I could not wait to get up and leave, but I didn't. I was now someone who loved talking about life, what makes people tick, where they came from, how they struggled, their strength, and their courage. I loved courageous people now; I had become a man full of courage. Many people told me I was full of courage, that I had integrity and was genuine and compassionate and could describe the struggle. This was the struggle I had been wrestling with in therapy for over twenty years. It was about finding who I was, walking through the pain, showing up when I did not want to, and doing the next right thing over and over again—just like I was doing sitting next to her at that moment.

It was one of the reasons I loved meetings and hearing people walk through their journey and talking about life. For years, I heard many toys at the broken toy store speak of coming out the other side. I loved their devotion to the truth, their courage to talk about themselves and their feelings. It is what I did, too. I wanted the self-hatred to vanish, the ego to diminish, to feel right-sized, to learn how to be grateful, and to know in my heart that I was loved. The biggest feat was learning how to love myself.

I look into my dog Ginger's eyes as I hug her and tell her she is lucky to have me. "No one would love you like I love you," I tell her. She concurs in her own way and probably tells me how lucky I am to have her.

There isn't a day when I don't tell that dog she is special, that she is the best. She loves those words. I never heard them, and now I know how to say them. Not to just Ginger, either, but also to my brother's children. The two girls get what my brother and I did not get: the words and the action, the holding, and the hugs.

Every day I left my mom in the nursing home, I would kiss her on the cheek and say those words, and she would say, "I love you too."

I sometimes thought back to when I met George's wife, Annette, and how she was with me. The short Italian woman was so loving with me and concerned about everything I talked about. I was interesting to her; she wanted me to find a good woman. When I had problems in relationships, she would sit and listen and almost always say the same thing: "They are frickin' nut jobs and you are better off without them." She never judged me, she always told me she loved me. Almost every birthday she and George called me and sang "Happy Birthday" to me on the phone. I always knew it was her idea even though I never asked.

I am not sure where I came up with the idea, but one day I decided I would bring a book to my Mom. I had been told to take someone else to help with conversation, but the book seemed right and I did not question it. We said our pleasantries, and I sat in the chair by her bed where I always sat. Eunie sat in the chair by the window, and I said, "I brought a book and would like to read to you. Is that okay?" Her eyes, no longer blue but a sort of gray, began to shine with excitement.

I opened *Homer and the Circus Train*. It was a children's book my father had read to me when I was a child. Right from the start she loved it. I read with excitement and enthusiasm. I would look up between pages and find her smiling like a five-year-old on the edge of her seat. I had found what I needed, and she loved that I read to her. It felt right. I remembered that my father read stories to my brother and me when we were young, but my Mom never did. I gave her what she couldn't give me.

She loved the children's books, and the time flew by. I felt good at the end of our visits. I can still remember the way she used to purse her lips together when I showed her picture of Homer, the caboose, about to come off the track in the book.

It was hard for me, not knowing what to say, what to do. I knew I could just be, sit there and read to her, and that is what I did for months.

JAIL BIRDS

I am not sure what was happening. George said I was changing. I think I was the last to know—maybe we all are.

I had spent close to fifteen years as chairperson for the recovery meeting at the Riverhead Jail on Tuesday nights. It was different there. There were real stories, with no whining, and I did more than just bring a meeting to the guys there. The inmates would sign up, and many times there would be a waiting list. It took men weeks to get on the list.

When I first took the commitment, I was unaware how it would go. That is, I thought that many of the inmates would be there for several years. This was not the case; many would be doing a county bullet as they called it, or nine months, and some awaited trial for a year or two. Some would be there for a few months then be shipped upstate to do their sentence.

Ten years ago there was a man awaiting trial—I will call Jim. He was in his thirties, maybe 5'4" with dark hair, and he was always polite and respectful. I had learned early on that these men were all human beings, no matter what they were in jail for, and I treated them with respect. Respect was something they never got from the guards or from the outside world. Jim used to help me with setting up the meeting and putting away the literature afterward. After a year, we got to know each other, and I wanted to ask why he was in jail. I made it a habit of not wanting to know—it was easier for me that way. It kept me from judging them in any way and treating them all as just another drunk wanting to get sober.

I asked Jim what he had done.

"They said I killed my fiancé," he said. "They say I stabbed her twenty-seven times. I don't remember doing it, I was in a blackout."

What the hell could I say to that? I was silent, so I said nothing. Afterward, I walked the hall toward the heavy steel door that led to freedom and felt that I could have said something to him. Shit, the guy was going away for a long time. Jim came to that meeting every week. He was not remanded to do so—he wanted to be there. In jail, everyone talks about what they did, and almost all of them say they were innocent. Some men wanted me to write letters for them, but most times I say it was not my job. If I did write one, I would never lie. I'd just write that they were attending the program and seemed sincere about wanting to recover. Jim left after two years; he never said he was innocent and was sentenced to twenty-five to life. He knew what alcohol had done. It had ruined the rest of his life. He would probably die in jail, or when he would be released, what would the world be like? How could he cope?

There were times early on at the jail when I would get close to the guys. I remember three guys became closer to me. They had a strong desire to be sober, and they were honest. I let them in, and they had dropped the walls and spoke from the heart at every meeting. They would share the shame they felt and how their families did not speak to them. One man had been in and out of jail for eighteen years. His mother had died while he was serving his sentence. The jail let him go to the funeral in shackles, and his family barely talked to him. He cried one night, sharing how he was looked at by his brothers and sisters. He wanted to find a better way. He wanted to make it all go away; the shame of it all was tearing him apart.

Not every meeting got to me like that night. My eyes filled with tears, and it brought me back to my life. I knew the shame he felt. I knew what the drugs and booze were doing to him. I could see the hopelessness on his face. Hell, some nights the room was filled with hopeless faces. Many nights before the meeting would start, I would look at each man, and the emptiness and sadness overwhelmed me some nights.

Many nights I would say that I had robbed, taking money from my father or mother, that I had stolen from a cleaning woman who had four children and cleaned my grandparent's house, and that I lied to people on a daily basis to make sure I had enough drugs or booze.

I often said, "The only difference between me and you guys is that you got caught and I didn't."

Another thing I often said was, "No one here is bad. You might have done some bad shit to get here, but none of you is bad. How many of you were high or drunk when you did your crime?" Every hand would go up. "Remember, God doesn't make junk. I was sick when I did what I did when I was active, and you were too. We are sick people getting well, not bad people getting good." I would tell them that it did not matter what I thought what was right or about them serving long sentences. I would tell them that I was not fond of the system and that I knew it would be harder for them to get sober than people on the outside, but that it was possible.

I would tell them about inmates I saw on the outside. They would approach me and ask if I remembered them. Most times I couldn't. Shit, I had seen hundreds of men, maybe thousands over the years, but they all wanted me to tell the guys inside that it was working for them, that they were working the program.

So those three men were friends there in the jail. They did several months each, and two were going upstate. The other man was released on probation. During their last meeting, they spoke one by one. Each man mentioned my devotion to come every Tuesday night and said how I had given them hope and treated them fairly and with respect. How I had not judged them and how I had been their friend and how important that was to them. Most of all, they told me they would always remember me. After the meeting, two of the men hugged me with tears in their eyes. I was impacted deeply and cried with them. Never did I question why I felt that way. I had only known these men for a year, some less, so why had they touched me so? It was just one of those special times for me, and I have had hundreds of them. I would feel connected and needed, and for that special period of time, it felt exactly as God intended it. Everyone benefited from each other. I benefited immensely. It gave me such self-esteem and a gratitude that would take me through life with a smile as long as I wanted it to.

I hurt for while after those men left. For a while, the room seemed different. I thought about them, wondering if they were working the program. Were they going to get back with their families? Would they be able to stay out of the system?

As time went by, there were new faces to replace the ones who had left. It has been a long time now, and while each man is different in some way, they are very much the same. Each one comes to my meeting on Tuesday night and listens to what I have to say. I watch them when they are new. I say, "I know what you guys are thinking. You are thinking, 'What the hell does this guy know? He does not know what I am feeling, what it is like struggling through life, being back and forth to jail, being full of guilt, remorse, and shame so deep that all I want to do is make it stop.'" Then I look around the room, and the room is silent as they begin to listen.

I try not to preach to them, but I do try to share my journey through the disease and talk about the things the program taught me. Most of all, I tell them that the old me would not give any part of myself to another human being without something in return. In other words, I would never spend several hours every Tuesday trying to help them if I was using.

I say, "I am here maybe because I was close to being inside, meaning jail, and sometimes I wonder how life would have turned out. I am here because I have been taught that when anyone asks for help, I need to reach out my hand to the sick and suffering. Trust me, this is helping me more than you can ever imagine."

That is the part the inmates will never get unless they are sober long enough to do something for another alky. George always told me that the jail meetings were changing me, making me a better man. My brother told me last week, "It is a good thing you do down there."

I leave there, drive home, park my truck in the front garage at my place, which I call the Plantation, and walk up to the house. I almost always look up at the stars with a smile, look up at my house sitting back in the woods, and know in my heart that I am living the dream.

I take my brother Eben to speak every few weeks. He knows what it is like. He spent several months in that jail and speaks about the pods where they sleep, the taste of the nasty food, how the officers talk to the inmates, when to shit, when to sit down, and when to do just about everything. The room is so quiet you could hear a pin drop. Those nights, I am so proud of him. Many nights when he speaks, my mind wanders back to the day the detective came looking for him. The detective swore to me they only wanted to see Eben in court to finish up his case, but there were so many I never asked which case. My brother got his last chance, and he has been sober for years now. It's amazing.

My mind comes back to the meeting, and I listen as my brother tells his story to the inmates. It's the story of how we used to both deal weed, how we used to drink and drug together, and how he felt so alone while I found the answer, how he hated the program for taking me.

He talks about all the calls I would get as he sat in jail. I remembered back when he would be in tears, pleading, "I need you to help me, the bail is $50,000." Then a week later, he'd call again and say, "They lowered the bail to $10,000. Please, you have to get me out of here." The calls always ended the same way, with me saying, "I'm sorry, I can't help you." If it was late at night, I could not sleep, and some nights I would lay there crying. When I was married, Mary T would hold me; when I was alone, I would sob myself to sleep.

He talked about how he lived less than a mile from my house with a drug dealer, how two years went by after our dad died before he even saw me.

I was never sure why that day was different than the others. He wanted no money. He just said, "I can't keep living like this, I need your help, please."

At that exact moment, I would have walked across the desert to find him. I knew in my heart it was the time. It was his "jumping off place." Every alky has one, and this was his. I felt it in my heart. When that moment comes, it is a miracle that sometimes only happens once in a person's lifetime, and I knew that. I had lived it and seen it happen over and over again with the sick and suffering.

And right this minute, the miracle is sitting next to me, talking about his two daughters. "They are my heart," he is saying. He's telling the inmates he owns his house, works hard to pay the mortgage, goes to meetings, sees a therapist, and most of all, he has me. My eyes well up with tears when he says that.

When I am there with my brother, I always feel the gift. It is the gift that someone you love has found the way, someone close to you does not have to suffer, and you feel comfortable when you go to sleep at night because you are not worried about getting the call saying they are in jail, hurt, or the worst, dead.

I never gave up hope with Eb. It was sixteen long years, and I kept praying. Would he make it and find the answer? Would he find out who he was and be an honest and sober man? There is not a day that goes by that I am not thankful. My brother found an easier, softer way. He is an example to many. He has become a miracle too.

Not long ago I met a man—his name in is not important—who is now awaiting trial. His life is every drunk's nightmare. He killed someone in a car crash while he was drunk over a year ago. He is full of guilt, shame, fear, and remorse, and yet each week he comes early and sets up the steps on the wall of the meeting room. He puts out the literature and is respectful of me and shakes my hand each week. That part always amazes me. Then at least half the guys in the meeting come up and thank me for coming and shake my hand.

The other night, he shared about what he may have to say at the trial to the family of the victim. I knew he would carry pain about this for the rest of his life. I asked, "If the man or woman you killed was sitting in this room right now, what would you say?" The inmate's eyes went glassy and filled with tears. "Just think about it," I said. "During your week, write that man or woman a letter, telling just how you feel about taking their life. Write as much as you need to and then destroy the letter." He said he would do it. Another man spoke up and said he had killed someone years before driving while drunk. He said he would write a letter too.

Those meetings are different from any meetings I go to. I try to give them hope. I tell them when I am away on vacation and my friend Eddie takes over the meeting. I have learned over the years not to get too close, but it is hard. Here, a man will share with tears rolling down his cheeks from the pain. In jail, they are taught not to be real, not to be vulnerable, to be tough, and not be scared. Yet many of the inmates are frightened to death and have no one.

Two years ago, an officer named Andy at the rehab where I hold the meeting was killed. He was doing security at a club in the Hamptons. It was a side job to make some extra money for his family. I had known him for several years and saw him when I came on Tuesdays. Andy was a good man. He wore glasses and stood at least 6'6". He used to like breaking my balls when I came through the door.

"Hey," he'd say. "It's happy Phil."

The inmates liked Andy. Some nights I did, and on the ones I didn't, I would send a couple comments back at him to even things up. We had a strange relationship, but I knew he respected me and the time I gave each week to the men in green.

When he was killed, it was tough for the people he worked with at the jail. He was loved by many. His children were now without a father. He was killed by a patron at a bar. The guy broke his windpipe during an argument. There was talk of the kid knowing martial arts, but I never knew for sure. It was sad the first time I came after his death. I asked the inmates to join me in a prayer for the officer at the end of the meeting.

A couple weeks later, I came to the meeting. Some of the inmates were painting a mural on the wall at the back of the room. It was of Andy in heaven. Blue sky surrounded his head, and it was an amazing likeness. I also heard that some of the inmates who came to the meeting donated their commissary money to his family.

It was an amazing thing. Here was this officer who would tell these guys what to do, when to sit, and when to talk, and he was now idolized. Any resentments or negative feelings were put aside by the men in green. It gets to me every time I think back. Forgiveness is powerful indeed.

I sit at the other end of the room when I chair the meeting, and Andy's huge face smiles down on that room. At times I look up and think about life. Why do some people get to stay, and some leave this earth unexpectedly, while still others choose not to go on anymore and chose their own way out?

At meetings on the outside, people clap for the coffee maker. They clap for a person who has gone back and forth for five years. It wasn't like that when I came in; no one gave you applause for doing your part. That was not the reason I made coffee for ten years.

Sometimes in our journey of being sober and enjoying life, the alky forgets how serious this disease is. I am guilty of it too, but I have been blessed to be in a meeting once a week that keeps the reality in my face. In the fifteen years I have been a chairperson bringing meetings to the jail, I have met some of toughest yet most honest men I could imagine. Many of them are honest and courageous. They are hurting from years of abuse and being stuck in the disease of addiction and alcoholism. They are trapped in the jail system and they feel their lives will never change.

The inmates come and go. Some nights I have many new faces. Some are sad, some are angry, but most of them show despair and hopelessness. They do not know me, they do not trust me, and many of them do not like me. When I introduce myself, I say, "My name is Phil. I am an alcoholic, and I run the Tuesday night meeting here at Riverhead Jail. I do not get paid for this. I volunteer my time as do all of my speakers who come each night to share their stories with you. I do not speak to the people who work here about what happens in this room, and don't bother to ask me to do a favor for you as it is not my job. If you interrupt the meeting, you may be asked to return to your cell and you won't be allowed to come back. It is a privilege to be here, not a right."

I say these words only a few times a year as most of the men in green are there six months to a year. Inmates share their hurt. Shame and guilt are powerful tools the disease uses to keep a good man down. They speak about their children. Some have only seen their kids twice in the last ten years because they have been incarcerated. These men have lots of time and spend much of it lifting weights to relieve the pain. Their arms are the size of most men's thighs. Many have tattoos, and some even have tattoos over their faces and necks. On occasion, a huge man will share his shame and humble himself with tears rolling down his cheeks. Some men come back over and over again. I may see the same faces four or five times in seven years. They are caught in the system and the disease won't let them stay free.

One such man named Jimmy was back last winter for the third time in a few years. I got to know him more, and he tried to let go of a lot of fear and hurt. Jimmy shared from the heart when he talked to the men there. Jimmy almost always gave me a hug. I liked him and wanted him to have what I had. He respected me and talked with me each time he came. He had a family with little kids, including a son who would want to play catch with him when he got out. His time was up, and when he left he said he was not coming back. He was going to go to meetings and would try to live a sober life.

Several months later, I went to the jail. I was setting up the meeting and Jimmy's friend, who was also an inmate there, came to me and said, "I don't know if you heard, but Jimmy came back to the jail Friday." He hesitated and looked down. "He hung himself on Saturday night." I was instantly angry. Why did this shit have to happen, especially to him? He was a good guy. I liked him, and most of all he was forty years old. I thought of his children—they didn't have a chance. It always throws me for a loop when someone takes their own life. Maybe it is because I had tried to do it many times myself. Many times I drove when I could not walk. Sometimes my foot would go to the floor and then would come that terrible noise of steel meeting steel, or in my case, steel meeting trees and telephone poles. I was lucky I didn't kill someone. I remember, sitting at my father's kitchen table trying to put together a shotgun that he had taken apart weeks before, fearing the worst would happen. I always knew when I was in bad shape when my guns were in pieces.

A few minutes later, another member named Bob came up to me. He had written the letter to the person he had killed in a hit-and-run accident. Two months before, he had shared about what he had done. He had killed a man while under the influence of drugs. His eyes filled with tears, and his face grimaced with shame and guilt. I had suggested he write a letter as if the man was sitting in the room with him. "Tell him what you feel," I said.

While my speaker qualified in the other room, Bob and I went to a room and sat down at a table. As Bob read through his letter, tears rolled down his cheeks. He was sobbing as the words stuck in his throat. My eyes were glassy with sorrow for this man. I thought about the man he had killed. The man had a wife and three children who would grow up with no father. I have no doubt that someone who is driving under the influence is like a madman with a fully loaded gun. I am unsure if jail is the answer for these repeat offenders; it is just a temporary answer for a very complicated problem. I do know that it is no coincidence that in the twenty-eight years I have been sober, I have not been in jail for alcohol- and drug-related accidents. I listened to the man's letter as he sobbed, choking on the guilt and remorse. I suggested that he destroy the letter, and we put it in the shredder together.

The system is better now. It is not fixed, and I think there have been only a little more than twenty years since Twelve Step programs have been allowed in the Riverhead Jail. Many jails across the country still don't allow meetings.

I heard years ago that fewer than one in thirty-six people who come through the doors of a Twelve Step meeting stay sober the first year. I do not think the odds are any better today. I tell the men in green that their recovery will be more difficult. They have shame and guilt to deal with from being incarcerated. Many of them try to live back in the problem, thinking that they are different and thus the situation will be different. My best suggestion to them is that whatever they have been doing, do completely the opposite. Most times, this is the best I can come up with.

I spoke with George that night when I left the jail. I told him about Jimmy, and I shared my feelings of being sad and angry at the same time.

"George, I know in my heart what I do there is more than carrying the message. I let the men know me. They trust me and know that I respect them as men, and they let me in just a little, but maybe it is more than they have let someone in their life, who knows. They change right before my eyes in the months we are together. A transformation takes place, and I know that I have something to do with that. I have been given a gift...not only sobriety, but a gift of caring to understand, to listen, and to give hope to someone who has no hope at all."

And I want all of them to receive what I have, but it is not my decision. Many will have to keep struggling through life as if it is some sort of punishment. That struggle of guilt, shame, abandonment, rejection, isolation, loneliness goes on and on, and until they come to terms that all they have to do is not drink or drug and go to meetings, they will be stuck on the merry-go-round. Many alkies never can believe that the way they feel about who they are and the train wrecks of their lives will work themselves out as long as they just don't use and go to meetings. Some families get closer, some get further apart, some married people divorce, some stay together, and some—like my family—get sober and can laugh about the crazy shit. My brother Eben and I have a relationship where we talk almost every day. He respects me, I respect him, and when we butt heads we can talk about it. I might be self-centered and wrong, or maybe it is his turn, but we can move on.

I have brought many guys from the local area there to speak. Each one carries a different message. Some are captivating to the inmates, like Eben and Eddie, who both did their time in jail, and the room is always quiet as they listen intently. Some speakers are new and speak from the heart about trying to live life without drinking, about being a better man, a better father, or a better husband. And some just tell it like it is. They stopped drinking and have been sober a year or so and their children still will not call them or meet them for a cup of coffee. They talk of how they just keep going. They pray for willingness. They pray for understanding. They try not to dwell on what they seek, but they try to be grateful for where they have come to.

It was what I wanted when I stopped drinking. I wanted so much for my friends and family to understand me, to be happy for my new way of life and my new way of looking at myself, and most of all to love me and accept me.

It did not happen as quickly as I wanted it. It never happens that way, and this alky wanted it yesterday. I was impatient and felt I deserved instant gratitude. I got resentful when I did not get it. I wanted my way to work out: my own timetable, my schedule, and my visions. It went on and on. Hell, I was and still am unreasonable many times when I think that I have a grip on the way things are supposed to happen. My life has not been easy. I have received gratitude, contentedness, self-worth, and self-love for thinking, acting, and doing for others, yet many times I am in the way.

My self-centeredness, fear, and lack of faith keeps me from those wonderful things we all seek.

I lack things in my life, and it troubles me when I think about it. I want to be with a woman who accepts me for me. I want us to be able to share our feelings and communicate without judgment.

Will it ever happen? The day when I just say, "The hell with it, I am going to take a leap of faith and see what happens…" That may be the day.

What keeps me from seeking out this hot woman with urgency is that I have reached a place in my life where I am very content. I am grateful for the little things. I see beauty in a lot, and I am getting to know more about me every day. I like what I am finding. I can feel when people love me; I know what my dog Ginger is feeling when we ride in the truck as she rests her head against my chest. I love it when my brother's daughter tells me in an e-mail that she misses me. I believe it now, when before I don't think I really did.

THE LITTLE GIRL IS GONE

So many things end. I had been seeing Mom for months. I had gotten used to the stale smell of the nursing home—at least it didn't make me want to barf anymore when I went there.

Just before the Fourth of July, I went through the security doors. A four-digit code had to be pressed to enter the hall and walk to the patient rooms. There was a little blue-haired lady sitting in a wheelchair. She was just inside in the hall, close to the doors, and I could tell she wanted to get out. I smiled as I passed, the doors slamming behind me. She said, "Could you let me out?"

I kept walking and said, "Sorry, maybe another time."

"Goddamn asshole!" she yelled. It made my day! I was laughing most of the day telling people about it. Hell, that would be my response too if someone did not let me out of that fucking place. "Ninety years old and full of piss and vinegar," I thought, good for her.

Mom was in the hall. She was sitting in a wheelchair with a half-dozen men and women. Their wheelchairs backed up to the wall. Some interacted, some ignored each other, and some stared vacantly. Some of the older women smiled. Many teeth were missing, but they did not know it. Some would comment about the food, wanting to go outside, or ask who the hell I was.

I always asked Mom if she would like to go back to her room. I had forgotten the book that day, so I picked a story to read out of *Reader's Digest*. I read to her, but it was hard to focus. My catering business was slower than I was used to, as June and July's bookings were off. The economy had taken a plunge and Bernie Madoff had wreaked havoc with many of the summer residents. Some had lost millions, and others were finished. I had read a story in a magazine and recognized many of the names of clients who used to spend thousands of dollars with my company each summer, entertaining their family and friends.

I read her the story, looking up before turning each page to see if she was listening to me or not. She hung on every word. Mom had been a big reader in her day, belonging to book clubs and reading several books each month. I think the last few years her concentration or eyesight had diminished, maybe both, but she showed much less interest in reading. She wouldn't read anything I brought her. Her face was thin that day, her skin a gray color, and her hands were even thinner than I remembered them. The bones and veins seemed more noticeable than usual. I had left a few hundred dollars with the office so they would make sure her hair was done each week. I could tell she had not had her hair done in a couple weeks. I made a mental note to talk to them at the desk and make sure it was taken care of and I kept reading.

Getting old is not for sissies. She was hanging on, if you call that hanging on. Frankly, I always said that I would head to Thailand when I knew the end was coming, get a couple of girls and a big ball of opium, and fade away.

Sometimes, I would ask Mom where I lived or where my brother lived, just to see how she was. She did not really remember her oldest daughter, and she did not know where she lived. But I kept her up to date anyway.

I spent an hour there that day. It was midafternoon and I needed to get back to work. I told her I loved her and that I would try to come see her next week, although I knew that I would not probably follow through with the visit. That was the last time I saw her.

On July 11, 2009, at 4:30 in the morning, my sister got the call. Eunice had died in her sleep. Even as I write this, I am not sure what I felt back then. Part of me felt relieved, and part of me was confused. If we knew it would be the last time we saw someone important in our lives, we would want something meaningful to happen. There would be something you wished you had told them. But you don't know. I went through the confusion and lack of sadness for a week. Even after the funeral, I was still not sure why I was not feeling more sadness and loss. Was I stuffing my feelings? Was I so unfeeling toward her, my own mother, as to not cry at her funeral. Like many things, in time I sorted it out the best I could. As always in these situations, it was complicated. I went through many years of my life wanting love and acceptance. I wanted her to say she was proud of me, that she loved me. I wanted her to show me, and I never felt that she showed me. She couldn't; she was broken. I got recognition and thanks, and I heard the words that she loved me near the end of her life. I said to myself that it was better than never hearing them at all, but the fact was that, at that point, maybe I had given up hope. Maybe it was too late. Maybe I had accepted the fact that she was unable to fulfill my needs and I had just let it go. I think it was all of this combined.

There was so much inconsistency growing up, but I always knew my father loved me. I knew it in my heart. Eunice would pull me in, and then push me away just to pull me back again. At times I would get the riot act, and other times there would be no reaction at all from her. She loved to work one of us kids against the other, manipulating us like a bunch of fucking puppets and pulling our strings until it would turn ugly. Then she would stand back smirk as if she had showed everyone how screwed up we really were. She did not like any of us children, or even my father, to get recognition or praise. She would cut our legs out from under us in a second, saying she was just kidding, that we were too sensitive, that it was all in fun. She found it amusing to humiliate us in front of family, her friends, or my stepfather. Wounds go deep, words are remembered for years, and actions are never forgotten.

Yes, I loved her for bringing me into the world. There were some things she taught me that I am grateful for, and I am thankful for all she did for me. There are many things I wished could have been different. I hate the way I can be with friends and coworkers. I hate the condescending tone that somehow rolls off my tongue and my inability to be intimate with a woman, which I now know is a result of my trust and self-esteem issues. I am not sure that one day I will get to a point when that fear of commitment, the fear of abandonment and rejection, does not raise its ugly head. I am fifty-five years old now, and my mother was just my mother. In almost all relationships, I have been drawn to the beautiful women who are elusive, unavailable, or inconsistent. I am drawn like a moth to a flame; I can't help myself. Maybe it is one of the reasons I have been without a relationship for the last three or four years, because it is easier.

They say that what you don't finish in this lifetime, you will be reborn to repeat. I believe that. Sometimes in a twisted way, I think I will get a redo and another lifetime on this earth to work on those things, and I feel some relief in that...

I know in my heart that I did the right thing by my mother. She was not able to take care of her own life, and I was able to let go of resentments and anger and be there in a responsible way. If I had been more involved in her finances and business decisions earlier, her life and all her children's lives would have been different. Would they have been better? Not really...just different. Money can't fix everything. Sometimes it creates more problems. Money is just a means to live. I know people who are worth millions, do not have to work, ski for months at a time, and are not really happy.

I worked hard for everything I have, and sometimes I look around my shop or my restaurant and see what I own. I own seven trucks with no payments, a restaurant, and a home in the Hamptons with a small mortgage, plus thousands of dollars of catering and kitchen equipment. I laugh sometimes, thinking that when I die it is going to take them years to sort out all this shit! Somehow, I am satisfied with the thought.

When I got sober, I was twenty-seven years old and in debt for ten thousand or more, which in 1981 was a lot of jing. All the things I have now came through my hard work and original ideas. I had just barely made it out of high school, and I never went to college. I remember not being able to balance a checkbook; now I have six checking accounts, retirement accounts, and accounts where I do some day trading. At times I see others with greater success and think I could have done more—but I have everything I need and more than I ever expected, so I leave that alone and just be grateful.

Sometimes, the people who have wealth fall into their lap do not appreciate it, and very often they end their lives with nothing or close to nothing.

Years of taking care of my mom's bills, upkeep on her house, and the endless phone calls and preparations for upcoming events was stressful, and I was tired at the end. It was all right for me to feel relieved, and yes, I did love my mother. I did not always like the way she was, especially the way she treated me and the rest of her children. I have listened to many members of the program tell their stories. Some were abused physically, some like me were abused emotionally, and some sexually, but all of us have had little or no spirituality. I think even though my mother went to church for many years, she had no spirituality. I know my dad and I used to love talking about it, and when he died I asked him to send me signs to let me know he was all right. I was the receiver of many signs from my father. They would send goose bumps up my neck when I shared them with friends and people in the program. Even if my mother was alert and aware near the end of her life, this was not a topic I would have brought up to her.

I had heard that something happens when both of your parents die, and now I know what people meant. I felt it as nine months approach after my mother passed—I was more alone than I had ever felt.

Not in a lonely way or a sad way…just knowing they weren't there anymore changed me.

When Dad died, I must have picked up the phone a hundred times to call him. It usually was when something good happened. I would be happy and want to share it with him. "He's not there anymore," a voice would tell me as I picked up the phone. He was so happy and proud of me when I got sober. I am so blessed he was here on this earth to be a part of that. He used to listen to my stories; he was the best listener. Since my mom died, I have not tried to call her once. As a matter of fact, I have barely had two dreams about her.

My father and I have been together in my dreams dozens of times in the nineteen years since his death. We are always working together, something we used to do when I was young. Most times we are at his place next door—the way it used to be, and not how the rich dude changed it with the fancy pool and pool house. In my dreams, he and I farm together. We build and repair equipment together, and one day I will join him I hope on the farm, wherever in heaven that is.

Until that time comes, I have unfinished business I need to take care of. There is lots of joyful memories, laughter, and good health left. I want to be there when the first poor young boys come over to my brother's house to take his daughters on a date—that should be interesting! I want the best for my brother. He needs me. My sisters will live life and walk through what they need to, and there will be many days for Ginger and I to go clamming, swim in the ocean, walk on the beach, and years and years of duck hunting for both of us.

And maybe, just maybe, I will fall in love one day with a beautiful woman and know what it is truly like to be loved by her.

The End

CPSIA information can be obtained at www.ICGtesting.com
Printed in the USA
BVOW012358040413

317371BV00010B/178/P